WOMEN, SEX, AND MADNESS

Covering a wide variety of subjects and points of inquiry on women's sexuality, from genital anxieties about pubic hair to constructions of the body in the therapy room, this book offers a ground-breaking examination of women, sex, and madness, drawing from psychology, gender and sexuality studies, and cultural studies.

Breanne Fahs argues that women's sexuality embodies a permanent state of tension between cultural impulses of destruction and selfishness contrasted with the fundamental possibilities of subversiveness and joy. Emphasizing cultural, social, and personal narratives about sexuality, Fahs asks readers to imagine sex, bodies, and madness as intertwined, and to see these narratives as fluid, contested, and changing. With topics as diverse as anarchist visions of sexual freedom, sexualized emotion work, lesbian haunted houses, and the insidious workings of capitalism, Fahs conceptualizes sexuality as a force of regressive moral panics and profound inequalities—deployed in both blatant and more subtle ways onto the body— while also finding hope and resistance in the possibilities of sexuality.

By integrating clinical case studies, cultural studies, qualitative interviews, and original essays, Fahs offers a provocative new vision for sexuality that fuses together social anxieties and cultural madness through a critical feminist psychological approach. Fahs provides an original and accessible volume for students and academics in psychology, gender and sexuality studies, and cultural studies.

Breanne Fahs is Professor of Women and Gender Studies at Arizona State University, US, and a practicing Clinical Psychologist. Her previous books include: *Performing Sex* (2011), *Valerie Solanas* (2014), *Out for Blood* (2016), and *Firebrand Feminism* (2018).

Women and Psychology

Series Editor: Jane Ussher
Professor of Women's Health Psychology, University of Western Sydney

This series brings together current theory and research on women and psychology. Drawing on scholarship from a number of different areas of psychology, it bridges the gap between abstract research and the reality of women's lives by integrating theory and practice, research, and policy.

Each book addresses a "cutting edge" issue of research, covering topics such as postnatal depression and eating disorders, and addressing a wide range of theories and methodologies.

The series provides accessible and concise accounts of key issues in the study of women and psychology, and clearly demonstrates the centrality of psychology debates within women's studies or feminism.

WOMEN, SEX, AND MADNESS

Notes from the Edge

Breanne Fahs

Routledge
Taylor & Francis Group

LONDON AND NEW YORK

First published 2020
by Routledge
2 Park Square, Milton Park, Abingdon, Oxon OX14 4RN

and by Routledge
52 Vanderbilt Avenue, New York, NY 10017

Routledge is an imprint of the Taylor & Francis Group, an informa business

© 2020 Breanne Fahs

British Library Cataloguing-in-Publication Data
A catalogue record for this book is available from the British Library

Library of Congress Cataloging-in-Publication Data
A catalog record has been requested for this book

ISBN: 978–1–138–61406–2 (hbk)
ISBN: 978–1–138–61408–6 (pbk)
ISBN: 978–0–429–46421–8 (ebk)

Typeset in Bembo
by Swales & Willis, Exeter, Devon, UK

For Eric Swank
All my stories, between the lines, bend toward you

Each sex has a relation to madness. Every desire has a relation to madness. But it would seem that one desire has been taken as wisdom, moderation, truth, leaving to the other sex the weight of a madness that cannot be acknowledged or accommodated.

—*Luce Irigaray*

CONTENTS

INTRODUCTION

Mad women, precarity, and the possibilities of sex

In the span of one week, I received two urgent calls at my psychotherapy clinic from two panicky mothers. Each needed a therapy appointment for their daughter, and each told me that a boy at school had sexually assaulted their girl, and that they had no idea how to care for their daughter through it. The parallels between these events were striking: I had known each of these girls many years before the assault, as I had seen each of their older brothers in therapy years ago. Each girl had a remarkable profile of overachievement, scholarly excellence, athleticism, beauty, self-assuredness, strong friendships, feminist attitudes, a robust social life, and a supportive family life. Each girl told me roughly the same story: A boy had sexually assaulted her, she had reported it, no one believed her, the boy spread rumors about her "wanting it" and being a "slut," and she now felt a mix of regret, shame, anger, self-blame, and disorientation about what had happened. Each had encounters with school officials who both claimed to feel supportive and blatantly blamed the girls for not giving clear signals, not running away, not yelling at the boys, and not ignoring the boys. Each girl described feeling depressed, anxious, overwhelmed, and uncertain whether she could rightly expect any support through this. And, notably, each of these assaults occurred directly in the wake of Brett Kavanaugh's Supreme Court confirmation hearing.

I begin the book with this brief story because it illustrates a key problem of how we study, understand, imagine, and write about women's sexuality. It is tempting to imagine these experiences as stories about sexual assault and rape culture, or to see the individuality of these girls' experiences as important and compelling, or to point out that boys and men seem increasingly enabled and emboldened to rape girls and women given the climate of normalizing sexual violence. All of these are true. But beyond that, I want to argue something more systematic and disturbing than even these already-disturbing claims. *We live in a culture of madness around sexuality*—one where the fundamental terms in which women learn to become sexual beings operates as if on a fault-line, shaking, ready to implode, forever precarious. We can try to understand these individual girls' psychological reactions to trauma—the so-called "madness" of post-traumatic stress disorder or the depressive and anxious disorders they may exhibit—but such an understanding fails to situate them in the broader sexual culture. And, of course, merely linking certain cultural or political events to women's sexual lives also falls far short of truly encapsulating the madness of the sexual culture in which women live.

The best of feminist psychology (see, for example, the work of Jane Ussher, Sara McClelland, Virginia Braun, Leonore Tiefer, Joan Chrisler, Abigail Stewart, and more) moves between these registers of individual experience and cultural context, between the micro and macro, the parts and the whole, the powerful psychological and the startling sociological. The whiplash of the versions of sexuality experienced in private versus the ones plastered on public billboards, TV screens, and magazines are both distinct and particularly vulnerable to feeding off of the worst qualities of the other. The most dysfunctional versions of our private lives draw from the more disturbing elements of so-called "sexual culture," and vice versa. And so, this is a book that understands women, sex, and madness not as interrelated individual phenomena but as a system, one where, much like a tornado, people and practices are drawn into an already-moving powerful storm. In this case, women and sex are continually drawn into the churning chaos of a culture that is frankly vicious in its relationship to sexuality. What people *do*, and *who* does those things matters far less than how they negotiate their sexual lives in this context.

Rethinking sex and madness

In her now-famous essay, "Thinking sex," Gayle Rubin (1984) wrote,

> It is precisely at times such as these, when we live with the possibility of unthinkable destruction, that people are likely to become dangerously crazy about sexuality ... Disputes over sexual behavior often become the vehicles for displacing social anxieties, and discharging their attendant emotional intensity. Consequently, sexuality should be treated with special respect in times of great social stress.
>
> *(p. 267)*

I imagine this book as both a response to these words of caution—giving a deeper understanding of the ways that we have (particularly in the U.S.) become "dangerously crazy about sexuality"—and also as a way to frame sexuality as a potential rebellion against displaced social anxieties.

Sexuality is seen here as a social force, a text larger than individual beings and bodies, a set of feelings and practices to be taken quite seriously in times of political and social turmoil. The madness that this book addresses is not one of individual psychopathology and individual reactions but instead one of *cultural* madness, a look at the frenzied, furious, panicky contexts in which people become sexualized. I conceptualize sexuality as a force of regressive moral panics and profound inequalities—deployed in both blatant and more subtle ways onto the body—while also finding hope and resistance in the possibilities of sexuality. In this way, sex is a mirror for our best and worst tendencies, our egregiously selfish and hideous impulses of destruction and the fundamental possibilities of joy, connection, and life itself. By moving through the various sites of tension and panic that underline sexuality, I emphasize cultural, social, and personal narratives about sexuality and see these narratives as fluid, contested, moveable, and changing.

At risk of sounding dismissive of the gains of the sexual liberation movement, I want to argue that the project of sexual liberation has largely failed to provide the kinds of so-called freedoms it promised to create (e.g., expansion of sexual possibilities, embrace of sexual diversity, fighting back against repression and oppression). These failures, however, may have unwittingly pushed scholarly inquiry *beyond* sexuality and into the broader political frameworks that govern sexuality. As Chris Chitty (2016) wrote,

> I'd like to ask how it is that the failure of the project of sexual liberation, which according to our analysis above has generated new modes of confinement through the extension of late capitalism into the very structure of sexual desire, might be the precondition for a politics beyond sexuality, for a desubjectifying or plebeianizing critical-diagnostic programme. If the antinomies which we have historicized above can be read as symptomatic failures for our ability to imagine a future and alternative modes of human relations outside the contradictions of late capitalism, how do we move to consider the synchronic or institutional aspects of the movements assembled under the inadequate heading of "sexual liberation"?
>
> *(p. 17)*

We find ourselves now in a quandary beyond simply the question of whether sex can be *liberating* for women. It is wholly insufficient to merely ask what kind of sex women have, with whom they have it, and, to a lesser degree, how they feel about it. Rather, we should instead ask: What possibilities are left for sexuality in a culture saturated in the worst qualities of late capitalism, racism, consumerism, misogyny, compulsory heterosexuality, and inequality? What can women's sexuality reveal about these conditions, and what happens if the stories revealed are deeply and profoundly different than the ones we would like to have or the ones we imagined were there?

Building on these difficult questions, I also want to pause to consider the ways in which the madness of sexuality—that is, the cultural contexts that unduly burden women's sexuality with anxiety—also draws from the culture of moral panics around sexuality. By this I mean that sexuality fuses together with clear notions of *moral threat*, sparking an especially vitriolic culture of hostility toward women who "deviate" from social norms (Fahs, Dudy, & Stage, 2013). As Saskia Eleonora Wieringa (2009) wrote of sexual moral panics,

> Sexuality is one of the most intoxicating elements with which to whip up social hysteria, and when it is mixed with religion and/or race, a particularly potent explosive mix is created … When a sexual moral panic is in full force, rational explanations are no longer heard as the floodgates are opened for ostracism, hate crimes, stigmatization, and violence.
>
> *(p. 209)*

In this sense, though I repeatedly ask women to narrate their sexual experiences *as individuals*, they also notably draw from these very panicky discourses in the broader sexual culture to understand their own lives. We can rightly imagine that concepts like sexual deviance, racialized (and hierarchical) understandings of bodies, social media frenzies, frank homophobia, and the pressures of capitalism all impact, to some degree, their way of *seeing* sexuality for themselves. As Janice Irvine (2009) wrote, "Sex panics are significant because they are 'the political moment of sex,' which Jeffrey Weeks and Gayle Rubin both describe as the transmogrification of moral values into political action" (p. 235). Moral panics of sexuality are, after all, strangely effective in reversing scripts about villains and victims, sexualizing the nonsexual, and subtly infecting mainstream thinking about sexuality both at the cultural and individual level (Fahs, Dudy, & Stage, 2013). Nobody seems to fully escape from the weighty baggage of the moral panics of sexuality, and this burden has only intensified over time.

To *re*think sex, I envision the intermingling of women, sex, and madness as intertwined, always feeding upon each other. Each of these—women, sex, and madness—constitutes a highly charged site for feminist interrogation, as women become linked (or saddled) to their bodies, and as women (and particularly women's sexuality) are so often accused of madness. Madness and sexuality— together and separately—follow women around. These themes are intentionally mixed up in order to interrogate how women see (or are driven to see) sexuality within the chaotic context of a culture that is often quite demented about sexuality. At the core of the book lies the claim that sex and bodies are subjected to, and become subjects of, discourses of madness and mental health. Again, I do not simply imagine madness as a claim about *abnormality* but instead as a framework for broader cultural stories that trickle down to individual people. For example, I look at the ways that sexuality becomes "dangerously crazy" in times of social stress, or the ways that bodies carry an undue burden from the labels of being "excessive" or "overly emotional," or how women react to men's near-fanatic quest for erectile functioning. These inquiries are decidedly feminist in their approach to understanding madness in a critical way—madness that is culturally-inscribed, or that haunts women and forces them to reckon with their own "too-muchness" in a diagnostic sense. I explore the inner workings of how these broader cultural frameworks are expressed, for women, in and through sexuality.

Perhaps we should also pause on the linguistic construction of madness—or more specifically, *madwomen*. Historically this has meant a wide swath of things: women locked in the attic, ranting and raving lunatic women, or women labeled as witches and burned at the stake (Earle, 2017; Gilbert & Gubar, 1980). Women have been labeled as mad for being *too* woman-like (e.g., emotional, passive, "hysterical," etc.) or for *not being woman enough* (e.g., angry, mouthy, violent, etc.) (Chesler, 2018). I have spent a rather large chunk of my career studying the life and work of Valerie Solanas, author of *SCUM Manifesto* and would-be assassin of Andy Warhol (Fahs, 2008, 2014). Notorious for both her actual madness and her identity as angry (and violent), Solanas perhaps embodies the crystallization of women and madness—she is mad (crazy) and mad (righteously angry). In the times we live in today, it is wise to consider the framing of madwomen (that is, women labeled as crazy) in tandem with mad women (that is, women who have become enraged). In this book, I am far more concerned with the latter than the former, though both inform each other and both haunt women's lives and women's stories about their sexualities.

In homage to mad (that is, angry) women, I also emphasize the central importance of looking at these themes during an age of such utter precarity, particularly for those already marked as vulnerable: people of color, women, sexual minorities, the poor and working-class, those with disabilities, and those with bodies marked as abject. It is, perhaps, a bizarre experience to think, read, and write about something so seemingly private and personal (or even arguably trivial) as sexuality when so many people are living on the edge. And yet, as Sara Ahmed has argued,

> I think fragility and precarity can be side-by-side, different accounts of related phenomena. If you think of a jug that is precarious, you might be referring to its position. Maybe it is too near the edge of the mantelpiece. Just a little push and it would fall right off. Precarity can be a generalized position; when we say a population is precarious we would refer to how much work has to be done just to maintain a position, how easy it is, because of how hard life is, for some to fall right off.
>
> *(Mehra, 2017)*

Sara Ahmed went on to talk about the necessity of taking on difficult struggles— intellectually and personally—in an age of precarity:

> I think there are many ways we are asked to rush over things that are hard— in politics and in life—and the writers who have taught me most, including Audre Lorde, especially Audre Lorde, have taught me to stay with what hurts however much it hurts, until you have worked something out about yourself

and the world. Audre Lorde also says that sometimes to survive we have to become stone. Sometimes to survive the weather you have to harden yourself. She invites us to embrace our imperfect broken bodies with bits and pieces missing. I think when the project is to survive heavy, hard histories, we do need multiple tactics; sometimes they are in tension with each other. Sometimes we need to lighten our loads, to laugh. Sometimes we need to be weighed down, to stop under the weight. We are not going to get it right when we are living with wrongs. We are not going to build a house that is light enough to accommodate everyone. It is an ongoing, unfinished project because it is a question: how to build a feminist world when the world we oppose is the world we still inhabit.

(Mehra, 2017)

Later, in a conversation between Sara Ahmed and Judith Butler (2016), Butler reframes the kinds of questions we should start to ask in light of such precarity:

How do we understand those desires that we might call abiding, persistent, and that for many define their basic sense of self? How do we even understand that basic sense of self, when it exists or when it struggles to exist? How is that sense formed, and when does it take hold, if it does? Under what conditions is it dismantled or even shattered?

(p. 491)

She adds later on,

What if we shift the question from "who do I want to be?" to the question, "what kind of life do I want to live with others?"? It seems to me that then many of the questions you pose about happiness, but perhaps also about "the good life"—very ancient yet urgent philosophical questions—take shape in a new way. If the I who wants this name or seeks to live a certain kind of life is bound up with a "you" and a "they" then we are already involved in a social struggle when we ask how best any of us are to live.

(p. 491)

Taking seriously these questions Butler poses, I want to add: How can we understand sexual precarity—that is, *being on the edge*—as a social phenomenon, something seen in relation to each other and our collective social struggle? What kind of *sexual* life do we want to have with each other? How can we reimagine the "good" life to minimize the sexual precarity of so many? By this, I do not mean the way that certain sexual *practices* operate as precarious, but rather the ways that individuals absorb and express their more general precarity *through and within* sexuality. This precarity can exist in multiple spheres: financial, emotional, social, psychological, collective, and existential.

More precisely, looking at women's sexuality in many ways speaks to larger stories about their immense precarity in this particular time and context. They express through stories of sexuality the precarity of being a woman (particularly as it intersects with other identities), as well as the precarity of living on the edge financially, bearing the weight of racism, or facing the looming threats of environmental destruction and climate change. The subtitle of this book *Notes from the Edge* means just that—these are stories and narratives that emerge while women are positioned, quite precariously, on the edge of sanity, stability, and existence itself. These are stories that also signal something about our future: What kind of world do we want to create for women, and how might we take seriously their current stories about the world they live in? *What kind of life do we want to live with others?*

Taking notes

I am a firm believer in the importance of narratives, oral histories, storytelling, and self-construction when addressing human experiences. This does not suggest that these kinds of stories are wholly accurate descriptions of the social world and are therefore absolutely true (in fact, many narratives reflect poorly on the "truth" of memory or the "realness" of speaking about the self), but narratives are nevertheless a powerful tool for understanding things as difficult and over-whelming as the *culture of madness* and *precarity of being a woman*. Oral histories have a long tradition in feminist histories, allowing collaborative knowledge-making and reciprocity to take center stage (Benson & Nagar, 2006). The trad-ition of *testimonio*, for example, situates narrative as an explicitly political entity in relation to identity formation and collectivity (Bernal, Burciaga, & Carmona, 2012). Feminist oral history (Geiger, 1990; Gluck & Patai, 2016; Sangster, 2002) and storytelling (McNamara, 2009; Parashar, 2015; Smith, 2013) have both sub-verted traditional understandings of knowledge-making and identity formation, particularly for women of color. More formally, qualitative inquiry in empirical work has yielded a robust array of studies that take seriously the stories and nar-ratives of women, particularly those who exist permanently on the margins (Braun & Clarke, 2013; Watts, 2006). And notes, or note-taking, have a prime place in the history of women's work—that of diaries (Martinson, 2003), ethno-graphic field notes (Oyewumi, 2000; Visweswaran, 1997), scribbles and margi-nalia (Jackson, 2002; McClelland, 2016; McHatton & May, 2013), or even being consigned to secretarial work (England & Boyer, 2009). Talking to women about their lives yields a wealth of new insights about the destructive and hopeful possibilities of sex, just as looking closely at stories of sex ensures that we see sexualities as *more* complex and *more* dissonant than ever before.

Thinking about women's sexuality as multiple, diverse, and wholly infused with broader cultural stories also allows for a careful consideration of how social rules about affect and emotion inform the core of women's sexual lives. The subfield of affect studies has created fertile ground for scholars to explore the relationship between emotions, individual life, and public culture (Ahmed, 2004; Berlant, 2008; Cvetkovich, 2012; Sedgwick, 2003). I draw from and build upon this work to ground the study of women's sexuality as, in some ways, a careful study of affect and its relationship to narrative. The case study method, for example, opens up new possibilities for looking carefully at the ways that individual lives intersect and thus generate new stories and nuance about under-studied subjects (e.g., the way that sex addict men imagine women). Case studies also allow for a close and in-depth examination of *emotional life*, particularly the emotions rooted in anxious cultural stories about sex and sexuality. I anticipate that clinical case studies have a far wider audience than clinical psychologists for this very reason, as they allow an intimate look at the relationship between emotions, narrative, and culture.

As an interdisciplinary text on sexuality, I imagine this book as drawing from multiple sources and frameworks. A good number of these chapters draw upon the traditions of qualitative feminist psychological research to explore women's sexual subjectivities, a subfield that much of my previous work has also addressed. That said, I also draw from a number of other methodological and intellectual traditions, including feminist and queer theory, cultural studies, clinical case studies, semiotics, sociological analyses, and polemical essays. The book moves through a range of unique perspectives and novel approaches to studying its subjects, many of which are overlooked and understudied: women's feelings about vaginal wetness, the fleshy body in the therapy room, the politics of rape language, and the urgent necessity of designing sex lives that move away from the intrusions of capitalism. While the merging of these different methodological approaches may feel jarring at times—moving from empirical work to cultural studies essays to clinical case studies to political rants—this movement allows greater exploration of the range of destructive and hopeful possibilities for women's sexual lives.

More precisely, in this book, I ask: What is at stake in situating sex as a *thinking* entity? How does critical feminist psychology teach us to see, find, and talk about things that are often obscured or silenced? What does it mean to be "dangerously crazy" about sexuality, and how might we imagine resistances to this madness? How can radical feminist performance artists create new stories about gender and sex? What sorts of power and knowledge exist in mundane sexual and social practices? What new visions exist for sex-positive politics, pleasured/pleasuring bodies, and anti-capitalist prescriptions for women, sex, and madness? How can women's narratives both diagnose sexual problems and create new visions for resistance and revolt?

Book organization

Women, Sex, and Madness approaches its subjects through critical frameworks that move the boundaries of how we typically see "feminist psychology." Rather than focusing only on psychological methods, or only on the study of women, this book instead features sections that take on clusters of ideas that interrogate various intersections of women, sexuality, and madness, including topics like lesbian haunted houses, sex addiction, emotional labor, and rabble-rousing/resistance. The book is organized into four parts, moving from how women see their partners through their own sexual experiences (Part 1) to how broader cultural narratives about sexuality get created (Part 2). The second half features chapters about how sexuality enters therapy and psychopathology discourses (Part 3) followed by an analysis of how sexuality can serve as a site of resistance and revolt, linking up with anti-capitalism, anarchism, and collective feminist struggles (Part 4). In all, this book offers different windows into the connection between women, sexuality, and madness, at times framing madness as a personal construct and at times seeing it as a larger cultural framework within which people construct their sexual lives.

Part 1: "Women explain things to me" includes three chapters that look at how women see their partners—particularly their current or former male partners—through their own sexual experiences. This approach allows a novel, critical look at how women see gendered scripts of sexuality and gives particular insight into how women see men as sexual partners and how this might differ from how men see themselves. This part of the book includes three interview-based studies of women's sexuality that draw from critical sexuality studies and critical heterosexualities work. First, I include a chapter that examines women's experiences with boring sex or sex that feels like labor or "a job." This is followed by a qualitative study of women's emotional labor in their sexual relationships (e.g., minimizing sexual pain, faking orgasm). The third chapter in this part looks at women's feelings about their vaginal lubrication and wetness. The women in these conversations are a community sample of women from diverse class, race, and sexual identity backgrounds, including a sizable percentage of women of color, sexual minority women, and working-class women.

Part 1 includes three chapters: Chapter 1: "Men, through women's eyes" is an essay that looks at women's experiences with sexual activities that they do solely to please a partner alongside women's experiences with sex as a form of labor. I look at how women talk about their male partners and what these experiences reveal about gender and sexual entitlement. I also consider the importance of studying masculinity through women's eyes, and use women's subjectivities to build a framework for the emerging subfield of critical heterosexualities. Following this, Chapter 2: "The other third shift? Women's emotion work in their sexual relationships" combines the sociological concept of "emotional labor" and "emotion work" with the psychological concept of sexual subjectivity. (Emotional labor refers to the ways that women suppress their subjective experiences of sexuality and instead prioritize their partners' needs and desired experiences.) I specifically look at women's experiences with minimizing sexual pain, faking orgasm, defining sexual satisfaction based on a partner's pleasure, and narrating sex they call "bad sex" as acceptable because of a partner's satisfaction, I do this in order to better understand how women engage in emotion work in their sexual and romantic relationships and how this work is often overlooked and understudied as a form of social oppression. As the last chapter of this part, Chapter 3: "Slippery desire: women's qualitative accounts of their vaginal lubrication and wetness" contrasts the immense amount of media and medical attention paid to men's erections and the minimal attention paid to women's vaginal lubrication, particularly in terms of sexual subjectivities. I speak with women directly about their feelings about vaginal wetness and look at how they moralize about their own wetness in diverse ways. Specifically, women describe their vaginal wetness as a form of pleasure and connection, a biological phenomenon, and as a source of anxiety about having "too much" or "too little" wetness.

Part 2: "Veering and queering" features three chapters on the ways that cultural narratives about women, sex, and madness are shaped, created, and maintained. That is, I look in this part of the book at the creation of stories and narratives that continue to move and shift in response to changing cultural contexts over time. For example, how people view sexual violence is often deeply connected to the cultural stories surrounding violence in addition to the personal experiences of actual violence. This part looks at the political language of rape, the way women imagine the vagina and vulva as a source of anxiety, and queer haunted houses as a means to examine narratives about queer theory, play, and humor.

The chapters in this part of the book include Chapter 4: "Killjoy's Kastle and the hauntings of queer/lesbian feminism," an essay that looks at the lesbian haunted house, "Killjoy's Kastle," and its implications for thinking about queer theory, performance art, and queer history. The utility of play and humor as a form of resistance, confrontation with lesbian feminist stereotypes, and the notion of queer "hauntings"—that is, the ways that queer identities and narratives function as a hidden, silenced, and spooky entity—are theorized. Following this, Chapter 5: "The politics of turning rape into 'nonconsensual sex'" examines the politics of language around rape as it has morphed into "nonconsensual sex" and what this means for imagining (and prosecuting) sexual violence. The ways that language about sexual coercion can serve as a tool of resistance and appropriation are considered, particularly in light of the contradiction of college campuses directing more attention to sexual assault while minimizing the role of men in assaulting women. As the final chapter in this part, Chapter 6: "Genital anxieties: using critical sexuality studies to examine women's attitudes about the vulva and vagina" looks at the ways that vulvas and vaginas can become a source of anxiety for women, particularly around "scary" sites of embodiment like sex during menstruation, genital surgeries, and pubic hair discourses. I consider moments where the stories about vaginas and vulvas become especially "abject" and how these stories infect women's own feelings about their genitals. Further, genital self-image and possible re-imaginings about the cultural and personal meanings of the vulva are considered.

Part 3: "On the couch" features three chapters that unite sex and madness, specifically looking at the ways that sexuality enters therapy and psychopathology discourses. These chapters, drawing from my work as a practicing feminist clinical psychologist, include one that examines discussions of erections in therapy with three different couples, followed by a chapter on male sex addicts and the framework for how sex addicts imagine women's lives. This part of the book concludes with a chapter about the physical, corporeal body in the therapy office and why it is important to theorize and understand the workings of corporeality (that is, the material conditions of the body) in therapy. These chapters highlight the importance of looking more deeply at the spaces in which sex and madness are most intimately intertwined on an interpersonal level, particularly as sex is treated, diagnosed, managed, and shaped in the therapy office.

This part of the book includes the following chapters: Chapter 7: "Compulsory penetration? A sex therapy romp" features three case studies with couples in sex therapy, where erections form a central role in their perceived distress. I look at how the erection functions as a symbol of masculinity, power, and sexual success, and how reducing the importance of the erection had positive outcomes for the couples. I also carefully consider the problems of how penile-vaginal penetration—and sexuality itself—have become compulsory (that is, required or mandated) aspects of heterosex rather than one of many options related to diverse sexual expression. Following this, Chapter 8: "Are women people? The lusty and chaotic world of sex addiction" features three case studies with men in treatment for long-term compulsive sexual behavior. After looking at some of the controversies surrounding sex addiction as a diagnosis, I examine the ways that these clients objectify women, and how feminist therapy interventions work not only to help with their compulsive behaviors but to reshape their views of women's sexual subjectivities. I also make links between cultural misogyny and the ways that sex addiction manifests toward women, combined with various feminist-minded interventions that may help sex addict patients in therapy. Finally, Chapter 9: "Therapy without bodies, or why fleshiness matters" looks at the corporeal, material, fleshy body in the therapy room, particularly the features of therapist and patient (age, size, sickness, menstrual status, etc.) to examine the materiality of the body and its impact on the therapy relationship for both clients and practitioners. By looking at leaky bodies, identity-marked bodies, and gendered bodies, I frame the body as an important "presence" in the therapy room. I also argue for more attention paid to both the therapists' and patients' body during the therapy process. I draw parallels with qualitative research in order to specifically look at how the body functions differently in the therapy room than in other similar spaces.

Part 4: "All riled up" highlights the ways that sexuality can serve as a site of resistance and revolt, particularly by using sexuality as a tool to contest social inequalities. These chapters imagine new possibilities for women, sex, and madness, while also thinking about the ways that women are mired in oppressive social structures. The part includes three chapters that look at how capitalism provides a deeply problematic framework for thinking about our sexual problems today, followed by two more hopeful chapters: one that looks at the anarchist arguments for sexual freedom, and one that examines ways to individually and collectively resist some of the most damaging constructs of sexuality women face today. The hazards and potentials of sexuality inform all three of these chapters.

This part of the book includes the following chapters: First, Chapter 10: "Warning: capitalism is destroying our sex lives" looks at how the operations of capitalism influence the ways that we have sex, and how an anti-capitalist critique of sexuality might be useful for imagining ways to decolonize the intrusions of neoliberalism and capitalism. Analyses of leisure and vacation time, pleasure, the product-oriented goals of sex, hierarchies produced between good and bad sexualities, and emotional and sexual labor are included. Next, Chapter 11: "'Freedom to' and 'freedom from': a new vision for sex-positive politics" draws from earlier anarchist principles that people must have freedom to do what they want, and freedom from having to do what they do not want to do. I apply these concepts to the notion of sexual freedom by specifically looking at gaps and problem areas in how women sometimes lack the "freedom to," and more often, how they lack the "freedom from." I argue for a new vision for sex-positive politics that moves from the call for women to do *more* sexually and instead includes far more attention to the "freedom from." As the final chapter in the book, Chapter 12: "Counter-erotics: sex as a form of resistance" emphasizes a justice-based perspective to how sex can become a form of resistance. Drawing from psychological frameworks of critical sexuality studies, sociological concepts of hidden and covert resistance, the complexities of sexual power, and contemporary and historical examples of collective sexual resistances (e.g., sex strikes, Masturbate-a-Thon, SlutWalk), this chapter argues for specific ways that feminist and antiracist resistance be enacted, from the highly individual/personal to the more collective.

Ultimately, in this book, I argue for an expansive understanding of the relationship between women, sex, and madness, moving away from the overly reductive notion of women *as mad*, and instead suggesting that having sex in a culture of sexual madness is complicated and difficult. By leaping across disciplinary and methodological boundaries, from qualitative psychological research to cultural studies analyses to clinical case studies to political and philosophical work on resistance, I want this book to serve as a guidebook for possibilities for what sexuality research can offer to the immensely messy political context in which we live. Further, I want to delve deeply into the problems and possibilities of sexuality for feminist resistance, looking at its more difficult manifestations (e.g., bored sex, capitalist-driven encounters, etc.) and its inspired, revolutionary potential (e.g., hidden resistance, collective strikes, anarchist relationship to sexual freedom). We owe it to each other and to ourselves to see the project of working toward sexual freedom as an ongoing struggle, one that will require renewal of our alliances, investment in vigorous and inventive research, desire for self-criticism and self-reflection, an unlearning of what we have been taught, and a true invigoration of our capacity to imagine differently.

References

Ahmed, S. (2004). *The cultural politics of emotion.* New York: Routledge.

Ahmed, S. (2016). Interview with Judith Butler. *Sexualities, 19*(4), 482–492.

Benson, K., & Nagar, R. (2006). Collaboration as resistance? Reconsidering the processes, products, and possibilities of feminist oral history and ethnography. *Gender, Place & Culture, 13*(5), 581–592.

Berlant, L. (2008). *The female complaint: The unfinished business of sentimentality in American culture.* Durham, NC: Duke University Press.

Bernal, D. D., Burciaga, R., & Carmona, J. F. (2012). Chicana/Latina testimonies: Mapping the methodological, pedagogical, and political. *Equity & Excellence in Education, 45* (3), 363–372.

Braun, V., & Clarke, V. (2013). *Successful qualitative research: A practical guide for beginners.* Thousand Oaks, CA: Sage.

Chesler, P. (2018). *Women and madness.* Chicago, IL: Chicago Review Press.

Chitty, C. (2016). Sex as cultural form: The antinomies of sexual discourse. *Blind Field: A Journal of Cultural Inquiry.* https://blindfieldjournal.com/2016/04/19/sex-as-cultural-form-the-antinomies-of-sexual-discourse/.

Cvetkovich, A. (2012). *Depression: A public feeling.* Durham, NC: Duke University Press.

Earle, H. E. (2017). "A convenient place for inconvenient people": Madness, sex and the asylum in *American Horror Story. The Journal of Popular Culture, 50*(2), 259–275.

England, K., & Boyer, K. (2009). Women's work: The feminization and shifting meanings of clerical work. *Journal of Social History, 43*(2), 307–340.

Fahs, B. (2008). The radical possibilities of Valerie Solanas. *Feminist Studies, 34*(3), 591–617.

Fahs, B. (2014). *Valerie Solanas: The defiant life of the woman who wrote SCUM (and shot Andy Warhol).* New York: The Feminist Press.

Fahs, B., Dudy, M. L., & Stage, S. (2013). Villains and victims: Excavating the moral panics of sexuality. In B. Fahs, M. L. Dudy, & S. Stage (Eds.), *The moral panics of sexuality* (pp. 1–23). London: Palgrave.

Geiger, S. (1990). What's so feminist about women's oral history? *Journal of Women's History, 2*(1), 169–182.

Gilbert, S. M., & Gubar, S. (1980). *The madwoman in the attic: The woman writer and the nineteenth-century literary imagination.* New Haven, CT: Yale University Press.

Gluck, S. B., & Patai, D. (Eds.). (2016). *Women's words: The feminist practice of oral history.* New York: Routledge.

Irvine, J. M. (2009). Transient feelings: Sex panics and the politics of emotion. In G. Herdt (Ed.), *Moral panics, sex panics* (pp. 234–276). New York: New York University Press.

Jackson, H. (2002). *Marginalia: Readers writing in books.* New Haven, CT: Yale University Press.

Martinson, D. (2003). *In the presence of audience: The self in diaries and fiction.* Columbus, OH: Ohio State University Press.

McClelland, S. I. (2016). Speaking back from the margins: Participant marginalia in survey and interview research. *Qualitative Psychology, 3*(2), 159–165.

McHatton, P. A., & May, S. (2013). Moving margins: Using marginalia as a tool for critical reflection. *International Review of Qualitative Research, 6*(1), 143–147.

McNamara, P. (2009). Feminist ethnography: Storytelling that makes a difference. *Qualitative Social Work, 8*(2), 161–177.

Mehra, N. J. (2017). Sara Ahmed: Notes from a feminist killjoy. *Guernica.* www .guernicamag.com/sara-ahmed-the-personal-is-institutional/.

Oyewumi, O. (2000). Family bonds/conceptual binds: African notes on feminist epistemologies. *Signs: Journal of Women in Culture and Society, 25*(4), 1093–1098.

Parashar, S. (2015). Anger, war and feminist storytelling. In L. Åhäll, & T. Gregory (Eds.), *Emotions, politics and war: Interventions* (pp. 93–107). New York: Routledge.

Rubin, G. (1984). Thinking sex: Notes for a radical theory of the politics of sexuality. In C. Vance (Ed.), *Pleasure and danger* (pp. 267–294). New York: Routledge & Kegan Paul.

Sangster, J. (2002). Telling our stories: Feminist debates and the use of oral history. In R. Perks & A. Thomson (Eds.), *The oral history reader* (pp. 101–114). New York: Routledge.

Sedgwick, E. K. (2003). *Touching feeling: Affect, pedagogy, and performance.* Durham, NC: Duke University Press.

Smith, L. T. (2013). *Decolonizing methodologies: Research and indigenous peoples.* London: Zed Books.

Visweswaran, K. (1997). Histories of feminist ethnography. *Annual Review of Anthropology, 26*(1), 591–621.

Watts, J. (2006). "The outsider within": Dilemmas of qualitative feminist research within a culture of resistance. *Qualitative Research, 6*(3), 385–402.

Wieringa, S. E. (2009). Postcolonial America: Sexual moral panics, memory, and imperial power. In G. Herdt (Ed.), *Moral panics, sex panics* (pp. 205–233). New York: New York University Press.

PART 1

Women explain things to me

1

MEN, THROUGH WOMEN'S EYES

When I was a 20-year-old rambunctious liberal arts student at Occidental College studying psychology and women's and gender studies, I wrote a rant-filled undergraduate thesis on women's orgasms entitled, "Dismembering orgasmic phallacies: Self-weaponry, potent fictions, and the blasphemous body." In this document, I tried to capture a problem that seemed to have paramount importance to me at that time: How could women understand their own sexuality if they were largely constructed as objects within a patriarchal society? What sort of sexual imagination could they have if their sexual practices, ideologies, feelings, and desires were created and constructed by a culture that hates women? And, of course, how would something as delicate, intricate, and complicated as women's orgasms stand a chance in a culture that overwhelmingly catered to men's sexual needs and desires? What could this tiny thing—the orgasm—teach us about the bigger things like power, oppression, and capitalism?

I mention this anecdote in part to demonstrate that my interests in the questions raised in this chapter—questions about how we can understand women and their sexuality in a patriarchal culture designed to minimize or strip away such understanding—have captivated me for over 20 years. These questions do not lend themselves to easy answers. I have spent much of my career as a researcher and teacher outlining the ways that women interpret their sexual experiences under conditions that stack the odds against them—conditions that require constant re-evaluation of their own desires and ideas, strip women of self-understanding and self-assertion, and diminish women's capacity for pleasure and satisfaction (particularly pleasure that is not wholly relational and directed toward pleasing others). Women's assertions of their sexual subjectivities tell only part of the story. When we live in a culture that deeply distrusts its own relationship to pleasure, that weaves its hatred of women into the mundane aspects of everyday life, storytelling about sexuality is painfully difficult.

Ultimately, I want to return again to the question of how women can understand themselves in a patriarchal culture, but I also want to ask a slightly different one: What can we understand about *men* by looking exclusively at what women say about men? What do the (voiceless) objects of patriarchal culture—the women rendered invisible and/or insignificant—tell us about the core of that patriarchal culture? How might we understand men better, or differently, through women's eyes, and how might women imagine different kinds of truths about men and sexuality?

To unpack these questions, I examine two common areas where women describe their personal sexual experiences of men: 1) sexual activities women perform solely to please a partner, and 2) women's experiences with sex as a form of labor. Together, these stories shed light on the ways that women's sexuality exists largely in relation to asymmetrical power structures that grant greater power to men than women. And, of course, these sexual narratives point toward more precise understandings of what it means to unite sex and madness not as *individual* madness ("being crazy") but as *cultural* madness ("living in a culture that is crazy"). These stories arrive after the second wave of feminism and after the sexual revolution, in a time that promotes the view of women as sexually empowered, agentic, and more satisfied than previous generations. And yet, reading between the lines, we see a far more complicated picture of so-called "sexual liberation" emerging.

Theoretical framework

The question of what it means to take up *sexual subjectivities*—that is, the telling of one's own sexual stories and the ability to imagine oneself as an agentic sexual being (Tolman, 2002)—carries immense weight in a culture that routinely strips women of power and agency. How can women talk openly about their sexual perspectives and desires if they live in a culture that denies them those very things? Further, in a historically Puritanical culture that is tremendously afraid of its own sexual impulses, and eager to quarantine sexuality and construct it a site of anxiety and chaos, understanding women's perspectives on sexuality becomes even more difficult. Much like Susan Bordo's (1997) claim that anorexia represents the crystallization of culture, that is the distillation of who we are as a people (e.g., a culture eager to imagine women as passive, small, and weak), I would argue that women's sexuality serves as a *symptom* of cultural stories about women and power. To closely examine how women's sexualities are shaped and molded to fit dominant, hegemonic ideas about men's power over women is to fashion a kind of self-portrait. In doing so, women's ideas and stories about men might help to unpack and better nuance the insidious ways that patriarchy operates, revealing aspects of men and masculinity that often remain unchecked, unspoken, and invisible.

As a key contribution of French feminist philosophy, the construction of women as commodities—and the shaping of subjectivity that results from men "trading" women on the sexual marketplace—helps to frame some of the conversations in this chapter and in the book more broadly. To understand how men feel about women, and how women perceive men's perceptions of them, the construction of women as sexualized commodities is essential. For example, Luce Irigaray (1985) stated,

> Women's bodies—through their use, consumption, and circulation—provide for the condition making social life and culture possible, although they remain an unknown "infrastructure" of the elaboration of that social life and culture. The exploitation of the matter that has been sexualized female is so integral a part of our sociocultural horizon that there is no way to interpret it except within this horizon.
>
> *(p. 171)*

Essentially, Irigaray argues that women come to understand their sexuality in relation to being "good" or "bad" commodities; as such, they imagine themselves in relation to how men evaluate or judge them. She wrote of this process:

> Woman is traditionally a use-value for man, an exchange value among men; in other words, a commodity. As such, she remains the guardian of material substance, whose price will be established, in terms of the standard of their work and of their need/desire, by "subjects": workers, merchants, consumers. Women are marked phallically by their fathers, husbands, procurers. And this branding determines their value in sexual commerce. Woman is never anything but the locus of a more or less competitive exchange between two men, including the competition for the possession of mother earth.
>
> *(Irigaray, 1985, pp. 31–32)*

She further argued that, in order to understand women as sexual commodities, both their physical bodies and their symbolic value must be accounted for. She wrote, "when women are exchanged, woman's body must be treated as an *abstraction*" (Irigaray, 1985, p. 175). And, when women become abstractions, men define women according to dominant definitions of power and virility, thus placing women along a continuum of more or less successful mirroring of men's sexual needs. She wrote, "Woman herself is never at issue in these statements: the feminine is defined as the necessary complement to the operation of male sexuality, and, more often, as the negative image that provides male sexuality with an unfailing phallic self-representation" (Irigaray, 1985, p. 70).

Similarly, American feminist legal scholar Catharine MacKinnon has argued that patriarchal conditions of sexuality foster a kind of permanent ignorance wherein men have no idea what women really experience, think, or feel. She wrote of this process:

Men's power to *make* the world here is their power to make us make the world of their sexual interaction with us the way they want it. They want us to have orgasms; that proves they're virile, potent, effective. We provide them that appearance, whether it's real for us or not.

(MacKinnon, 1987, p. 58)

In this sense, women's perceptions about heterosex (and men in general) exist within a culture that *demands* a lack of self-knowledge and constructs women around men's fantasies and desires. Put differently, Achille Mbembe (2001) argued about men's phallic power:

In fact, the phallus has been the focus of ways of constructing masculinity and power. Male domination derives in large measure from the power and the spectacle of the phallus—not so much from the threat to life during war as from the individual male's ability to demonstrate his virility at the expense of a woman and to obtain its validation from the subjugated woman herself.

(p. 13)

If men experience validation from the subjugation of women, how, then, do women speak about this process?

Women's sexual subjectivities

Many social constructionists of sexuality have convincingly argued that women's sexuality does not exist in a vacuum; the notion of "my sexuality" is impossible on an individual level unless we account for the social processes that *make* sexuality (Plante, 2014; Tiefer, 2004). Women's sexualities are made and remade through a process of disavowal ("you must like what I like"), colonization ("my reality is superior") and mirroring ("show/tell me what I want to hear") and enter a matrix where patriarchy, misogyny, and racism construct "good," "moral," and "healthy" sexualities. Sexual scripting theory, developed by Gagnon and Simon (1973), posited that people construct sexual selves through intrapsychic scripting that draws on fantasies, memories, feelings of arousal, and ideas about desirable and undesirable sex. Later, Rebecca Plante (2007) argued that sexual scripts also extend widely into the realm of the social:

"The Story" is the narrative of the many. It is the way in which Western citizens make sense of the need to make sense, to develop and sustain a continuous self. There are rape stories, gay and lesbian "coming out" stories, and recovery/self help stories.

(p. 33)

Sexual scripts and sexual subjectivities come alive most poignantly in the context of women's sexual satisfaction, a seemingly innocuous term upon which an enormous number of assumptions are built about sexuality. What is a satisfied woman? What makes a sexual encounter satisfying? Many sex researchers have assumed that sexual satisfaction for women can be measured using single-item questions that make generalizations about how satisfied women are (Barrientos & Páez, 2006; Meston & Trapnell, 2005; Sprecher, 2002), often ignoring the complexity and possible contradictions of physical and emotional satisfaction, as well as the complex ways that women gauge their satisfaction in relation to their partners. Notably, women described sexual satisfaction most often in relation to pleasing their partners and cared more about whether they have satisfied another person than whether they have themselves felt physically satisfied (McClelland, 2010, 2014), while men described sexual satisfaction as "getting off" (Bancroft, Loftus, & Long, 2003; Nicolson & Burr, 2003). Similarly, in a small study of English women, Nicolson and Burr (2003) found that partner satisfaction mattered *more* than personal satisfaction when women defined their sexual satisfaction. This distinction has supreme importance for understanding women's sexual lives, as women consistently construct their notions of satisfaction around *the other*, caring less about their own feelings and more about the satisfaction of their partners.

This attention to emotional and physical caretaking—and the prioritization of a partner over themselves—has deep roots in traditional gender roles and socialization processes that teach women to value men's needs over their own (Beauboeuf-Lafontant, 2007; Katz & Tirone, 2009). That said, sexual satisfaction is also connected to who *expects* to feel satisfied and who feels *entitled* to pleasure, as those who felt more entitled to satisfaction and pleasure reported more sexual satisfaction (Braun, Gavey, & McPhillips, 2003). Not surprisingly, sexual minority youth and *all* women reported lower rates of sexual satisfaction than did heterosexual youth and men in general (Diamond & Lucas, 2004; Sanchez, Kiefer, & Ybarra, 2006). Recent research has framed sexual satisfaction instead as a combination of frequency of orgasm, emotional satisfaction, emotions about sex, and physical satisfaction (Fahs & Swank, 2011) in an attempt to broaden overly narrow definitions of sexual satisfaction and capture elements of women's satisfaction beyond partner pleasure. Further, several sexual satisfaction inventories have pushed to broaden how researchers measure sexual satisfaction in order to avoid an overly simplistic single-item assessment of something as complex as sexual satisfaction (Pinney, Gerrard, & Denney, 1987; Štulhofer, Buško, & Brouillard, 2010; Ter Kuile, van Lankwd, Kalkhown, & Egmond, 1999).

In my earlier work on women's orgasms, I found that women also felt satisfied when their partners felt sexually successful, leading to epidemic rates of women faking orgasm (Fahs, 2011; see also Muehlenhard & Shippee, 2010). Women reported that their own physical experiences of sex (e.g., having an orgasm) mattered less than what they reflected back to their partners (e.g., their partners perceiving that women had an orgasm). Certainly, the prevalence of women faking orgasms is startlingly high, with studies consistently showing that over half of women have faked orgasm (Darling & Davidson, 1986; Fahs, 2011, 2014; Muehlenhard & Shippee, 2010; Opperman, Braun, Clarke, & Rogers, 2013; Wiederman,

1997), particularly with male partners while engaging in penile-vaginal intercourse (PVI) (Fahs, 2011; Muehlenhard & Shippee, 2010). Most men did not know when women faked their orgasms (Knox, Zusman, & McNeely, 2008).

When asked why they faked orgasms, women most often replied that they wanted to protect their partners' ego, followed by feelings of wanting sex to end and a general sense of fatigue—both of which also suggest that women prioritize others' needs over themselves. They also reported feeling that they *must* have intercourse and that they did not expect their own orgasm and, at times, women also faked orgasm in order to avoid conflict, none of which bode well for positive and healthy relationships of sexual mutuality (Fahs, 2011; Frith, 2013; Muehlenhard & Shippee, 2010). Another study found that women often felt uncomfortable talking about bad sex with male partners and that women often resorted to faking orgasms rather than voicing their concerns (Thomas, Stelzl, & Lafrance, 2017). Faking orgasm also occurred more often when women perceived partner infidelity (Kaighobadi, Shackelford, & Weekes-Shackelford, 2012) and when they felt love for their partner (Mialon, 2012), suggesting that women's priorities included "keeping their man" and ensuring their partner's satisfaction. Feminist psychologists have begun to ask larger social questions about whether women get the "fair deal" in stories about orgasm reciprocity (Braun, Gavey, & McPhillips, 2003) and whether orgasm has become a symbol of a (male) partner's "hard work" that must be validated by women's orgasms, real or fake (Frith, 2013).

Sociologist Paula England has convincingly argued that, while gender equity has made significant strides in the public realms (e.g., workplaces), women have achieved far less progress in the private realms (England, 2010). This may explain why, both historically and currently, women's sexuality is rife with stories about profound inequalities and deeply-felt power imbalances with men. Returning to the construction of women as commodities (Irigaray, 1985), these power imbalances appear vividly when women construct sexuality as a kind of labor or job. For example, many women regularly have sex when they do not want to (Katz & Tirone, 2009; Vannier & O'Sullivan, 2010) in order to please their partners or meet a partner's demands or needs (Cacchioni, 2015). Younger women, less educated women, poorer women, and women of color engaged more often in unsatisfying sex than did other (higher status) groups of women (Fahs & Swank, 2011), just as women's ideas about what they "deserved" differed greatly from what men's ideas about deservingness, with women emphasizing other-directedness more than men (McClelland, 2010; Nicolson & Burr, 2003). Married women often reported that men "needed" sex and that as women they had to overstate their sexual desire and have more sex than they wanted to in response to this (Elliott & Umberson, 2008). Further, women reported feeling distrust, anger, anxiety, and fear when talking to their partners about their sexual needs (Faulkner & Lannutti, 2010) and often agreed to unwanted sexual activities to please their partners, including threesomes, performing as bisexual at parties, denying the seriousness of their coercive experiences of sex, and agreeing to watch pornography at their partner's request (Fahs, 2011).

Given the findings in the literature about women's relationship to sexual satisfaction and sexual labor, the work in this chapter on women's sexual subjectivities raises many questions: What kinds of stories and scripts arise for women who live in a deeply misogynistic and patriarchal culture that is "dangerously crazy" about sex? What does it mean to make stories about sexuality when women's subjectivities are often governed by scripts that prioritize men's pleasures, needs, desires, and bodies over their own?

Method[1]

In this chapter, I utilized qualitative data from a sample of 20 adult women (mean age = 35.35, SD = 12.01) recruited in 2014 in a large metropolitan Southwestern U.S. city. Participants were recruited through local entertainment and arts listings distributed free to the community as well as the volunteers section of the local online section of Craigslist (for the benefits of using Craigslist to recruit participants see Worthen, 2014). The advertisements asked for women aged 18–59 to participate in an interview study about their sexual behaviors, practices, and attitudes. Participants were selected only for their gender, racial/ethnic background, sexual identity, and age; no other pre-screening questions were asked. I utilized a purposive sample to provide for greater demographic diversity in the sample: Sexual minority women and racial/ethnic minority women were intentionally oversampled, and a diverse range of ages was represented (35%, or seven aged 18–31; 40%, or eight aged 32–45; and 25%, or five people, aged 46–59). The sample included 60% (12) white women and 40% (8) women of color, including two African-American women, four Mexican-American women, and two Asian-American women. For self-reported sexual identity, the sample included 60% (12) heterosexual women, 20% (4) bisexual women, and 20% (4) lesbian women. All participants consented to having their interviews audiotaped and fully transcribed, and all received USD $20.00 compensation. Identifying data was removed, and each participant received a pseudonym to ensure anonymity. Participants reported a range of socioeconomic and educational backgrounds, employment histories, and parental and relationship statuses.

Participants were interviewed using a semi-structured interview protocol that lasted for approximately 1.5 to 2 hours, where they responded to 32 questions about their sexual histories, sexual practices, and feelings and attitudes about their sexuality and their bodies. This study and the specific interview protocol were both approved by the Institutional Review Board (local ethics review). All participants were interviewed by me in a room that ensured the privacy and confidentiality of responses. Questions related to this chapter emphasized women's experiences when engaging in boring or dull sex to please a partner, and engaging in sex that felt like labor or a "job." Women were specifically asked: "Have you ever had boring or dull sex to please a partner?" They were also asked, "Some women describe sex as a kind of job or a form of labor. What are your experiences with feeling like sex is a form of labor?" These questions were scripted, but served to open up other conversations and dialogue about related topics, as follow-up questions, clarifications, and probes were free-flowing and conversational. For this chapter only, women's sexual experiences with women were excluded. Only their sexual experiences with men were included.

Responses were analyzed qualitatively using a critical phenomenologically-oriented form of thematic analysis that draws from feminist theory and gender theory (Braun & Clarke, 2006). This type of analysis allowed for groupings of responses based on women's responses to the questions about their sexuality (e.g., sexual compliance). To conduct the analysis, I familiarized myself with the data by reading the transcripts thoroughly, and I then identified patterns for common interpretations posed by participants. In doing so, I reviewed lines, sentences, and paragraphs of the transcripts, looking for patterns in their ways of describing their sexual experiences (Braun & Clarke, 2006). I selected and generated themes through the process of identifying logical links and overlaps between participants. After creating these themes, I compared them to previous themes expressed by other participants in order to identify similarities, differences, and general patterns. I then refined and reworked the themes until saturation was complete.

Results

Part 1: pleasing a partner

Sixteen of the 20 women reported having boring or dull sex to please a partner, though two had only had those experiences with women and were excluded from the study. Fourteen women reported tedious or alienating sexual experiences with men, with four key themes noted in the transcripts: 1) feeling used by men, 2) sex as mundane and routine, 3) feelings of betraying themselves, 4) sexual compliance. As evident in the descriptions below, some participants' responses overlapped between themes in that one participant's responses could fit into multiple themes.

Theme 1: feeling used by men

Four women described feeling used sexually by men, particularly as their own experiences and subjectivities were largely ignored by male partners. Rachel (39, White, Bisexual) described having disappointing sex with a man who overvalued his own sexual skills and devalued her experience:

> He thought that he was the shit, and I was just like, "We're doing it missionary," and he was like, "Oh yeah!" He was a total douchebag, and I'm like, "This is *horrible*." I started in my mind thinking of different things that I could

be doing and felt that, "No, he's not worth it. I'm going to tell him to get off." He was kind of mad that he didn't get to orgasm—he didn't get to ejaculate—and I was like, "Yeah but you were having so much fun by your-self you forgot what I was here for."

Zari (43, African-American, Heterosexual) also had the experience of being used and coped with it by disappearing mentally during sex: "With my ex-husband, I had sex out of obligation to the person, you know what I mean? He wasn't paying attention and just used me, so I started blocking him out and pretending that he's somebody else."

As another example of feeling used, Yvonne (41, Latina, Heterosexual) described that she felt used during sex with her boyfriend and that this merged with feelings of sexual obligation:

> He asks and I'm not really in the mood, and I just say "Okay, here." I haven't been a good girlfriend in the past couple of weeks or whatever it's been. Kind of like, "Here you go," and he knows this. He'll be like, "Did I just totally use you?" and I'm like, "Yeah." It's kind of more of a chore.

Here the implications of men feeling entitled to sex and women often feeling that they *owe* sex to men (being a "good girlfriend") is quite vivid.

Theme 2: sex as mundane or routine

Three women also described sex mostly as mundane or routine and described it as something they do like any other banal household chore. In these narratives, the stories of women feeling sexually excited or having mutual pleasure are absent. For example, Emma (42, White, Heterosexual) described sex as mechan-ical and mundane: "Lots of times sex bores me. It's very boring. Missionary, done in five minutes, roll over, go to sleep." Martha (52, White, Heterosexual) likened sex to other unpleasant household chores: "I just put up with it. It's just boring, like another chore. You know, it's like loading the dishwasher or some-thing." As a final example, Trish (19, White, Lesbian) described a previous experience with men as routine and absent of any feeling: "It's when I didn't feel good or just didn't want to put in the effort or I'm tired. It's unsatisfying, maybe, kind of like, 'Okay, we did that.' It's just having sex to have sex."

Theme 3: feelings of betraying themselves

Four women described boring sex as a betrayal of their own needs and wants, with sex as a way of going against themselves in order to please men. Gail (46, White, Bisexual) described having sex without following her intuition:

Generally boring sex just means that I either didn't follow my instincts for what I wanted because either of time or I didn't feel that the other person would be open to me leading, or someone else didn't do more and I didn't follow up by saying, "Hey, I want something different." Sex is just very plain Jane and not very exciting.

Daphne (33, White, Heterosexual) described engaging in sex to please a partner rather than following her own needs: "Giving oral sex often feels like it's just for him and not for me, but again there's also that old man who wanted me to pee on him and I couldn't. I attempted to but I couldn't do it." Kathleen (49, White, Heterosexual) felt that she had to have regular boring sex to keep her man:

Lovemaking gets a little monotonous. But the fact that I really do adore him and he adores me, I don't want to scare him off again. It's like I've got him on a sort of track right now and I don't want to scare him off so I do things I really don't feel like doing.

Theme 4: sexual compliance

Five women described scenarios where they complied with sex they frankly did not want and often felt regret afterward. Gretchen (52, White, Heterosexual) talked about having sex that was not fun or appealing because she felt she had to:

They want sex and you're like, "Oh, this is not fun, but I'll go along with it." Like my ex-boyfriend came out and there was this expectation that we were gonna have sex. I felt like I owed him and then afterwards it's like, "This was not worth it."

Lila (36, White, Heterosexual) felt averse to having sex with an uncircumcised man but did it anyway:

He was uncircumcised, and I hated it but had sex anyway. I wasn't a very strong person at the time. I didn't really have any confidence or any will to say, "I'm not interested." I was just more embarrassed. I just felt so inadequate that I just went along.

Two women described having anal sex in an attempt to please their boyfriends even though they found it awkward, listless, and mostly pleasureless. Corinne (21, White, Bisexual) talked about having anal sex without feeling any interest in it:

The anal thing is like that. I tried because he wanted to, but I wasn't really interested. I used a strap-on with him anally, and at first I was like, "Uh, this is kinda weird," but I did it even though I wasn't into it. It was boring.

Naomi (18, White, Bisexual) described a similar experience where she responded to a request for anal sex but eventually found it dull: "When I first started playing anally with my committed boyfriend I was into it, but then I just did it to pleasure him. I'm like, 'Okay, if that's what you want.'" This sense of going along with men's sexual requests or demands and feeling less able to shape sexual experiences to fit women's own desires suggests deep power imbalances between men and women.

Part 2: sexual labor

In the previous theme, I have outlined how women imagined the metaphorical labor implications of sex as a job; that said, many women also talked more explicitly about using sex as a means to gain financial resources or escape possible violence. This meant that sex was seen as a more frankly transactional process in exchange for the performance of sexual acts. The question about whether women have experienced sex as a kind of job or a form of labor yielded a wide variety of responses that centered on three themes: 1) paid sex work experiences, 2) unpaid transactional or survival sex, 3) sex as an obligation. Fifteen women said that they had, in one way or another, engaged in sex that felt like a kind of job or a form of labor.

Theme 1: paid sex work

Six women disclosed that they had, at one point, taken money for sex in some capacity, though they did so in different ways and for many different reasons. Rachel (39, White, Bisexual) had some experience with paid dominatrix work and paid phone sex:

> I did a little pro-dom work for a short time, and I did it for pay. It was not penetrative sex. It was more role-play, fantasy, dominant-submission. Guys would specifically want to be playfully tied up, spanked, worship my feet, and that was about it. I never had any physical penetrative sex with any of them, and they paid me $200 an hour. I did phone sex during a long period of unemployment, and a friend of mine said, "Hey, will you help me?" and I was like, "Sure!" It was good money, but it was annoying because people would want to do the phone sex thing and they would try to get something for nothing. They thought they were keeping their monogamy promise because it was okay if they didn't pay for it. They thought it didn't count as cheating on their wives.

Notably, Rachel felt that unpaid transactional sex felt inauthentic, saying,

> It comes down to active consent. When two people meet at a bar, and I'm enjoying our conversation, maybe we've had two drinks, and I'm

feeling it and like, "Hey, do you want to go back to my place?" and you say yes, I never bought you a drink or gifts. You are coming because you want to, not because I swooned you with my financial resources. That's more meaningful and honest than the people who do three dates before sex. That's what I find repulsive, like a commodity exchange.

Several other women had engaged in various sexual things for money as well. Gretchen (52, White, Heterosexual) said that she was paid to give handjobs to "ordinary" men:

The guy wanted me to masturbate him while I smoked, and it was like 50 bucks or something. That was exciting to do. There was the fear element because it's like meeting in cars, in the back of motel parking lots and stuff. But it was also surprising how completely normal these guys are. Like these are the things that gets these guys off!

Corinne (21, White, Bisexual) felt eager to engage in paid sex work, seeing it as liberating:

I kind of feel like, "Why not?" As long as it's consensual, I'm gonna do it. Why not get paid for it? Really, you're gonna give me $1,200 to go to dinner with you and sleep with you? You're pretty attractive, and you could find some girl over there, but sure, I'll take it! That's great. $1,200 was the minimum. It was usually between $1,500 and $1,800 a night. I would only work three or four nights a month and was doing good. I had my own apartment, my own car, eating out, going out, buying whatever I wanted. I was making about $5,000 a month, and my rent was only like 700 bucks and my car payment was like 400 bucks. I felt *smart* doing it. I can work four nights and make enough to support myself. I could be busting my ass at a minimum-wage job for 40 hours a week to pay rent and drive and shitty car and struggle? That sucks.

Three other women also took money from acquaintances or strangers for sexual things in order to survive and pay their bills. Felicity (20, White, Heterosexual) described her experiences on a "sugar daddy" website as something she was fine with as long as she could survive on the money:

I have taken money for providing companionship. I have done some of it naked, and I will continue to do it. It doesn't feel wrong to me. I am on the sugar daddy website as a broke college student, and I do need money desperately. If someone wants to have a good conversation about sex, great that's cool; I can do that. My boyfriend is chill with it, but it might be affecting him and our physical relationship. I tell him that the other guys don't count. I'm just doing that for money.

It's just pretend. I get about 50 bucks each time because I'm only talking to them naked rather than putting out.

Similarly, Zari (43, African-American, Heterosexual) worked for a time as a stripper and described the experience as helping her to "market" herself more effectively:

I danced in a topless club. I like to dance and I got to wear different costumes, and I had a whole other personality. It was like acting in a way. I did it for three and a half years off and on, during my summer breaks and stuff for school. It was a lot of fun. It taught me a lot, how to market myself, so that's one thing I can say about that job. You actually make all your money off of your personality, not how you dance or how you look. People pay for your personality, so I had to talk to everybody and learn how to talk to anybody.

Naomi (18, White, Bisexual) said that she worked as a "cam girl" for a few months right after she turned 18, but that she stopped because it soured her perceptions of men:

I had to masturbate to get paid. I got paid by tokens and tips, so every paycheck I got about $600.00. I didn't do it for very long. I just got creeped out by it, because it was like all of these old men watching me masturbate and they only liked me because I was so young. At first, it was really fun and empowering, but then it just made me not like men. I had to stop. They grossed me out.

Theme 2: unpaid transactional or survival sex

Five women talked about having transactional or survival sex that was unpaid but felt like a means to an end. Gail (46, White, Bisexual) felt that sex was required to keep her man happy and to make sure he did not cheat on her:

Society does place that burden on us, and I think we also place it on ourselves, especially when you are in a committed relationship. You have that thing—"I've got to keep my partner satisfied," and it is true that if two partners aren't satisfying each other, it's definitely going to increase the odds that someone's going to look for sex elsewhere. We have to find out what he's missing and give it to him.

Martha (52, White, Heterosexual) also said that she had to keep having sex in order to keep herself and her children financially secure:

I know women in my mom's generation, that's what you had to do when you get married. Do laundry, vacuum the floor, have sex. It was a chore for that generation. I've felt like that too, like I had to have sex. I was so concerned about the kids and stuff. It was like something I had to do at this point, not really a chore, but there was no emotion there. I did it because he wanted it and a lot of times I just dealt with it. I wanted him to be happy and go to work. It wasn't that bad. It was just so impersonal.

Gretchen (52, White, Heterosexual) also described transactional sex as a normal and intuitive means to get things she wants from a man:

There are times I have sex when I don't necessarily want to just like I go to work and don't necessarily want to. The payoff was a better relationship, more intimacy, more security. Once I was having sex with a guy and he said, "What do you want? I'll give you anything," and I didn't ever think to say, "A new BMW might be nice!" In all seriousness, women used to be taught that their only skill is their sex and sexuality is the vagina, and that's in high demand. If you're married and you have sex to keep your husband and get a fur coat, everyone is better off. If you want it and they want it, they want to pay you for it. Instead of being a volunteer, you're doing it for real.

Veronica (49, African-American, Heterosexual) also normalized transactional sex:

Sometimes sex isn't for you, it's for him. You do it because you know that's what he wants and if you don't do it, you may lose him. And if you lose him, there goes your financial security. I know that sex is sometimes something you just gotta get through.

These descriptions of accepting survival sex as a reality of gender and power imbalances suggest a deep internalization of the transactional relationship between men and women.

Theme 3: sex as an obligation

Seven women framed sex as an obligation and said that it often felt like labor because of this. Emma (42, White, Heterosexual) described having sex when she was tired in order to please her boyfriend:

It used to feel like a job, especially when I'd get home and I was tired because I knew it would be a fight. "You don't love me anymore! You don't want to have sex!" he'd say. I enjoy sex very much, but yeah, it did become labor.

Antonia (25, Latina, Lesbian) said that she has heard that sex is a job from lots of her female friends:

> When a girl has sex with a guy, from what I hear, guys don't know how to do it right and are just in it for themselves. They don't care whether women have an orgasm or not, or what she gets out of it. It's very much a chore for them.

Lila (36, White, Heterosexual) echoed this experience, saying that she sometimes had sex because it felt compulsory: "It's definitely something that feels required sometimes, like there are times I'm with somebody long enough and we're close, and I just do it because it's been a while. I just give in."

Other women more explicitly admitted to feeling like sex was owed to men as a kind of labor, suggesting that some women perceived that this was a requirement of being in a long-term committed relationship. Daphne (33, White, Heterosexual) felt like she had to fake orgasms in response to men's labor:

> There's a lot of work involved if the individual's not getting off. It may feel cumbersome. That's where I'd fake an orgasm, like come on, get over it. I definitely believe that I've got this idea that I can't leave him feeling unfulfilled if he doesn't get off.

Yvonne (41, Latina, Heterosexual) described having obligatory sex and that her boyfriend picked up on it:

> If I feel like that then something needs to change in the relationship. I've felt like, "Oh god, it's a chore," but if that continues then I think something's wrong and I'll try to stop doing it … My boyfriend and I would joke about it 'cause he was letting me borrow money for something and we joked about me having sex with him in exchange for the money. He knew I was doing it as a chore even though we were only joking about the money.

Discussion and conclusion

These rather unflattering portraits of women having sex with men—from the boring and dull sex to sex that functions as transactional or as a form of overt labor—reveals much about the more difficult, contradictory, and power-imbalanced aspects of sexuality today. And, while these stories show some of the intricate ways that women talk about, think about, and narrate their sexual experiences, they also show much about men themselves. We hear about men "needing" sex and, more disturbingly, feeling entitled to women's sexual labor. While this may seem like a typical and mundane narrative of American sexual life—that men have more testosterone and need sex, or that women feel they should provide sex to men—this rhetoric has dangerous implications for women's well-being. Recently, a man named Alek Minassian in Toronto killed ten people by driving a van through a crowd of people; in his Facebook post just prior to this event, he identified himself as a leader of the "incel rebellion" (that is, "involuntary celibate") and derided women for denying him sex. The Reddit group for "incels" advocated violence against women as well as justifying and encouraging rape (Chavez, 2018). Stories of women "owing" sex to men thus can have deadly consequences and should be treated with the utmost seriousness, both individually and culturally.

The portrayal of men as going forward with sexual encounters that involve tired, disengaged, disappointed, and bored women as sexual partners suggests a range of possibilities about contemporary sexual life that are deeply problematic. Are men aware of women's disinterest and simply ignoring it? Does men's feeling of sexual entitlement overshadow women's feelings of displeasure? Is the push to have more and more and more sex, no matter its quality, leaving people with the sense feeling sexually "normal" matters more than mutuality or happiness? Are people unable to communicate about sexuality or support each other's differing levels of interest and desire? These narratives raise many questions not only about "bad sex"—and arguably, many of these narratives are not even extraordinarily bad—but also how sex has been taken up as yet another compulsory aspect of domestic life. The consistent links women drew between sex and obligation (e.g., sex is like doing the dishes, sex is yet another thing on a to-do list) suggests that transactional and obligatory sex is not an outlier but a relatively *mainstream* experience.

It is crucial that we contemplate this reality: *women have a lot of sex with men that they do not want to have.* What does this mean on a deeper level? Catharine MacKinnon warned us that men create the sexual reality they want at the expense of listening to and valuing women's sexual subjectivities. Luce Irigaray argued that women have become sexual commodities, traded on a sexual marketplace. Those studying sexual scripting theory have argued that the scripts about sexuality have become increasingly narrow and more conventional for heterosexual scripts—and that things like pornography and sexual education often reinforce narratives of women's sexual powerlessness and men's sexual power. Historian Michel Foucault warned that,

> There is no binary division to be made between what one says and what one does not say; we must try to determine the different ways of not saying such things, how those who can and those who cannot speak of them are distributed, which type of discourse is authorized, or which form of discretion is required in either case. There is not one but many silences, and they are an integral part of the strategies that underlie and permeate discourses.
>
> *(Foucault, 1978, p. 27)*

There is the temptation, I think, to imagine that women have arrived at a place of sexual empowerment in this modern age, that they have garnered momentum from the sexual revolution and the women's movement and have sprouted selves that have unlimited sexual choices and newfound sexual freedoms. In this chapter, I suggest that quite a different story has emerged, that we have not progressed terribly far from the sexual realities of our grandmothers and great-grandmothers' generations. In many ways, this should not surprise us. Women have made advancements in economic and political opportunities, but these have been inconsistent, especially for poorer and working-class women and women of color (Browne, 2000). Women have entered the workforce in greater numbers and have taken on more new obligations, but this has also created the economic imperative for women to *do more and more* (Hochschild, 2012). At the very least, this leaves less time for sex and creates more obligatory burdens on women's time and energies. (This also applies to men, who are, like women, working more hours and have taken on more responsibilities than ever before.) With this framework in mind, sex as *labor*, sex as *dull*, sex as *boring*, sex as a *job* all make more sense. (And, in Chapter 10, I go into more detail on how capitalism is slowly and viciously destroying people's sex lives.)

This returns us to the question posed at the beginning of this chapter: What do women's sexual narratives tell us about *men and masculinity*? Taken collectively, women's descriptions of obligatory, boring, dull, labor-filled sex suggest that, *through women's eyes*, contemporary masculinity can be characterized by a willful blindness to the experiences of women. In other words, men do not seem to notice, care, or respond to the many signals of distress and obligation that women feel during sex. In women's eyes, men play many roles when sex becomes obligatory, and none of these are very flattering. Men pay women for sex and seem to find it acceptable to control women's sexuality with money. Men demand (or imply the demand) for sex—and seem oblivious to women's displeasure at this. Men joke about using women, or even frankly use them, for their sexual needs. These portrayals only present part of the picture, but they still suggest a robust, old-fashioned story about sexuality: men as takers, women as givers; men as owed, women as owing; men as buyers, women as sellers; men as needing, women as serving. Traces of these painful dichotomies permeate the stories in this chapter and serve as a sobering reminder of the limits of sexual empowerment rhetoric. While women's sexual lives are certainly more complicated than this—and they can experience joy, enthusiasm, and pleasure from sex—too often the more painful aspects of sexuality are obscured by sexual empowerment rhetoric.

Ultimately, the data in this chapter suggests some important new directions for critical masculinity studies and for feminist sex research more broadly. In the same way that critical whiteness studies takes black subjectivities seriously (Nayak, 2007), a sophisticated understanding of men and sexuality may require a close and detailed examination of how women experience sex with men. After all, women have much to say about how they perceive men's sexual needs, wants, and practices; listening to women yields new and interesting information about the relationship between sexuality and power (among other things). Further, integrating critical sexuality studies—particularly material that critically examines heterosex—into existing research is crucial (Fahs & McClelland, 2016), as it forces serious consideration of heterosexuality and heteronormativity and better integrates voices from the margins.

These results stand at a fascinating intersection between shocking and mundane, between extraordinary and ordinary versions of sexuality. We see a hefty number of women engaging in paid sex work while also hearing about how many women feel obligated to have unwanted sex (something mundane and normalized). Women described dead ends ("I just gave in") and crafty and inventive modes of claiming agency when faced with other disempowering circumstances. Most importantly, these stories push consideration of the material, economic, and gendered conditions that exist when sex moves away from mutuality, pleasure, and joy, and instead into the more depressing aspects of modern American life: fatigue, boredom, resentment, resignation, and (over)working. Whether we can recover sex from these places of inequality—ones that reinforce rather than subvert gendered inequalities—is a question with profound implications for our collective sexual future.

Note

1 This study's methods also apply to Chapter 3 and draw from the same 2014 sample. Chapter 2 uses similar methods but draws from a different sample collected three years earlier in 2011. I note in those future chapters only the areas of difference (e.g., exact wording of questions).

References

Bancroft, J., Loftus, J., & Long, J. S. (2003). Distress about sex: A national survey of women in heterosexual relationships. *Archives of Sexual Behavior, 32*, 193–208.

Barrientos, J. E., & Páez, D. (2006). Psychosocial variables of sexual satisfaction in Chile. *Journal of Sex & Marital Therapy, 32*(5), 351–368.

Beauboeuf-Lafontant, T. (2007). You have to show strength: An exploration of gender, race, and depression. *Gender & Society, 21*(1), 28–51.

Bordo, S. (1997). Anorexia nervosa: Psychopathology and the crystallization of culture. In C. Counihan, & P. Van Esterik (Eds.), *Food and culture: A reader* (pp. 226–250). Florence, KY: Psychology Press.

Braun, V., & Clarke, V. (2006). Using thematic analysis in psychology. *Qualitative Research in Psychology, 3*(2), 77–101.

Braun, V., Gavey, N., & McPhillips, K. (2003). The "fair deal"? Unpacking accounts of reciprocity in heterosex. *Sexualities, 6*(2), 237–261.

Browne, I. (Ed.). (2000). *Latinas and African American women at work: Race, gender, and economic inequality*. New York: Russell Sage Foundation.

Cacchioni, T. (2015). *Big Pharma, women, and the labour of love*. Toronto: University of Toronto Press.

Chavez, N. (2018). Toronto van attack suspect's Facebook post linked to anti-women ideology. *CNN*. www.cnn.com/2018/04/25/americas/toronto-van-attack/index.html.

Darling, C. A., & Davidson, J. K. (1986). Enhancing relationships: Understanding the feminine mystique of pretending orgasm. *Journal of Sex & Marital Therapy, 12*(3), 182–196.

Diamond, L. M., & Lucas, S. (2004). Sexual-minority and heterosexual youths' peer relationships: Experiences, expectations, and implications for well-being. *Journal of Research on Adolescence, 14*(3), 313–340.

Elliott, S., & Umberson, D. (2008). The performance of desire: Gender and sexual negoti-ation in long-term marriages. *Journal of Marriage and Family, 70*(2), 391–406.

England, P. (2010). The gender revolution: Uneven and stalled. *Gender & Society, 24*(2), 149–166.

Fahs, B. (2011). *Performing sex: The making and unmaking of women's erotic lives*. Albany, NY: State University of New York Press.

Fahs, B. (2014). Coming to power: Women's fake orgasms and best orgasm experiences illuminate the failures of (hetero) sex and the pleasures of connection. *Culture, Health & Sexuality, 16*(8), 974–988.

Fahs, B., & McClelland, S. I. (2016). When sex and power collide: An argument for critical sexuality studies. *Journal of Sex Research, 53*(4–5), 392–416.

Fahs, B., & Swank, E. (2011). Social identities as predictors of women's sexual satisfaction and sexual activity. *Archives of Sexual Behavior, 40*(5), 903–914.

Faulkner, S. L., & Lannutti, P. J. (2010). Examining the content and outcomes of young adults' satisfying and unsatisfying conversations about sex. *Qualitative Health Research, 20* (3), 375–385.

Foucault, M. (1978). *The history of sexuality* (Vol. 1). Trans: Robert Hurley. New York: Pantheon.

Frith, H. (2013). Labouring on orgasms: Embodiment, efficiency, entitlement and obliga-tions in heterosex. *Culture, Health & Sexuality, 15*(4), 494–510.

Gagnon, J. H., & Simon, W. (1973). *Sexual conduct: The social sources of human sexuality*. Chi-cago, IL: Aldine Publishing.

Hochschild, A. (2012). *The second shift: Working families and the revolution at home*. New York: Penguin.

Irigaray, L. (1985). *This sex which is not one*. Ithaca, NY: Cornell University Press.

Kaighobadi, F., Shackelford, T. K., & Weekes-Shackelford, V. A. (2012). Do women pre-tend orgasm to retain a mate? *Archives of Sexual Behavior, 41*(5), 1121–1125.

Katz, J., & Tirone, V. (2009). Women's sexual compliance with male dating partners: Asso-ciations with investment in ideal womanhood and romantic well-being. *Sex Roles, 60* (5–6), 347–356.

Knox, D., Zusman, M., & McNeely, A. (2008). University student beliefs about sex: Men vs. women. *College Student Journal, 42*(1), 181–185.

MacKinnon, C. A. (1987). Desire and power. In C. A. MacKinnon (Ed.), *Feminism unmodi-fied: Discourses on life and law* (pp. 48–62). Cambridge, MA: Harvard University Press.

Mbembe, A. (2001). *On the postcolony*. Berkeley, CA: University of California Press.

McClelland, S. I. (2010). Intimate justice: A critical analysis of sexual satisfaction. *Social and Personality Psychology Compass, 4*(9), 663–680.

McClelland, S. I. (2014). "What do you mean when you say that you're sexually satisfied?" A mixed methods study. *Feminism & Psychology, 24*(1), 74–96.

Meston, C., & Trapnell, P. (2005). Development and validation of a five-factor sexual satis-faction and distress scale for women: The Sexual Satisfaction Scale for Women (SSS-W). *The Journal of Sexual Medicine, 2*(1), 66–81.

Mialon, H. M. (2012). The economics of faking ecstasy. *Economic Inquiry, 50*(1), 277–285.

Muehlenhard, C. L., & Shippee, S. K. (2010). Men's and women's reports of pretending orgasm. *Journal of Sex Research, 47*(6), 552–567.

Nayak, A. (2007). Critical whiteness studies. *Sociology Compass, 1*(2), 737–755.

Nicolson, P., & Burr, J. (2003). What is "normal" about women's (hetero)sexual desire and orgasm? A report of an in-depth interview study. *Social Science & Medicine, 57* (9), 1735–1745.

Opperman, E., Braun, V., Clarke, V., & Rogers, C. (2013). "It feels so good it almost hurts": Young adults' experiences of orgasm and sexual pleasure. *Journal of Sex Research*, *51*(5), 503–515.

Pinney, E. M., Gerrard, M., & Denney, N. W. (1987). The Pinney Sexual Satisfaction inventory. *Journal of Sex Research*, *23*(2), 233–251.

Plante, R. F. (2007). In search of sexual subjectivities: Exploring the sociological construction of sexual selves. In M. S. Kimmel (Ed.), *The sexual self: The construction of sexual scripts* (pp. 31–48). Nashville, TN: Vanderbilt University Press.

Plante, R. F. (2014). *Sexualities in context: A social perspective*. New York: Routledge.

Sanchez, D. T., Kiefer, A., & Ybarra, O. (2006). Sexual submissiveness in women: Costs for sexual autonomy and arousal. *Personality and Social Psychology Bulletin, 32* (4), 512–524.

Sprecher, S. (2002). Sexual satisfaction in premarital relationships: Associations with satisfaction, love, commitment, and stability. *Journal of Sex Research*, *39*(3), 190–196.

Štulhofer, A., Buško, V., & Brouillard, P. (2010). Development and bicultural validation of the new sexual satisfaction scale. *Journal of Sex Research*, *47*(4), 257–268.

Ter Kuile, M. M., van Lankwd, J. J., Kalkhown, P., & Egmond, M. V. (1999). The Golombok Rust Inventory of Sexual Satisfaction (GRISS): Psychometric properties within a Dutch population. *Journal of Sex & Marital Therapy*, *25*(1), 59–71.

Thomas, E. J., Stelzl, M., & Lafrance, M. N. (2017). Faking to finish: Women's accounts of feigning sexual pleasure to end unwanted sex. *Sexualities*, *20*(3), 281–301.

Tiefer, L. (2004). *Sex is not a natural act & other essays*. Boulder, CO: Westview Press.

Tolman, D. (2002). *Dilemmas of desire: Teenage girls talk about sex*. Cambridge, MA: Harvard University Press.

Vannier, S. A., & O'Sullivan, L. F. (2010). Sex without desire: Characteristics of occasions of sexual compliance in young adults' committed relationships. *Journal of Sex Research*, *47*(5), 429–439.

Wiederman, M. W. (1997). Pretending orgasm during sexual intercourse: Correlates in a sample of young adult women. *Journal of Sex & Marital Therapy*, *23*(2), 131–139.

Worthen, M. G. (2014). An invitation to use craigslist ads to recruit respondents from stigmatized groups for qualitative interviews. *Qualitative Research*, *14*(3), 371–383.

2
THE OTHER THIRD SHIFT?

Women's emotion work in their sexual relationships

Feminist psychologists and sociologists have both devoted much attention to the problem of gender inequalities. While gender equity has made significant strides in public realms (e.g., women having access to education and traditionally male jobs), women have achieved far less progress in the private realms (England, 2010). Famed sociologist Arlie Hochschild (1989) argued in her classic, *The second shift*, that women in the workforce faced a burden not only of their "first shift," that is, working an eight-hour day outside of the home, but also the "second shift": eight hours of domestic labor once they got home. Further, persistent gender essentialism, or the belief in men and women as fundamentally different, has expanded gender inequities in the home and in the workplace (England, 2010), making women's "shifts" all the more difficult to bear. In particular, expectations that women continue to provide most of the domestic and child-rearing labor alongside the emotional labor in the household have left women with a paradoxical reality in their sexual lives.

I propose this emotion work required during women's sexual lives is an additional "third shift," building on the previously conceptualized third shift that requires women to spend hours weighing, balancing, and reconciling their choices and decisions in light of their first two shifts (Bolton, 2000; Hochschild, 1997). That is, while women apparently have more sexual freedoms than previous generations (Bell, 2013; Fahs, 2011a), they still perceive the need to engage in (demanding and taxing) emotion work with their intimate partners, including dating partners, cohabitation partners, and spouses (Daniels, 1987; Erickson, 2005; Hochschild, 1983). That emotion work is obligatory, without discretion, and in some ways standardized in order to support their romantic relationship's demands and to survive the various power imbalances present in these relationships.

Hochschild defined "emotional labor" as labor that "requires one to induce or suppress feeling in order to sustain the outward countenance that produces the proper state of mind in others" (1983, p. 7), and argued that women must manage and suppress their emotions and direct them according to corporate and workplace expectations (Hochschild, 1983, 2012). Much of this labor is necessary because women internalize social roles that demand friendliness, deference, and positive outlooks that affirm, enhance, and celebrate the well-being of others. Surface acting—where women behave in friendly and "nice" ways even if they feel bored, angry, or frustrated—differs from deep acting; in the latter, women go beyond surface performance and try to convince themselves that they really *are* feeling the emotions required of them (Hochschild, 1983).

Regarding women's intimate lives, there is less research on this performative element, though Sinikka Elliott and Debra Umberson (2008) have noted that emotional labor, deep acting, and "feeling rules" appeared most intensely during sexual relationships for married women. We can also glean information from sexuality research that does not overtly study emotional labor. For example, we know many gendered scripts of sexuality demand that women direct attention away from their own needs and instead prioritize their partner's needs, resulting in a variety of problematic symptoms of gender inequality such as faking orgasm (Fahs, 2011a; Muehlenhard & Shippee, 2010; Wiederman, 1997); sexual compliance (Impett & Peplau, 2003; Kaestle, 2009; O'Sullivan & Allgeier, 1998); sexual extortion and violence (DeMaris, 1997); tolerating sexual pain (Elmerstig, Wijma, & Berterö, 2008; Elmerstig, Wijma, & Swahnberg, 2013); and the prioritization of their partner's pleasure over their own (McClelland, 2011; Nicholson & Burr, 2003). Ultimately, when women broke such passive stances, whether through adopting feminist sexual scripts or expecting more personal satisfaction, this ultimately led to better outcomes interpersonally, sexually, and socially (Bay-Cheng & Zucker, 2007; McClelland, 2010, 2011; Schick, Zucker, & Bay-Cheng, 2008; Yoder, Perry, & Saal, 2007).

Using the sociological literature on emotional labor and emotion work as a framework, in this chapter I examine the contexts where emotional/sexual labor appeared in their sexual lives. Despite the diversity of women's sexual identities, I most closely examined women's experiences of emotional/sexual work with *men* and in the context of longer-term romantic relationships rather than "hookups" or one-night stands. In short, I examined the social contexts surrounding women's accounts of sex that demanded emotion work and why they nevertheless endured this sex for the sake of their relationships.

Literature review

The concept of emotional labor has appeared in both sociological and psychological literature, with attention directed primarily to emotional labor in the domestic sphere (Daniels, 1987; Erickson, 2005; Hochschild, 1989); sex work (Sanders, 2005); the transfer of racial and classed scripts to children (Froyum, 2010); and jobs that require physical pampering and emotional caretaking (Brotheridge & Grandey, 2002), often exacting a great toll on women's physical and emotional well-being (Judge, Woolf, & Hurst, 2009; Pugliesi, 1999). Within marriages, this emotion work may appear as offering encouragement and affirmation, showing empathy, demonstrating affection, or putting the partner's needs above one's own needs (Erickson, 2005; Hochschild, 1983).

In the domestic sphere, women's emotional labor (most often called "emotion work") often applies to caring for their partner and children's emotional needs such as comforting them when distressed, caring for them while sick, and managing the emotional needs of the household (Erickson, 2005; Hochschild, 1983). Married women overwhelmingly engage in more domestic labor than their husbands, often because this divide fits into their husbands' notions of the gendered self (Twiggs, McQuillan, & Ferree, 1999). This gender gap also influenced how married couples felt about each other (Voydanoff & Donnelly, 1999), as wives reported less marital satisfaction when they perceived a more unequal division of gendered labor (Piña & Bengtson, 1993).

Most often, sociologists have pointed out the deleterious effects of emotional labor on working people, particularly those in jobs that demand emotional performance or that require emotional caretaking such as service workers, teachers, medical workers, beauticians, psychologists, and flight attendants (Hochschild, 1983; Wharton, 1999); for example, flight attendants must engage in fake smiles and cheerfulness, while teachers must soothe anxious parents and students. Emotional labor has been linked to job dissatisfaction, burnout, high turnover, decreased work performance, low productivity, and emotional exhaustion (Morris & Feldman, 1996; Wharton, 1999). In particular, the denial of self-needs while being other-focused increased job stress, decreased job satisfaction, and increased personal distress (Pugliesi, 1999). Similarly, "surface acting"—that is, the need to explicitly perform emotional labor to another person or group—resulted in emotional exhaustion and decreased job satisfaction, even for extroverts (though extroverts fared better than introverts) (Judge, Woolf, & Hurst, 2009). Notably, even for jobs with supposedly high job satisfaction, including nonprofit work and academia, emotional labor taxed workers via expectations that they suppress disappointment, tolerate low pay and unreasonable demands for productivity, and engage in caretaking of the populations they served (e.g., students reporting sexual trauma, sexist colleagues, et al.) (Eschenfelder, 2012; Gill, 2009).

In this chapter, however, I directed attention to women's emotion work *within their sexual lives*, as they managed the dual demands of maintaining their identities as daughters of post-second-wave "sexual liberation" while also supporting their partners' emotional needs. While this topic has mostly been conceptualized in the abstract and not by looking at numerous aspects of sexuality (as I do in this chapter), some research has addressed the connection between emotion work and sexuality. Elliott and Umberson (2008) addressed married couples' sexual labor and found that married women worked to perform more desirously than they truly felt. Further, the researchers found that many husbands expected their wives to perform desire, whether in the form of acting more interested in sex or having more sex.

Managing feelings during sex

The relationship between the self and other, between women and their partners, was felt not only in the context of orgasm—where meaning-making often revolves around orgasm as the ultimate goal of sex and/or something that must be performed and, for the partner, achieved (Fahs, 2011a; Opperman, Braun, Clarke, & Rogers, 2014)—but also as women managed their own and their partners' feelings during sex. Women's ability to both express their sexual needs and manage their partners' feelings frequently led to sexual ambivalence. Women often felt distrust, anger, and fear about talking to their partners about their sexual needs (Faulkner & Lannutti, 2010), all while trying to ensure that their partners enjoyed sex and felt comfortable and loved (Fahs, 2011a). Elliott and Umberson (2008) described this as "emotion work" within marriages around the performance of sexual desire, while my previous work (2011a) articulated that women perform emotion work around a variety of sexual events including not labeling coercion as rape, performing as satisfied, and engaging in "performative bisexuality."

The kinds of emotion work women performed during (hetero)sex ranged from engaging in (unwanted) sex in exchange for their male partners doing the housework to women expressing a sexual desire to their partners even when they would rather not have sex (Elliott & Umberson, 2008). Particularly given the strong imperative for orgasmic reciprocity during sex (Jagose, 2013), many women across a range of backgrounds felt obligated to both have an orgasm and to provide their partners with pleasure (Braun, Gavey, & McPhillips, 2003; Fahs, 2011a, 2014). Further, women who valued gender conformity often based their sexual satisfaction on their partners' approval, leading to lower sexual autonomy (Sanchez, Crocker, & Boike, 2005).

Women also engaged in emotion work when managing their bodies and bodily fluids during sex, in part because women's bodies are often labeled as leaky, troublesome, messy, disgusting, and difficult to manage. For example, women managed their partner's perceptions of menstrual blood as "gross," felt they must clean up after having menstrual sex, and emphasized their partner's feelings about menstrual sex, often at the expense of their own pleasure (Fahs, 2011b). This labor emphasized how women manage others' perceptions of their body alongside their own perceptions of themselves as "gross." Another study on menstrual sex found that one-third of women said that they would *never* engage in it, often because it threatened their partners, though women in relationships more often engaged in menstrual sex than those who were not (Allen & Goldberg, 2009).

Interestingly, women's need to manage their partner's feelings during sex may also extend into their empathic experiences with pornography viewing. One study found that women's strongly ambivalent feeling about watching pornography reflected their perception of women's emotional labor in pornographic production. Concern for, and disgust about, the female actor's need to perform their enjoyment—symbolized by excessive moaning or "fake" orgasms—lessened women's desire to watch the pornographic films (Parvez, 2006). Further, those with feminist values reported far less pornography viewing than those without feminist values (Burnham, 2013). In addition, Croatian men who watched porn-ography reported lower sexual satisfaction and suppression of intimacy (Štulho-fer, Buško, & Landripet, 2010), while women who watched pornography designed with male-centered sexual scripts felt less responsive and aroused com-pared to female-centered scripts (Mosher & MacIan, 1994), raising questions about identification, empathy, and enjoyment of pornography. Ultimately, women's perceptions of emotional labor and identification with other women's emotional labor in pornography shows how such labor permeates multiple spheres outside of intimate relationship dynamics.

Sexual (dis)satisfaction

While people often tout the goal of sexual reciprocity (that is, the goal of mutual orgasm and mutual pleasure during sex) in their sexual relationships, recent feminist work has started to question sexual reciprocity in light of entitle-ments (male) and obligations (female) patterned along gender lines (Braun, Gavey, & McPhillips, 2003). Many women engaged in sex despite not feeling satisfied emotionally or physically, particularly for younger, less educated, and poorer women as well as women of color, raising questions about the relation-ship between social justice and social identities (Fahs & Swank, 2011). Several studies have shown that women, particularly younger women, prioritized the sexual pleasure of their partners over their own (McClelland, 2011; Nicholson & Burr, 2003), indicating that their feelings of "deserving" and entitlement to orgasm and sexual pleasure often received less priority than other-directed sexual behaviors (McClelland, 2010).

Thea Cacchioni (2007) has theorized that women often engage in "relational sex work," that is, the unacknowledged effort and continuing monitoring women devote to managing theirs and their partners' desires and activities, which may influence their definitions of themselves as sexually functional, powerful, or having agency. What women *expected* to feel often differed from what men *expected* to feel from sex, something no doubt fed by interpersonal scripts and cultural constructions about sexual satisfaction (Armstrong, England, & Fogarty, 2012; McClelland, 2010; Ott et al., 2006).

As a way to describe engagement in sexual activity despite *not* wanting it, studies of sexual compliance have also revealed deep-seated gender inequalities that occurred within coupled sexuality. A review essay on sexual compliance found that women engaged in unwanted sex to avoid sexual violence, maintain relationships, and "sacrifice" for their male partners (Impett & Peplau, 2003). While one study of over 4,000 young women found that 8% engaged in unwanted sex at their partner's insistence (12% of whom repeatedly engaged in sex acts they did not enjoy) (Kaestle, 2009), another study of 80 college women found that 38% of women engaged in unwanted sex with their partners (O'Sullivan & Allgeier, 1998), most often to satisfy their partner's needs, meet their perceived obligations to their partner, promote intimacy and love, and avoid relationship tension (Kaestle, 2009; O'Sullivan & Allgeier, 1998) and violence (DeMaris, 1997). Further, certain types of sexual behavior, particularly anal sex, occurred more often in physically violent relationships for young women (Hess et al., 2013), suggesting that sexual compliance may also be linked to sexual extortion, emotional abuse, and physical violence as well as engagement in painful or more high-risk sexual behaviors (DeMaris, 1997; Impett & Peplau, 2003).

Studies on sexual pain also reveal notable links between gender and power, as women reported tolerating sexual pain in order to please their partners (Dewitte, Van Lankveld, & Crombez, 2010; Elmerstig, Wijma, & Berterö, 2008; Elmerstig, Wijma, & Swahnberg, 2013). One study of 16 young Swedish women found that they associated sex with resignation, sacrifice, and feeling guilt, leading them to construct the "ideal sexual woman" as one who willingly had sexual intercourse, was perceptive of their partner's needs, and could satisfy their partner; further, having penile-vaginal intercourse made women feel "normal" regardless of pain or discomfort (Elmerstig, Wijma, & Berterö, 2008). Another study of Swedish teenagers found that one-third reported experiencing pain during intercourse and a full 47% continued to have vaginal intercourse despite feeling pain, most often because they did not want to spoil sex or hurt their partner's feelings (Elmerstig, Wijma, & Swahnberg, 2013).

In contrast, some studies have looked at "sexual agency," finding that women who engaged in assertiveness, refusal of unwanted sex acts, proactive engagement in what they want, and interrogative practices tend to feel more agentic during sex (Maxwell, 2012). A handful of studies have found links between feminist attitudes and sexual satisfaction as well as the ability to assert agency, challenge double standards, and feel sexual motivation, while nonfeminist attitudes predicted endorsement of traditional gender roles around sexuality, less assertiveness about condom use, and less initiation of sex (Bay-Cheng & Zucker, 2007; Schick, Zucker, & Bay-Cheng, 2008; Yoder, Perry, & Saal, 2007).

Given the notable lack of research that integrates seemingly disparate aspects of women's experiences of emotion work in their sexual relationships, and the ways that both psychological and sociological research has largely ignored the *emotional narratives* present in discourses of sexuality, I ask several questions to guide this chapter: First, in what ways do women's narratives about sexual (dis) satisfaction, orgasm, and pleasure contain stories about the performance of emotion work? What does "emotion work" in the context of sex look like, and how does it connect to patterns about gender and power? How do women manage their own, and others', emotional experiences of sex, and what toll, if any, does this take on women? Finally, how does emotion work around "bad sex" (variously defined) appear for women engaging in sex with men, and how do these descriptions map onto issues of sexual entitlement and reciprocity (Braun, Gavey, & McPhillips, 2003)?

Method[1]

Women were asked one primary question about sexual satisfaction—"There are many different definitions and motivations for sex. What do you consider to be satisfying sex?"—along with several follow-up probing questions about motivations for sex and sexual satisfaction. Women were also asked a question about faking orgasms ("What are your experiences with faking orgasm or with faking your experience of pleasure?") and one question about their experiences with sex as a whole ("Women often report conflicted emotions about different sexual acts they have tried. Can you talk about your experiences with anal sex, oral sex, intercourse, and other acts that you would consider to be 'sex'?"), each with a series of follow-up questions.

Results

Emotion work appeared as normative in women's sexual lives, as all but one woman referenced emotion work—either directly or more subtly—as a part of their current or past sexual experiences, particularly during their sexual experiences with men. Direct references to emotion work included claims about sacrificing one's own needs to please a partner (e.g., painful intercourse); subtle emotion work occurred more around engaging in emotion work that may or may not have been displeasing to women (e.g., faking orgasm). In this chapter, I identified four key areas where emotion work in women's sexual experiences appeared: 1) faking orgasms, 2) tolerating sexual pain, 3) defining sexual satisfaction based on the partner's pleasure, and 4) narrating sex that they call "bad sex" as acceptable because of a partner's satisfaction. As evident in the descriptions below, some participants' responses overlapped between themes in that a participant's responses might fit into multiple themes. For example, the same women sometimes reported faking orgasm and tolerating sexual pain.

Theme 1: faking orgasms

Fifteen of the twenty women (75%) interviewed reported that they had faked an orgasm at least once, with nine women (45%) saying that they faked orgasm regularly during their sexual encounters. Notably, faking orgasms did not appear more often for married women, but definitely appeared more often for women engaging in heterosex. (While women in same-sex relationships described *having* more orgasms with women, they did endorse feelings that faking orgasm was necessary; see Fahs, 2011a.) Most women framed this as the need to reinforce their male partner's sexual skills and avoid hurting their feelings. Shantele (30, African-American, Heterosexual) described faking orgasm as emotion work that helped to manage her male partners' feelings of disappointment:

> I fake my orgasms, I do, yes. Sometimes some guys are very insecure, and they feel like if I'm not coming they didn't do their job. They make me

> feel like if I don't orgasm then I didn't enjoy sex, so sometimes I have to pretend just to perform it. Sometimes I take too long and just tell them I'm about to come and then they come.

Note that she also engages in a variety of small moments of emotion work (e.g., worrying about taking too long, trying to hurry, trying to have an orgasm to please a partner). Similarly, Jane (59, White, Heterosexual) felt that men were *entitled* both to their own and to her orgasm even if it was faked:

> I usually have my eyes closed and I just fake it. I felt that my partner was entitled to it, or I wanted to give that to him. I felt it was important because he would be disappointed if I didn't have an orgasm.

The pressure to assist men's arousal, or not disappoint them, appeared strongly in these narratives; notably, this perception was not something women merely perceived, as three women described the actual consequences of them not having an orgasm. Hannah (57, White, Bisexual) described her male partner as getting "furious" when she did not orgasm and told him so in an honest way:

> I remember he just sulked about it when I straight up said, "It didn't happen." He got angry and flipped it around with, "Why was *she* [referring to her ex-girlfriend] good enough and I can't do it for you?" I felt so guilty.

Other women described faking orgasm as a validation of the labor their partners had invested in them, as they worried about their partner's efforts "not going anywhere" (an interesting reference to sexual labor in itself) and wanted to validate their sexual skills. Cris (22, White, Lesbian) mentioned that she faked orgasm both with her former male partners and with her current female partner:

> With guys I faked it all the time. Now, with her, I've faked it occasionally pretty much because I was really tired and I just couldn't do it, and I felt bad because she was trying like really hard and so I didn't want her to think she wasn't doing anything good.

Angelica (32, Mexican-American, Heterosexual) used faking orgasm both to end the encounter and to encourage her sexually insecure partner:

> Sometimes just because I want to get it over with, and I know they're trying to wait for me to go, I just make them feel better. Like, "YAAAAAY," or whatever. I want them to feel like they accomplished something with me.

This language of accomplishment, trying hard, and investing labor into orgasms represented a major theme for many women, as the notion of sexual energies "going nowhere" felt threatening, especially during heterosex. This also implies linkages between capitalism, labor, and sexuality, as women prize sexual efficiency, labor, production, and an orgasm-based economy over meandering non-productive pleasurable sex.

Women also faked an orgasm to end sexual encounters altogether. Keisha (32, African-American, Bisexual) admitted to faking orgasms when she reluctantly agreed to sex:

> I've been there, faked it, just to obviously agree with him, like "Oh, he was good!" or make him seem that he isn't incompetent or bad. I fake it mostly during the times when you're agreeing to have sex when you don't really feel like it.

Inga (24, White, Bisexual) described faking it to end sex because she believed he would not otherwise take seriously her desires to be done with sex:

> I faked orgasm to get the guy off of me, just because I was done and just wasn't into and I just didn't want him there anymore, so I did that to get him off of me. He wouldn't listen to me otherwise.

Inga's description combined faking orgasm with resistance, as she pushed away an unwanted male partner, while Keisha seemed to feel more trapped by the endurance of unsatisfying sex.

Theme 2: tolerating sexual pain

In line with the "sexual compliance" literature (Impett & Peplau, 2003), some women, particularly those in current or previous heterosexual long-term relationships and marriages, demonstrated their emotion work by tolerating physical sexual pain (nine women, or 45%), particularly as they hid their pain and feigned enjoyment for their partners. Though different sexual acts bring different levels of pain, this phenomenon arose primarily for women during anal intercourse, as women felt pressured to engage in anal sex despite their feelings of displeasure. Rhoda (57, White, Heterosexual) recalled that she agreed to anal sex as a sexual "chore": "I tried it once or twice. It was painful, not satisfying whatsoever to me. It was more like a chore, but it was kind of like 'Okay, I'll do it.' He requested it." Similarly, Tania (25, White, Heterosexual) recalled that she continued to have anal sex with her boyfriend even though she strongly disliked it: "Sometimes there's not enough lubrication, and it really hurts. Once it hurts, it's painful, and you don't feel anything. You don't feel aroused, but you just keep going." (Note her use of "you" instead of "me/I" to distance herself from the experience.) The willingness to endure pain in favor of prioritizing men's fantasies about anal sex appeared repeatedly in women's narratives.

Three women also tolerated physical, sexual pain during their vaginal sex experiences, often due to lack of sexual arousal and lubrication prior to their male partners wanting to begin PVI. April (27, Mexican-American, Lesbian) put up with PVI pain in order to "save" her previous heterosexual relationship while also normalizing traditional gender roles: "Penetration is uncomfortable. It just hurts, or it feels good for a while, and then it's just like a strain or pressure. I tried to just get through it to save my relationship because he needed sex." Pain also arose in response to women agreeing to sexual acts with men they did not truly want to engage in, a repeated theme of heterosexual experience. Sylvia (23, White, Heterosexual) agreed to act out pornographic scenes with her boyfriend, tolerating physical, sexual pain to keep the peace:

> He watched a lot of porn, so he wanted to try every little single thing out there that had to do with anything that he'd seen. It went from ropes and gags to meeting people on Craigslist to having sex with couples to anal sex ... A lot of times it hurt, but as long as he was happy, then I would try whatever. I think it's a deep-seated thing that we just want to please our significant others. I just have to get used to it.

Theme 3: defining sexual satisfaction based on the partner's pleasure

When asking women about what satisfied them sexually, many women (seven women, or 35%) mentioned that their partner's pleasure (specifically, their partner having an orgasm) mattered more in terms of emotional satisfaction than their own orgasm. Inga described herself as a "giver" and said explicitly that her partner's orgasms were more important than her own:

> I am very much a giver so I would say when my partner or the person I'm with gets off, I am satisfied. When they have an orgasm or when they're happy and satisfied, I'm satisfied. You can see it in their eyes that they feel good.

Shantele, too, said that she felt satisfied primarily by her partner feeling pleasure rather than reveling in her own pleasure:

> I actually don't get off with sex, but I do enjoy watching a guy get off, knowing that he's satisfied. The sound of him coming, the look on their face—most men are really quiet when they're doing it, but then when they're about to come they're a little louder and their face is more expressive. It looks like it hurts but it doesn't.

The experience of watching her partner's face during orgasm and not experiencing her own orgasm reveals the differences in how women define sexual satisfaction for themselves versus their partners and the emotion work women often engage in to help men achieve satisfaction.

Two women described conflicted feelings between their satisfaction about pleasing a male partner and their worry about feeling sexually used. Kelly (23, White, Heterosexual) noted this conflict in her feelings about oral sex:

> I have sometimes done things I didn't really want to do just to please someone else. I often feel like oral sex is a service. You're doing them a service and giving your power away. I feel like if you're not in a trusting relationship, you're giving too much power away. You should only do things you don't like in a serious relationship and then it's okay because it makes them happy.

She resolves this tension by seeing the behavior as exploitative while not in a committed relationship, but generous/giving while in a relationship, and highlights the costs of emotion work during sex.

Theme 4: narrating "bad sex" as acceptable

Eight women (40%) who described sexual encounters with their partners as "bad sex" indicated this was an acceptable and normal part of their lives. In particular, some women did not *expect* to have "good sex" and did not feel entitled to ask for what they wanted sexually. Leticia (41, Mexican-American, Bisexual) described many of her (hetero)sexual experiences as disappointing but would never tell her male partners about her feelings:

> I often just lay there, and they're thinking they're doing the greatest thing on earth and it's not, so I had to fake my orgasms just to make him stop. I always want the guy to think that they did their part, just to make them feel good. I don't know. I should probably say something more, but it's just like I don't see the point. There are not a lot of men that will sit there and listen to what you want. Or they'll listen, but they won't do it, so there's no point. I would like for a man to pay attention to my breasts and some men don't really do that, or I'd like kissing on my neck, but I can't ask for that. I don't really have orgasms through the actual intercourse part.

This feeling of having no voice and feeling alienated from the sexual act while allowing a man to think his sexual moves are "the greatest thing on earth" reveals Leticia's expectation of emotion work during sex.

Four women (20%) also tolerated feeling emotionally distressed during their sexual encounters with men, even while sometimes covering it up. Patricia (28, African-American, Heterosexual) recalled feeling fear, sadness, and intense vulnerability during most of her sexual exchanges:

> I cry a lot when I have sex, or afterwards. I tell him I'm happy. I know you're not supposed to be thinking things like, "If this person leaves me what am I going to do?" but those are some of the things that I actually consider when I'm having sex. I have abandonment issues. I'll be in a relationship and I may not really want to have sex but I'll be like "okay" just to shut him up. I'll be mad but I'll agree anyway.

Her inability to synchronize her inward and outward emotions—instead putting on a "happy face"—showed the depth of her emotion work.

Two divorced women discussed that they "put up with" bad sex in their former marriages. Abby (26, White, Heterosexual) recounted the process of disclosing to her ex-husband after years of marriage that she had faked all of her orgasms:

> I didn't want to tell him right away that I was faking orgasms. I don't think it's something they need to know right away. I'd rather they know just that they're doing a good job until I can break it to them. When I did finally tell my husband, he was furious. Later, after we split up, I saw him one day and he asked me, "Does [your new partner] give you orgasms?" Like that was all important to him all of a sudden. During our whole relationship, he didn't care but now it was on his mind.

Likewise, Jean (57, White, Heterosexual) talked about enduring bad sex as a normal condition of her sexual life:

> Sometimes I just go blank. It happens mostly because you're doing it on somebody else's timeline and somebody else's demand. You're performing, and sometimes you can perform well. But you're still thinking, "When is this going to be over so I can be who I really am?" I just endure it I guess.

Jean's belief that, during bad sex, she cannot "be herself" and her explicit use of the word "performing" reflected the performative core of emotion work, where women suppressed emotions such as boredom, frustration, or fear in favor of the socially acceptable emotions they felt they could express.

Discussion

By combining sociological theories of emotional labor and emotion work with qualitative psychological narratives about sexuality, the data in this chapter provided a fuller picture of the kinds of emotion work women performed during their sexual experiences, particularly during experiences in which they did not expect sex to be pleasurable. As such, these data raise the question of what it means to have sex outside of pleasure, and what is at stake in continuing to have unpleasurable sex. Though this chapter included a diverse sample of women from multiple sexual identities—heterosexual, bisexual, and lesbian—women overwhelmingly described emotion work occurring in their relationships with men (current and past), though women differed about how this work manifested in these relationships. In fact, emotion work appeared in some form for nearly all women as part of their current or past sexual experiences, as women described frequently enduring unsatisfying sex and lack of orgasm in order to provide their (typically male) partners with feelings of power, sexual skillfulness, and dominance.

That said, women in heterosexual, longer-term relationships seemed particularly prone to discuss emotion work and its consequences for their lives, implying that romantic long-term heterosexual relationships may be particularly demanding in ways that other relationships are not (e.g., quick college hookups, queer relationships, etc.). While emotion work did occur in same-sex dynamics, women spoke of that work with less intensity than when describing their experiences with men; that said, women having sex with women often felt pressured to perform sexual labor as *both* the "giver" and "receiver" of orgasm (for a longer discussion of this, see Fahs, 2011a).

Much of women's emotion work centered on performance around the desire for sex ("wanting sex") and satisfaction during sex ("feeling satisfied"). These two forms of emotion work—telling a partner that they want to have sex, feel desirous of them, and feel excited for sex—alongside women's shallow acting performance (that is, performances where women are aware of acting, as contrasted to deep acting, where women no longer recognize that they are acting) of satisfaction during or after sex (e.g., orgasm, moaning, or the "YAAAAAY" expressed by Angelica) portrayed the varying demands that women perceived in their sexual lives. In particular, the strong emphasis on orgasm, despite women often needing to fake orgasm, suggests that orgasm signified a key form of emotion work for women (hearkening Hochschild's description of flight attendants' fake smiles). Women's multiple reasons for faking orgasms—to stop the encounter, support a partner's ego, validate the partner's sexual labor, and not hurt their partner's feelings—indicated that women's emotion work around fake orgasm met multiple goals. Moreover, rather than viewing men as generous for seeking to bring them to orgasm (a gift to the woman), women typically viewed men as demanding women's orgasms as validation of the men's sexual prowess (a gift to the man). This distinction, and the hazards of framing orgasm as a sexual goal, has been discussed in feminist work on orgasm reciprocity and who gets the "fair deal" (Braun, Gavey, & McPhillips, 2003). To add to this complexity, studies on masculinity and "sovereign selfhood" suggest that heterosexual masculinity often configures women around their own needs, desires, and self-images rather than imagining women as having needs of their own (Waldby, 1995).

Women's tendencies toward faking orgasm—a strikingly common occurrence in this sample—also fit with women's inclinations to define sexual satisfaction based on their partners' pleasure rather than their own. These narratives suggest that heterosexual sexual reciprocity is less about mutual enjoyment and more about women feeling they must confirm men's masculinity through heterosexual prowess (e.g., "I made my partner orgasm") (Braun, Gavey, & McPhillips, 2003). Constructions of women as "givers" or as wanting their partner's orgasm more than their own (or seeing their own orgasm as a physical impossibility) shows a clear gender and power difference in who *expects* to orgasm, who *does* orgasm, and interpretations of *meaning* surrounding orgasm. Shantele's especially poignant description of watching with delight the facial expressions of her male partner during orgasm, all while giving up on the possibility of her own orgasm, symbolized much larger themes in women's sexual lives: they witnessed, watched, or felt joy in seeing another's pleasure, but did not expect (authentic) reciprocity for themselves. This again suggests that women's so-called "sexual liberation" has quite a long way to go in order for men and women to truly experience sex on a similar plane (Bell, 2013; Fahs, 2011a).

The data in this chapter also suggests that there are real costs to women for the emotion work they engage in. For example, the various performances of satisfaction may extend not only into their physical performance of moaning or fake orgasms, but also into their arousal patterns themselves (as emotion work potentially could lead to a fusion between shallow acting and deep acting and thus becomes internalized as "what is" rather than as a performance, though this is only a theoretical claim rather than a claim based on our data). Thus, multiple layers of emotion work—shallow and deep—permeate women's sexual lives. Trying to assess how women feel exploited (or whether exploitation seems like "the way it is" and thus does not even feel exploitative any longer), or the ways that women feel properly "compensated" for emotion work in sex (Money? Security? Relationship stability? Emotional satisfaction? Pleasing the other? Pleasing the self?) present complicated challenges to feminist sex researchers. Further, assessing how women manage their own, and others', emotional experiences, and how that impacts their relationships, will require a series of studies.

These narratives also provided a starkly different image of masculinity compared to most popular-culture depictions of male sexuality. Rather than living up to masculine ideals of men as hard, tough, secure, self-sufficient, and sexually skilled, women described acting toward men in their sexual lives (particularly longer-term sexual partners) in ways that suggested a view of those men as low in sexual self-esteem and quite needy. Research into men's *actual* emotional needs in sex is an urgently needed next step to have a fuller picture, particularly given how much emotion work women do on behalf of those purported needs. Abby's description of "breaking the news" presented a particularly poignant and interesting construction of power imbalances, as she endured non-orgasmic sex for years and then used that information to ultimately demonstrate power over her (ex-)husband. Women's narratives of tolerating sexual pain, particularly during (unwanted) anal sex with men, further entrenched this rather negative portrayal of men as self-centered, inattentive, and even cruel. Sylvia's "acting out" of her boyfriend's pornographic fantasies also suggests that women sometimes felt pressured to engage in painful sexual actions of another's choosing rather than to assert their own preferences. Overall, women seemed more invested in devoting emotion work to their longer-term romantic relationships than to shorter "hookup" or casual sex relationships, implying that the emotion work might be more "worth it" for sustained relationships. (Similar dynamics appear in the literature on oral sex, as people construct cunnilingus as more appealing in longer-term relationships and less appealing in shorter-term ones; see Chambers, 2007.)

Perhaps most interestingly, nine women (40%) described tolerating "bad sex" to meet their partner's needs and standards for sex. This extends the previous three themes even further, as women's expectations for what sex *can be* also rapidly diminished (and these mental acrobatics clearly illustrates how deep these emotional rules go). Jean's resignation around "not being herself" during sex, Leticia's frank giving up on hopes that a partner would listen to her, or Patricia's crying over the fear of her partner leaving her all suggest, in different ways, that women sometimes no longer expected sex to feel pleasurable. This kind of emotion work seemed especially dangerous as women had uninspiring and laborious sex without hope that the social contract of sex would in turn provide them with sexual pleasure as well. As ten of the twenty women in the sample clearly struggled to prioritize their own needs during sex, often instead directing their priorities outward toward others, this is something practitioners, researchers, and scholars should bear in mind when measuring and studying the "self" in self-reports of sexual satisfaction (McClelland, 2011).

Future research could look at this other "third shift"—that is, the emotion work women devoted to their sexual relationships—in relation to the emotion work devoted to the workplace and to the family (Elliott & Umberson, 2008). More work on emotions in both the psychological and sociological literature is crucial to understanding women's experiences of sexuality. Intersections between the types of emotion work women exert have only recently been examined (Wharton & Erickson, 1995), so adding sexual emotion work to these intersectional studies could provide more detail about the taxing and draining qualities of emotion work across different facets of life. Clearly, research shows that many women devote an overwhelming amount of emotion work to their jobs, partners, children, and (now) sexual lives; researchers need to determine how to minimize the negative consequences of this labor while amplifying its positive consequences and/or lessening the emotion work altogether. More research on intersections between feminist identity and emotion work could help to further explore the protective benefits of challenging traditional gender roles (Yoder, Perry, & Saal, 2007). Additionally, teasing apart how much pressure women receive from their (male) partners to have orgasms, tolerate sexual pain, and deprioritize their own orgasms, and how much pressure they receive from cultural norms in the media for these things (e.g., magazine articles highlighting the importance of constant desire) also seems crucial to better understanding women's sexuality.

Ultimately, the data in this chapter suggests that Paula England's (2010) claims about the "stalled" gender revolution may also extend into women's sexual lives. While women have made progress in many areas—destigmatizing sex before marriage and same-sex relationships, exploring new avenues to sexual pleasure, working to negotiate power in their relationships, and socializing their friends/daughters/partners about how to better address their needs (Bell, 2013; Maxwell, 2012)—they also struggle in these areas, particularly as men's sexual needs and entitlement to orgasm and pleasure often seem more powerful than their own. Perhaps the sexual revolution inadvertently "freed men first" from the constraints of traditional gender and sexuality roles (English, 1983), or allowed women to *be desired* rather than *have desire* (evoking "cathexis," or the gendered characteristics of sexual desire, see Connell, 2005), leading to some complicated quagmires of how to effectively sexually liberate women in today's culture. While I focused on emotion work in longer-term romantic relationships, women's emotional/sexual labor has also extended into "hookup" experiences and casual sex as well (particularly faking orgasms) (Armstrong, England, & Fogarty, 2012; Kitroeff, 2013), giving renewed salience to the feminist analysis of such labor.

The data in this chapter also raises questions about contemporary claims to empowerment and agency broadly defined, as even those women with more socially-inscribed sexual "power" reported a vast amount of emotional/sexual labor they devoted in their heterosexual and hetero-gendered sexual experiences. Providing emotion work in their sexual relationships thus makes sense as a strategy for enduring relationships with lopsided power dynamics, but it also invites interrogation of how we will envision sexual empowerment and agency in light of these emotion work tactics (Gill, 2007). That said, helping women to feel more entitled to reciprocity, authentic orgasms, assertions of their own needs, and sexual power are important goals for partners, practitioners, parents, and scholars, just as working with men to feel more secure about their (imperfect) sexual selves will hopefully result in less emotion work, greater authenticity, and more positive sexual experiences for all.

Note

1   The method for this chapter is similar to Chapter 1. It draws from a different group of women from data collected in 2011 (mean age = 35.35, SD = 12.01). The sample included 35% or 7 ages 18–31; 40% or 8 ages 32–45; and 25% or 5 ages 46–59, as well as 60% (12) white women and 40% (8) women of color, including two African-American women, four Mexican-American women, and two Asian-American women. For self-reported sexual identity, the sample included 60% (12) heterosexual women, 20% (4) bisexual women, and 20% (4) lesbian women. All other methodological choices are the same.

References

Allen, K. R., & Goldberg, A. E. (2009). Sexual activity during menstruation: A qualitative study. *Journal of Sex Research*, 46(6), 535–545.

Armstrong, E. A., England, P., & Fogarty, A. C. K. (2012). Accounting for women's orgasm and sexual enjoyment in college hookups and relationships. *American Sociological Review*, 77(3), 435–462.

Bay-Cheng, L. Y., & Zucker, A. N. (2007). Feminism between the sheets: Sexual attitudes among feminists, nonfeminists, and egalitarians. *Psychology of Women Quarterly*, *31*(2), 157–163.

Bell, L. C. (2013). *Hard to get: 20-something women and the paradox of sexual freedom*. Berkeley, CA: University of California Press.

Bolton, M. (2000). *The third shift: Managing hard choices in our careers, homes, and lives as women*. New York: Jossey-Bass.

Braun, V., Gavey, N., & McPhillips, K. (2003). The "fair deal"? Unpacking accounts of reciprocity in heterosex. *Sexualities*, *6*(2), 237–261.

Brotheridge, C. M., & Grandey, A. A. (2002). Emotional labor and burnout: Comparing two perspectives of "people's work." *Journal of Vocational Behavior*, *60*(1), 17–39.

Burnham, L. E. (2013). *Feminist values and pornography consumption amongst women and its relationship to sexual self-esteem and body esteem* (MSW Thesis). Smith College.

Cacchioni, T. (2007). Heterosexuality and "the labour of love": A contribution to recent debates on female sexual dysfunction. *Sexualities*, *10*(3), 299–320.

Chambers, W. C. (2007). Oral sex: Varied behaviors and perceptions in a college population. *Journal of Sex Research*, *44*(1), 28–42.

Connell, R. W. (2005). *Masculinities* (2nd ed.). Berkeley, CA: University of California Press.

Daniels, A. K. (1987). Invisible work. *Social Problems*, *34*(5), 403–415.

DeMaris, A. (1997). Elevated sexual activity in violent marriages: Hypersexuality or sexual extortion? *Journal of Sex Research*, *34*(4), 361–373.

Dewitte, M., Van Lankveld, J., & Crombez, G. (2010). Understanding sexual pain: A cognitive-motivational account. *Pain*, *152*(2), 251–253.

Elliott, S., & Umberson, D. (2008). The performance of desire: Gender and sexual negotiation in long-term marriages. *Journal of Marriage and Family*, *70*(2), 391–406.

Elmerstig, E., Wijma, B., & Berterö, C. (2008). Why do young women continue to have sexual intercourse despite pain? *Journal of Adolescent Health*, *43*(4), 357–363.

Elmerstig, E., Wijma, B., & Swahnberg, K. (2013). Prioritizing the partner's enjoyment: A population-based study on young Swedish women with experience of pain during vaginal intercourse. *Journal of Psychosomatic Obstetrics & Gynecology*, *34*(2), 82–89.

England, P. (2010). The gender revolution: Uneven and stalled. *Gender & Society*, *24*(2), 149–166.

English, D. (1983). The fear that feminism will free men first. In A. Snitow, C. Stansell, & S. Thompson (Eds.), *Powers of desire: The politics of sexuality* (pp. 477–483). New York: Monthly Review Press.

Erickson, R. J. (2005). Why emotion work matters: Sex, gender, and the division of household labor. *Journal of Marriage and Family*, *67*(2), 337–351.

Eschenfelder, B. (2012). Exploring the nature of nonprofit work through emotional labor. *Management Communication Quarterly*, *26*(1), 173–178.

Fahs, B. (2011a). *Performing sex: The making and unmaking of women's erotic lives*. Albany, NY: State University of New York Press.

Fahs, B. (2011b). Sex during menstruation: Race, sexual identity, and women's qualitative accounts of pleasure and disgust. *Feminism & Psychology*, *21*(2), 155–178.

Fahs, B. (2014). Coming to power: Women's fake orgasms and best orgasm experiences illuminate the failures of (hetero)sex and the pleasures of connection. *Culture, Health & Sexuality*, *16*(8), 974–988.

Fahs, B., & Swank, E. (2011). Social identities as predictors of women's sexual satisfaction and sexual activity. *Archives of Sexual Behavior*, *40*(5), 903–914.

Faulkner, S. L., & Lannutti, P. J. (2010). Examining the context and outcomes of young adults' satisfying and unsatisfying conversations about sex. *Qualitative Health Research, 20* (3), 375–385.

Froyum, C. M. (2010). The reproduction of inequalities through emotional capital: The case of socializing low-income black girls. *Qualitative Sociology, 33,* 37–54.

Gill, R. C. (2007). Critical respect: The difficulties and dilemmas of agency and "choice" for feminism. *European Journal of Women's Studies, 14*(1), 69–80.

Gill, R. C. (2009). Breaking the silence: The hidden injuries of neo-liberal academia. In R. Ryan-Flood, & R. Gill (Eds.), *Secrecy and silence in the research process: Feminist reflections* (pp. 39–55). London: Routledge.

Hess, K. L., Javanbakht, M., Brown, J. M., Weiss, R. E., Hsu, P., & Gorbach, P. M. (2013). Intimate partner violence and anal intercourse in young adult heterosexual relationships. *Perspectives on Sexual and Reproductive Health, 45*(1), 6–12.

Hochschild, A. R. (1983). *The managed heart: Commercialization of human feeling.* Berkeley, CA: University of California Press.

Hochschild, A. R. (1989). *The second shift: Working families and the revolution at home.* New York : Penguin.

Hochschild, A. R. (1997). The time bind. *WorkingUSA, 1*(2), 21–29.

Hochschild, A. R. (2012). *The outsourced self: Intimate life in market times.* New York: Metropolitan Books.

Impett, E. A., & Peplau, L. A. (2003). Sexual compliance: Gender, motivational, and relationship perspectives. *Journal of Sex Research, 40*(1), 87–100.

Jagose, A. (2013). *Orgasmology.* Durham, NC: Duke University Press.

Judge, T. A., Woolf, E. F., & Hurst, C. (2009). Is emotional labor more difficult for some than for others? A multilevel experience-sampling study. *Personnel Psychology, 62*(1), 57–88.

Kaestle, C. E. (2009). Sexual insistence and disliked sexual activities in young adulthood: Differences by gender and relationship characteristics. *Perspectives on Sexual and Reproductive Health, 41*(1), 33–39.

Kitroeff, N. (2013). In hookups, inequality still reigns. *New York Times Blogs.* http://well.blogs. nytimes.com/2013/11/11/women-find-orgasms-elusive-in-hookups/?_php= true&_type=blogs&_r=0.

Maxwell, C. (2012). Bodies and agentic practice in young women's sexual and intimate relationships. *Sociology, 46*(2), 306–321.

McClelland, S. I. (2010). Intimate justice: A critical analysis of sexual satisfaction. *Social and Personality Psychology Compass, 4*(9), 663–680.

McClelland, S. I. (2011). Who is the "self" in self-reports of sexual satisfaction? Research and policy implications. *Sexuality Research and Social Policy, 8*(4), 304–320.

Morris, J. A., & Feldman, D. C. (1996). The dimensions, antecedents, and consequences of emotional labor. *The Academy of Management Review, 21*(4), 986–1010.

Mosher, D. L., & Maclan, P. (1994). College men and women respond to X-rated videos intended for male or female audiences: Gender and sexual scripts. *Journal of Sex Research, 31*(2), 99–113.

Muehlenhard, C. L., & Shippee, S. K. (2010). Men's and women's reports of pretending orgasm. *Journal of Sex Research, 47*(6), 552–567.

Nicholson, P., & Burr, J. (2003). What is "normal" about women's (hetero)sexual desire and orgasm? A report of an in-depth interview study. *Social Science & Medicine, 57*(9), 1735–1745.

O'Sullivan, L. F., & Allgeier, E. R. (1998). Feigning sexual desire: Consenting to unwanted sexual activity in heterosexual dating relationships. *Journal of Sex Research, 35*(3), 234–243.

Opperman, E., Braun, V., Clarke, V., & Rogers, C. (2014). "It feels so good it almost hurts": Young adults' experiences of orgasm and sexual pleasure. *Journal of Sex Research, 51*(5), 503–515.

Ott, M. A., Millstein, S. G., Ofner, S., & Halpern-Felsher, B. L. (2006). Greater expectations: Adolescents' positive motivations for sex. *Perspectives on Sexual and Reproductive Health, 38*(2), 84–89.

Parvez, Z. F. (2006). The labor of pleasure: How perceptions of emotional labor impact women's enjoyment of pornography. *Gender & Society, 20*(5), 605–631.

Piña, D. L., & Bengtson, V. L. (1993). The division of household labor and wives' happiness: Ideology, employment, and perceptions of support. *Journal of Marriage and Family, 55*(4), 901–912.

Pugliesi, K. (1999). The consequences of emotional labor: Effects on work stress, job satisfaction, and well-being. *Motivation and Emotion, 23*(2), 125–154.

Sanchez, D. T., Crocker, J., & Boike, K. R. (2005). Doing gender in the bedroom: Investing in gender norms and the sexual experience. *Personality and Social Psychology Bulletin, 31*(10), 1445–1455.

Sanders, T. (2005). "It's just acting": Sex workers' strategies for capitalizing on sexuality. *Gender, Work & Organization, 12*(4), 319–342.

Schick, V. R., Zucker, A. N., & Bay-Cheng, L. Y. (2008). Safer, better sex through feminism: The role of feminist ideology in women's sexual well-being. *Psychology of Women Quarterly, 32*, 225–232.

Štulhofer, A., Buško, V., & Landripet, I. (2010). Pornography, sexual socialization, and satisfaction among young men. *Archives of Sexual Behavior, 39*(1), 168–178.

Twiggs, J. E., McQuillan, J., & Ferree, M. M. (1999). Meaning and measurement: Reconceptualizing measures of the division of household labor. *Journal of Marriage and Family, 61*(3), 712–724.

Voydanoff, P., & Donnelly, B. W. (1999). The intersection of time in activities and perceived unfairness in relation to psychological distress and marital quality. *Journal of Marriage and Family, 61*(3), 739–751.

Waldby, C. (1995). Boundary erotics and reconfiguration of the heterosexual male body. In E. A. Grosz, & E. Probyn (Eds.), *Sexy bodies: The strange carnalities of feminism* (pp. 266–277). Florence, KY: Psychology Press.

Wharton, A. S. (1999). The psychosocial consequences of emotional labor. *Annals of the American Academy of Political and Social Science, 561*, 158–176.

Wharton, A. S., & Erickson, R. J. (1995). The consequences of caring: Exploring the links between women's job and family emotion work. *The Sociological Quarterly, 36*(2), 273–296.

Wiederman, M. W. (1997). Pretending orgasm during sexual intercourse: Correlates in a sample of young adult women. *Journal of Sex & Marital Therapy, 23*(2), 131–139.

Yoder, J. D., Perry, R. L., & Saal, E. I. (2007). What good is a feminist identity? Women's feminist identification and role expectations for intimate and sexual relationships. *Sex Roles, 57*(5–6), 365–372.

3

SLIPPERY DESIRE

Women's qualitative accounts of their vaginal lubrication and wetness

The FDA approval of Addyi (Flibanserin) on August 18, 2015, signaled a shift in thinking about women's sexual function and dysfunction in the United States. Despite clear evidence that the drug barely increased numbers of "sexual events" during an average month, that the placebo effect was uncommonly strong for this drug, that it posed serious health risks, and that the alcohol interactions were tested overwhelmingly on men instead of women (Boseley, 2015; Kroll, 2015; Streicher, 2015), the drug is now widely available and heavily advertised. The highly conflictual FDA approval process for Flibanserin revealed a number of underlying tensions about what scientists know, how they conceptualize sexual "failure" and adequate research designs, and what they never thought to ask about women's sexuality. In particular, clear notions of sexual dysfunction as located within the individual woman rather than within the context of a couple or partnership seemed to underlie lobbying efforts for Flibanserin. Further, pharmaceutical companies largely avoided studying women's subjective accounts of sexual pleasure, desire, lubrication, arousal, and interest, instead aiming for "brain chemicals" that they could alter (Boseley, 2015; Cacchioni, 2015; Streicher, 2015). After failed attempts to artificially induce women's vaginal lubrication with "female Viagra" in 2004 (Harris, 2004), Flibanserin has now bypassed increased blood flow and arousal for women and has instead targeted the interplay between dopamine, norepinephrine, and serotonin to induce sexual desire, moving the pharmaceutical lens from vaginal lubrication to the brain's desire for sex.

When looking at the existing literature on women's subjective accounts of vaginal lubrication and wetness, shockingly few studies appear, though it does seem clear that vaginal lubrication is constructed in the existing literature as a tangible indicator of women's "normal" sexual functioning and of sexual arousal. In the shadow of the near cultural obsession with male erections in the Western world—not only in academic writing about sexuality but also in the symbolic realm (Gohr, 2018)—women's vaginal lubrication has primarily been framed as a sexual dysfunction issue rather than something connected to desire, pleasure, satisfaction, or partner connection. When researchers have studied or measured vaginal lubrication, they have approached it as a physical response rather than a social one (for a critique of this, see Tiefer, Hall, & Tavris, 2002) and have largely ignored any vaginal lubrication that occurs outside of the context of penile-vaginal intercourse (e.g., masturbation, same-sex sexual contact). These oversights not only promote the idea that vaginal lubrication exists for intercourse, but they also overwhelmingly ignore women's subjective stories about how they feel about their wetness.

In an effort to move away from highly clinical interpretations of vaginal wetness and instead ask women to narrate their complex experiences with their vaginal lubrication, in this chapter I examine women's feelings about, and subjective interpretations of, vaginal lubrication and wetness. These discussions provide a crucial link between women's understanding of wetness, feelings of self-worth, and satisfaction with their partners. Conversations with women illuminated four themes that appeared in women's responses while showcasing the powerful complexities of how women locate the "cause" of wetness within themselves, their partner's connection with them, their personal joy, or in biology.

What do we know about vaginal wetness?

While no studies have used interviews to study women's experiences with vaginal lubrication and wetness, a small handful of studies have examined, using quantitative measures, vaginal wetness as an indicator of biological sexual function (Hilber et al., 2010; Leclerc-Madlala, 2001; Leiblum, Seehuus, & Brown, 2007; Tanner et al., 2009). Other related work has examined women's experiences with synthetic lubricants. For example, one study found that the majority of women in the US have used lubricants (65% have ever used them, 20% have used them in the past 30 days), primarily to increase pleasure and decrease discomfort (Herbenick, Reece, Schick, Sanders, & Fortenberry, 2014). Another recent study of 2,451 US women found that they preferred penile-vaginal intercourse to feel more wet, were more easily orgasmic when sex was wet, and thought their partner preferred sex to feel more wet than dry; further, women in their 40s felt more positively about using synthetic lubricants than women under the age of 30 (Jozkowski et al., 2013). Three studies mentioned vaginal wetness in relation to condom use and public health (Higgins, 2007; Higgins & Hirsch, 2008; Skafte & Silberschmidt, 2014), while one study found that women with sexual pain also reported more frequent use of synthetic lubricants than did women without sexual pain (Sutton, Boyer, Goldfinger, Ezer, & Pukall, 2012). Still, these studies tell us very little about women's subjective feelings about vaginal lubrication or how they experience their natural lubrication.

A somewhat larger body of studies have examined women's loss of vaginal wetness in relation to aging, medical problems, or taking medications. Older, post-menopausal women experienced decreased vaginal lubrication and more sexual dryness compared to younger women (Hayes & Dennerstein, 2005; Meston, 1997), while women with high blood pressure reported less vaginal lubrication and more problems achieving orgasm than women with normal blood pressure (Franklin, Kanigel, & Lehrman, 1998). Women who took inject-able contraception also reported problems with vaginal wetness as a side effect of the drug (Smit, McFadyen, Zuma, & Preston-Whyte, 2002).

Some cross-cultural work has examined women's experiences and perceptions of vaginal wetness and dryness as cultural ideals. One large-scale cross-cultural study of 11 countries (UK, Germany, Japan, Australia, Canada, Spain, Italy, Mexico, Argen-tina, Brazil, and Thailand) found that perceptions of vaginal dryness varied from a minimum of 5.8% in Italy to a maximum of 19.7% in Brazil; perceptions of whether it bothered women varied from 5.6% in the UK to 26.4% in Germany, with women over age 50 reporting more dryness than women under 50 (Leiblum, Hayes, Wasner, & Nelson, 2009). In sub-Saharan Africa, many women practice "dry sex" by inserting various substances to dry up their normal lubrication fluid and give the impression that the vagina is "virginal" and "tight"; such practices often lead to damage to the cervix and vaginal canal, condoms breaking, and can increase the risk of HIV transmission (Civic & Wilson, 1996; Levin, 2005). These risks are especially concerning for sex workers who must practice "dry sex" to please clients (Schwandt, Morris, Ferguson, Ngugi, & Moses, 2006).

The problem of sexual function and dysfunction

Research on sexual dysfunction has largely blamed women for the problem and located the problems as medical, biological, and physiological rather than social (e.g., lack of desire, as about the body "failing" rather than about relationship or communication problems). To address this, The New View, a group dedicated to challenging the medicalization of sex, argued that sexual problems connect to sociocultural, political, and economic factors, partner and relationship factors, psychological factors, and medical factors (Tiefer, Hall, & Tavris, 2002). Some feminist critics have also challenged the assumed overlap between desire and arousal, particularly in relation to language in the DSM about women's arousal and desire as essentially the same thing (Graham, 2010).

Debates exist about whether there are gender differences in how women experience arousal within their genitals and arousal within their minds. One study that measured women's subjective arousal and physiological arousal after exposing participants to erotic stimuli found that these were largely in sync for women (Rellini, McCall, Randall, & Meston, 2005), while another study found that, compared to men, women had far greater discrepancies between self-reported and genitally-measured sexual arousal (Chivers, Seto, Lalumiere, Laan, & Grimbos, 2010). This implies that women's sexual desire and arousal may or may not match their physiological responses. Women also desired shorter periods of intercourse compared to men (Miller & Byers, 2004), perhaps due to discomfort with intercourse once their natural lubrication becomes dry.

Researchers who study sexual dysfunction have noted that women attach feelings of shame, guilt, and depression to various sexual dysfunctions. One study of women's sexual distress found that emotional problems (individually or with a partner) predicted sexual distress far more than physical aspects of sexual dysfunction related to vaginal lubrication and arousal (Bancroft, Loftus, & Long, 2003). One study of vulvodynia (chronic vulvar pain) found that most women blamed themselves as "failures" when they experienced pain during penile-vaginal intercourse, resulting in feelings of shame, guilt, and decreased sexual desire (Ayling & Ussher, 2008). Problems with lubrication were associated with distress, depression, and lower partner communication (Hayes et al., 2008). Further, while most sexual problems for women decreased with age, vaginal dryness increased with age, causing marked distress in older women who experience lack of vaginal lubrication (Laumann, Paik, & Rosen, 1999). Connections between pressure to orgasm, women's self-blame, lack of reciprocity, and power imbalances between men and women have also been noted in the literature (Braun, Gavey, & McPhillips, 2003; Fahs, 2014; Jackson & Scott, 2002), suggesting numerous avenues for women to feel distressed about their sexual practices, arousal patterns, and sensations.

Hard versus soft: erections and wetness

The relative lack of attention to women's narratives about vaginal lubrication, particularly those outside of penile-vaginal intercourse, starkly contrasts the near cultural obsession with men's erections found in popular, medical/pharmaceutical, and research literature. An abundant number of studies have directed attention to men's erections, seeing them as a benchmark for sexual health and well-being (Adams, Wright, & Lohr, 1996; Rosen, 1996; Rowland, Georgoff, & Burnett, 2011), while a smaller body of work has criticized this obsession with erections and sperm as problematic for sexual health, feminist politics, and relationship well-being (Loe, 2004; Moore, 2008; Potts, Grace, Vares, & Gavey, 2006).

Very few studies have asked men to narrate their experiences with erections and sexual arousal. One study of men in New Zealand found that the cultural stories of "sex for life" that encourage older men to have penetrative sex during old age often stand in contrast to men's wishes to relate sexually to their partners in other ways that they consider healthy, normal, enjoyable, and satisfying (Potts et al., 2006). Further, men who used Viagra did not experience it as a mechanistic intervention into a "disorder" but saw it in much more complicated and emotional terms (Potts, Grace, Gavey, & Vares, 2004). This suggests that both vaginal lubrication and erections are constructed more as medical, clinical entities rather than complicated subjective experiences of arousal and connection.

Given the relative lack of studies examining women's narratives about vaginal lubrication and wetness, I ask several questions to guide this chapter: First, what do women say about their vaginal wetness and how do they frame vaginal wetness in relation to themselves, their partners, and their biology? How do women's ideas about vaginal lubrication map onto, and differ from, clinical understandings of "sufficient" and "insufficient" lubrication for intercourse and the focus on penile-vaginal intercourse? Is wetness a source of shame, embarrassment, and anxiety, or is it a source of pleasure, joy, and satisfaction? Finally, how do women's ideas about vaginal lubrication and wetness connect to bigger stories around gender, power, and sexual scripts?

Method[1]

Women were asked four questions: "Tell me about your experiences with vaginal wetness or lubrication"; "What does it feel like to be wet?"; "Does wetness happen easily or is it more difficult for you?"; and "What emotions do you have about wetness?"

Results

All participants had something to say about their experiences with vaginal wetness and lubrication, though how women discussed their feelings about this aspect of their bodies differed in notable ways. While most women framed wetness in positive terms, conflicts about its meaning also arose. I identified four themes associated with women's feelings about vaginal lubrication and wetness: 1) wetness as pleasure, joy, and connection, 2) wetness as a physical and biological phenomenon, 3) anxiety about insufficient wetness, 4) having excessive or "too much" wetness. As evident in the descriptions below, some participants' responses overlapped between themes in that one participant's responses fit into multiple themes.

Theme 1: wetness as pleasure, joy, and connection

The majority of women identified feeling wet as a pleasurable experience. Specifically, nine women discussed wetness as primarily about pleasure, joy, and connection rather than about feelings of anxiety, partner problems, or excessiveness. Three women felt that wetness signaled connection to a partner and an awareness of positive relationship dynamics. Daphne (33, White, Heterosexual) felt that wetness helped her to get in touch with her own body and understand connections to others:

> Sometimes I can notice there's some kind of secretion and it makes me check in, like "What's going on with my body?" With someone I'm having sex with, it's even more of a turn on when you're playing around, and then they touch down in that area and discover that you're wet. Everything is so inner with us, so it's almost like they have to go a bit further within to really find out what's going on.

Joyce (21, Filipino, Bisexual) described wetness as a way of knowing she felt desire for someone:

If there's a connection with the person that comes with eye contact, dialogue, conversation, competition, if someone impresses me in some shape or form then I do feel more wet and I have more desire for that person. With the mind/body connection, I don't restrain my mind from having desire for people, so I think my body responds to that.

Iris (22, Mexican-American, Lesbian) connected wetness to feelings of love and satisfaction:

It's a big factor in creating pleasure and then also knowing that your partner is pleasured. I like wanting it. It's a lot of arousal. I don't feel arousal if I'm not emotionally connected to someone, so I guess when I'm wet, it's *love* that I feel. I don't get that arousal without feeling love.

Connection to partners and desire for others represented a primary way that women imagined their feelings about wetness, as powerful emotional feelings of connection inspired arousal.

Wetness also signaled a way for women to feel pleasure and comfort in their own bodies. Antonia (25, Mexican-American, Lesbian) felt that wetness allowed her to feel normal, content, and aware of her body:

It is what it should be. I'm never embarrassed about it. I think that you can just feel it. There's the constant normal day-to-day quality, just feeling normal. You can kind of feel like a vaginal discharge in a way when you're around arousing thoughts, images, people. Their actions sometimes, depending on who it is, and the way they touch me can do that for me, or the way somebody dances can do that for me.

Bea (37, Filipina, Heterosexual) described feeling wet easily and how that connected to her anticipation of pleasure:

I can get pretty wet pretty fast. So if we are not going to have it, then I don't want him playing with me! I'm like, "Don't go touching those areas if you don't plan on following through." It's like walking around in a wet diaper almost. I like the feeling though, imagining that something's going to happen.

These two examples emphasize women's sense of connection to their bodies, awareness of how to get wet, and pleasure from feeling arousal.

Theme 2: wetness as physical, biological phenomenon

As a second theme, four women described wetness as a physical, biological phenomenon and did not relay any particular feelings about it aside from its functionality. For example, Yvonne (41, Mexican-American, Heterosexual) described her lack of emotions about it when I asked her about her emotions about wetness: "That's a weird question. I don't think I have any emotions about it. I don't dislike it, but I don't know how to describe any feelings about it. It's just wet and warm." Emma (42, White, Heterosexual) also described it in highly physical and biological terms rather than emotional terms: "It feels slippery. I've always been ready to go when I needed to be. It doesn't take much. I don't have any real emotions about it. It's just my body. It tells me I'm ready." In these narratives, wetness did not necessarily connect to women's emotions but instead to their sense of readiness for sex.

Two women also described wetness as connected to their bodies behaving normally. Zari (43, African-American, Heterosexual) described wetness as normal and not worth much analysis:

> I think you're supposed to be that way. I figured it's normal. That's the only feeling I have is that you're supposed to be that way. I always seem to be wet when I'm supposed to be and dry when I'm supposed to be, so I don't have a problem with it. I think it's just a normal thing I guess.

Veronica (49, African-American, Heterosexual) also described wetness as a straightforward biological response that signaled good health: "I see it as something that's there when I'm healthy and in good physical shape. It's the body's way of showing that you're ready to have sex. It's how I know I'm normal." This language of health, biology, and normality differed from other women's constructions of wetness as about relationships, personal body image, and identity.

Theme 3: anxiety about insufficient wetness

Eleven women mentioned having anxiety about insufficient wetness, sometimes in relation to what they saw as their own bodily failure to become wet and sometimes in relation to partner dynamics, though such a line was not always easily drawn in their accounts. Six women mentioned feelings of anxiety related to their vaginal lubrication and wetness, blaming lack of wetness on their failing personal bodies rather than partner dynamics. For example, two middle-aged women mentioned that going through menopause had negatively impacted the ease of becoming wet. Kathleen (49, White, Heterosexual) said of her post-menopausal state:

> It's frustrating as a woman when you know your desire is there, but your body is like "Nope, sorry, it's not there." It's not a good feeling. I think it's more hormonal rather than lack of interest. Like all of a sudden, it's just not there when it was there a minute ago. Where'd it go?

Gretchen (52, White, Heterosexual) also described frustration about not getting wet as easily following menopause:

> Now that I've gone through menopause, it kind of makes me sad. I was
> never ashamed of it before. It was always a good thing and things were
> working the way they should. Now, it's one of the side effects of meno-
> pause. Less estrogen and less vaginal fluid production, and I'm not happy
> with it because it is signaling the end of reproduction but it's also like
> "Oh you, you're old, you've become invisible."

This sense of becoming invisible after menopause and its connection to losing
the ease of vaginal wetness shows how wetness connects to ideas about aging,
self, and value as well as sexual desire.

Three younger women also struggled with vaginal wetness because they felt
that their bodies did not work. The relationship between this perceived lack of
function and its impact on partner dynamics was tricky as these women saw the
problem as an individual one. Corinne (21, White, Bisexual) talked about her
difficulty with wetness related to her own body:

> Wetness is more difficult for me. I have no idea why. I've always wondered.
> I went to the doctor and talked to her about it because even sometimes when
> we're going to have sex it's hard for me, but she said that it's normal. For
> some people it's easy and sometimes it's harder. Some people have to use
> lubrication. When I have sex without enough lubrication, it feels like scrap-
> ing, forceful, too much rubbing and friction.

Trish (19, White, Lesbian) felt that alcohol impaired her vaginal wetness:

> Sometimes it's frustrating when you can't get as excited, especially if
> there's drinking involved and so you get this super horny feeling but that
> alcohol stops you from getting wet. I'm like, "Wait, why am I not
> excited? I feel exactly like I am. I feel like I should be wet, but I'm not."

In these examples, women located their difficulties with wetness as failing to
measure up to what they *should* feel, however perceived. Five women mentioned feeling that they had insufficient lubrication because of certain dynamics
that happened with their sexual partners, assigning responsibility to the couple
rather than to themselves for their wetness (though again, such a line is tricky to
define in a definitive sense). Some women described this as a problem with the
technical aspects of partnered sex. Gretchen (52, White, Heterosexual) remem-
bered that even when she did feel wet, her male partner would insist on having
vaginal sex for too long and she would then dry up:

> With one boyfriend, he would go on for hours and hours, and it was just
> like my body had kind of run out of fluid and hadn't had a chance to
> reload yet. The pleasure was gone, and then it became more friction and
> rubbing, like I was dehydrated.

Lila (36, White, Heterosexual) felt that partnered sex had to involve a certain kind of manual stimulation or else she would not become wet:

> I just need some digital fingers and I'm good to go, like on the top, not in. I'll tell them right away to go counter-clockwise and I will place their fingers right where they need to be. If they don't do that, I won't become wet. If they're doing it correctly, I'll become wet, but otherwise if they're far off I won't.

In these examples, women assigned responsibility for lack of wetness to a lack of partner skill or awareness of their sexual wishes.

Two women described having insufficient lubrication for pain-free intercourse, but they still wanted to proceed in order to please a partner. Rachel (39, White, Bisexual) discussed her feelings about having painful sex with her partner:

> When I'm not wet, it's painful sex. It doesn't feel comfortable. I think to myself, "Okay, this is uncomfortable. My body's slow. Things aren't happening like I want them to." It feels like a mind-body disconnect, but he wants it so I try it. My husband and I have kids, so it's like there are kids around all the time, so when we have a moment it's like five minutes is all we got. I can't necessarily have the ten-minute warm-up I would love so I'll take what I can get. But I'll tell you, I pay for it later.

Naomi (18, White, Bisexual) said that she kept having sex despite not wanting to and became dry:

> It was really hard. We were doing it a lot, and I got dry after a while and it hurt so bad. I kept going because he was hot, and I knew that I wasn't gonna be able to see him very much after that.

This sense of settling for less-than-ideal partner dynamics also contributed to women's lack of vaginal lubrication and wetness.

Theme 4: excess: having excessive or "too much" wetness

As another way that women criticized themselves for their wetness, three women described feeling like they had excessive or "too much" wetness, with one believing that this connected to her ability to ejaculate and two others believing that they produced too much lubrication. Gail (46, White, Bisexual) worried that something was wrong with her because of her excessive wetness:

> Sometimes I wonder, "Is there something wrong with me?" because I'm very, very lubricated and wet depending on what time of the cycle I'm in.

Sometimes I wonder, "Is that something I need to get checked out?" or "Is that normal and I should just be happy that I have it?"

Felicity (20, White, Heterosexual) also felt some anxiety about her extreme wetness combined with worrying about how she tasted to her boyfriend:

I tend to be pretty damp. I have a *lot* of lubrication. My boyfriend usually complains because I don't drink a whole lot of water and he can taste it. For him, sex can be bad if I taste really bitter and sometimes I do taste really bitter and that's something I've tried really hard to control.

These feelings about "excessive" wetness connected to other anxieties about being normal or tasting bad to a partner, again revealing how "noise" from other aspects of women's sexuality impacts their feelings about vaginal lubrication.

One woman also expressed uncertainty about her body's production of vaginal lubrication in relation to the idea of "peeing" or "squirting." Martha (52, White, Heterosexual) described feeling embarrassed by her wetness during arousal: "It was embarrassing. I squirt. When I did it with my husband, he was like, 'You just peed on me,' and I said, 'No I didn't.' And he got up and took a shower. I thought, 'Well, this must be bad.' But my husband likes it. It means I had an orgasm. I feel water gushing out of me, sometimes too much water." This sense of wanting a partner to validate the "embarrassment" of too much lubrication and/or "squirting" signaled her awareness of not only her own pleasure but also her partner's experience of sex.

Discussion

Wetness is an often-overlooked aspect of women's sexuality, hidden beneath the more performative or measurable or well-studied dimensions of orgasm and (for men) erections. Women's sexual subjectivities about sexual "function" overlap here with sexual performance and sexual desire, making women's feelings about wetness an interesting subject of inquiry for feminist-minded critical sexuality studies researchers. In this chapter, I found that women's attitudes about their vaginal lubrication and wetness showed great diversity in how women interpreted their body's arousal responses, revealing new insight about women's subjective feelings about embodiment, arousal, and sexual functioning. The divide between women immediately seeing wetness as a sign of their anxiety about wetness—either personal anxiety related to their own bodies or couple anxiety related to partner dynamics—compared to women seeing wetness as a sign of pleasure, joy, connection, or biological normality/health shows the diversity women have when thinking about their physical arousal responses. Because researchers have not studied this subject beyond its connection to highly clinical notions of sexual dysfunction (and the related area of pharmaceutical "interventions" to treat low sexual arousal in women), these varied responses reveal the importance of soliciting women's narrative responses in tandem with, or instead of, their physiological arousal patterns. Because women cannot compare their own wetness to many other women's bodies (except for women who have sex with many other women), most women seem to have internalized some ideal version of wetness that they evaluated themselves against; we do not yet know whether partner attitudes impacted women's feelings about vaginal wetness (Hoffman et al., 2010) or whether women self-generated notions of "proper" lubrication.

Women's stories about wetness highlighted some key tensions that exist in the study of women's sexuality more broadly. For example, are "problems" with arousal located in the individual or in the couple? Should women be "treated" for problems with arousal, or should they work on their couple dynamics, communication, expression of sexual needs, and relationship issues? The data in this chapter suggested that women who struggled with wetness sometimes assigned responsibility to their own bodies (e.g., menopause impacting ability to become wet) and sometimes saw it as related to partners (e.g., not having enough time to become aroused because of a partner rushing). The implications of this for clinical practitioners, medical providers, and (particularly in light of Addyi/Flibanserin's release onto the market), the pharmaceutical industry seem notable. How women understand their sexual arousal patterns and wetness, and what emotions they attach to wetness, can connect to how they view their sexual relationships and their bodies more broadly. For example, those women who chose to have vaginal sex despite feeling "dry" often did so to please a partner, which relates directly to the literature on sexual compliance (Katz & Tirone, 2009; Vannier & O'Sullivan, 2010).

Further, women sometimes saw their vaginal lubrication as "excessive," signaling yet another area where stories of excess and being "too much" follow women around. Women already struggle with accusations of "excess" in relation to their emotional lives (Sachs & Blackmore, 1998), menstrual cycles (Stubbs & Costos, 2004), body hair (Fahs, 2011), and body weight (Spitzack, 1990); notably, even something as personal and intimate as vaginal lubrication also seemed to absorb these narratives of excess. That women imagined their wetness as "too much" or even as medically concerning (see Gail's narrative) connected to a larger cultural story of women's bodies "failing" either by being "insufficient" or by being "too much."

On a more positive note, many women seemed to experience their vaginal lubrication and wetness as a sign of connection, pleasure, and joy, finding ways to feel comfortable in their bodies and close to their partners. Women imagined their arousal in relation to not only sex per se, but also people, activities, moods, anticipation, imagination, states of mind, or even dancing. This description of the erotic—of what women imagined as connected to their body's responses of excitement—went far beyond the notion of mere "stimulation." Rather, women talked at length about arousal as connected to things that extended far beyond sexual technique (e.g., being looked at in a certain way, emotional connections, taking time or feeling rushed, desiring and feeling desired, use of alcohol, etc.), complicating and refuting the idea that wetness merely arises from certain kinds of touching or stimulation alone.

For women who imagined their wetness as connected to physical and biological processes, an emphasis on health and well-being appeared. Seeing wetness as a biological response did not preclude their appreciation of it as a sign of health and wellness. The sense that women's bodies are wet and dry on demand, that they can control their body's responses and their experiences of sexual arousal, showed women as embracing agency, empowerment, and control, even when they did not frame wetness using emotion language. Feeling at ease with sexual arousal also contrasts with the stories that the pharmaceutical industry promotes, as comfort, satisfaction, pleasure, and relaxation (emotions women seemed to feel about their wetness quite often in this data) cannot serve as good marketing points for an industry hell-bent on medicalizing women's sexual desire and framing all women as "deficient." In this regard, this chapter's results are reasonably hopeful and present a counter-narrative to the story that women find their sexual arousal universally distressing and troubling.

In general, these findings suggest that women's experiences of "wet embodiment," that is, imagining wetness, having emotions about wetness, giving a narrative to wetness, or discussing the meaning of wetness, is largely without a pre-existing script. Unlike the later questions I asked in the study about menstruation (another bodily fluid with clearly scripted meanings around "grossness" and needing "management"), wetness seemed more difficult for women to discuss in an emotional sense in part because it is largely invisible (or, more accurately, *made* invisible) in mainstream culture. This status impacts how women described wetness as their reference points were more diffuse and difficult to access compared to other bodily fluids like menstrual blood, urine, feces, and breast milk.

Ultimately, in this chapter, I emphasized the importance of women's qualitative narratives about wetness in an age where pharmaceutical companies are seeking to medicate and "normalize" a reductive vision of women's sexual arousal and desire to have sex. Further, given that emphasis on men's arousal is often constructed as primary and important, while women's arousal is seen as secondary and forgotten (often because synthetic lubricants can seemingly substitute for the functionality of wetness), the data in this chapter suggest that attention to wetness both within and outside of medical discourses is crucial to understanding women's sexuality. As these narratives reveal, women's ideas about wetness extend far beyond notions of feelings stimulated and aroused by specific actions, as they instead focused on complicated notions of body image, partner communication, desire to please partners, feelings about aging, concerns about excessiveness, joy in being with a partner, and appreciation of the body's natural processes (among others) to describe vaginal lubrication. These aspects of women's arousal will continue to evade and elude the reach of what pharmaceutical companies can medicate, and as such, reveal the power and complexity of women's sexuality as a flexible, fluid, and defiant entity.

Note

1 The method for this chapter is the same as Chapter 1 and draws on the same 2014 group of 20 women.

References

Adams, H. E., Wright, L. W., & Lohr, B. A. (1996). Is homophobia associated with homo-sexual arousal? *Journal of Abnormal Psychology*, *105*(3), 440–445.

Ayling, K., & Ussher, J. M. (2008). "If sex hurts, am I still a woman?" The subjective experience of vulvodynia in hetero-sexual women. *Archives of Sexual Behavior*, *37*(2), 294–304.

Bancroft, J., Loftus, J., & Long, J. S. (2003). Distress about sex: A national survey of women in heterosexual relationships. *Archives of Sexual Behavior*, *32*(3), 193–208.

Boseley, S. (2015). FDA approval of "female Viagra" leaves bitter taste for critics. *The Guardian*. www.theguardian.com/science/2015/aug/19/fda-approval-female-viagra-critics-addyi-us-licence.

Braun, V., Gavey, N., & McPhillips, K. (2003). The fair deal? Unpacking accounts of reci-procity in heterosex. *Sexualities*, *6*(2), 237–261.

Cacchioni, T. (2015). *Big pharma, women, and the labour of love*. Toronto: University of Toronto Press.

Chivers, M. L., Seto, M. C., Lalumiere, M. L., Laan, E., & Grimbos, T. (2010). Agreement of self-reported and genital measures of sexual arousal in men and women: A meta-analysis. *Archives of Sexual Behavior*, *39*(1), 5–56.

Civic, D., & Wilson, D. (1996). Dry sex in Zimbabwe and implications for condom use. *Social Science & Medicine*, *42*(1), 91–98.

Fahs, B. (2011). Dreaded "otherness" heteronormative patrolling in women's body hair rebellions. *Gender & Society*, *25*(4), 451–472.

Fahs, B. (2014). Coming to power: Women's fake orgasms and best orgasm experiences illuminate the failures of (hetero) sex and the pleasures of connection. *Culture, Health, & Sexuality*, *16*(8), 974–988.

Franklin, D., Kanigel, R., & Lehrman, S. (1998). High pressure isn't sexy. *Health*, *12*(1), 24.

Gohr, M. A. (2018). Cult of the penis: Male fragility and phallic frenzy. In B. Fahs, A. Mann, E. Swank, & S. Stage (Eds.), *Transforming contagion: Anxieties, modalities, possi-bilities* (pp. 160–172). New Brunswick: Rutgers, University Press.

Graham, C. A. (2010). The DSM diagnostic criteria for female sexual arousal disorder. *Archives of Sexual Behavior*, *39*(2), 240–255.

Harris, G. (2004, February 28). Pfizer gives up testing Viagra on women. *The New York Times*. www.nytimes.com/2004/02/28/business/pfizer-gives-up-testing-viagra-on-women.html?_r=0

Hayes, R. D., & Dennerstein, L. (2005). The impact of aging on sexual function and sexual dysfunction in women: A review of population-based studies. *The Journal of Sexual Medi-cine*, *2*(3), 317–330.

Hayes, R. D., Dennerstein, L., Bennett, C. M., Sidat, M., Gurrin, L. C., & Fairley, C. K. (2008). Risk factors for female sexual dysfunction in the general population: Exploring factors associated with low sexual function and sexual distress. *The Journal of Sexual Medi-cine*, *5*(7), 1681–1693.

Higgins, J. A. (2007). Sex feminisms & sexual health: Theorizing heterosex, pleasure, and constraint in public health research. *Atlantis*, *31*(2), 72–81.

Higgins, J. A., & Hirsch, J. S. (2008). Pleasure, power, and inequality: Incorporating sexuality into research on contraceptive use. *American Journal of Public Health, 98*(10), 1803–1813.

Hilber, A. M., Hull, T. H., Preston-Whyte, E., Bagnol, B., Smit, J., Wacharasin, C., & Widyantoro, N. (2010). A cross cultural study of vaginal practices and sexuality: Implications for sexual health. *Social Science & Medicine, 70*(3), 392–400.

Hoffman, S., Morrow, K. M., Mantell, J. E., Rosen, R. K., Carballo-Diéguez, A., & Gai, F. (2010). Covert use, vaginal lubrication, and sexual pleasure: A qualitative study of urban U.S. women in a vaginal microbicide clinical trial. *Archives of Sexual Behavior, 39*(3), 748–760.

Jackson, S., & Scott, S. (2002). Embodying orgasm: Gendered power relations and sexual pleasure. *Women & Therapy, 24*(1), 99–110.

Jozkowski, K. N., Herbenick, D., Schick, V., Reece, M., Sanders, S. A., & Fortenberry, J. D. (2013). Women's perceptions about lubricant use and vaginal wetness during sexual activities. *Journal of Sex Research, 10*(2), 484–492.

Katz, J., & Tirone, V. (2009). Women's sexual compliance with male dating partners: Associations with investment in ideal womanhood and romantic well-being. *Sex Roles, 60* (5–6), 347–356.

Kroll, D. (2015). More complicated than "Pink Viagra": What you should know about Flibanserin (Addyi). *Forbes.* www.forbes.com/sites/davidkroll/2015/06/04/more-complicated-than-pink-viagra-what-you-should-know-about-flibanserin-addyi/

Laumann, E. O., Paik, A., & Rosen, R. C. (1999). Sexual dysfunction in the United States: Prevalence and predictors. *JAMA, 281*(6), 537–544.

Leclerc-Madlala, S. (2001). Virginity testing: Managing sexuality in a maturing HIV/AIDS epidemic. *Medical Anthropology Quarterly, 15*(4), 533–552.

Leiblum, S. R., Hayes, R. D., Wasner, R. A., & Nelson, J. S. (2009). Vaginal dryness: A comparison of prevalence and interventions in 11 countries. *Journal of Sexual Medicine, 6*(9), 2425–2433.

Leiblum, S. R., Seehuus, M., & Brown, C. (2007). Persistent genital arousal: Disordered or normative aspect of female sexual response? *The Journal of Sexual Medicine, 4*(3), 680–689.

Levin, R. (2005). Wet and dry sex—The impact of cultural influence in modifying vaginal function. *Sexual and Relationship Therapy, 20*(4), 465–474.

Loe, M. (2004). *The rise of Viagra: How the little blue pill changed sex in America.* New York : New York University Press.

Meston, C. M. (1997). Aging and sexuality. *Western Journal of Medicine, 167*(4), 285–290.

Miller, A. S., & Byers, S. E. (2004). Actual and desired duration of foreplay and intercourse: Disordance and misperceptions within heterosexual couples. *Journal of Sex Research, 41* (3), 301–309.

Moore, L. J. (2008). *Sperm counts: Overcome by man's most precious fluid.* New York : New York University Press.

Potts, A., Grace, V. M., Gavey, N., & Vares, T. (2004). "Viagra stories": Challenging "erectile dysfunction". *Social Science & Medicine, 59*(3), 489–499.

Potts, A., Grace, V. M., Vares, T., & Gavey, N. (2006). "Sex for life"? Men's counter-stories on "erectile dysfunction," male sexuality, and ageing. *Sociology of Health & Illness, 28*(3), 306–329.

Rellini, A. H., McCall, K. M., Randall, P. K., & Meston, C. M. (2005). The relationship between women's subjective and physiological sexual arousal. *Psychophysiology, 42*(1), 116–124.

Rosen, R. C. (1996). Erectile dysfunction: The medicalization of male sexuality. *Clinical Psychology Review, 16*(6), 497–519.

Rowland, D. L., Georgoff, V. L., & Burnett, A. L. (2011). Psychoaffective differences between sexually functional and dysfunctional men in response to a sexual experience. *The Journal of Sexual Medicine*, *8*(1), 132–139.

Sachs, J., & Blackmore, J. (1998). You never show you can't cope: Women in school leadership roles managing their emotions. *Gender and Education*, *10*(3), 265–279.

Schwandt, M., Morris, C., Ferguson, A., Ngugi, E., & Moses, S. (2006). Anal and dry sex in commercial sex work, and relation to risk for sexually transmitted infections and HIV in Meru, Kenya. *Sexually Transmitted Infections*, *82*(5), 392–396.

Skafte, I., & Silberschmidt, M. (2014). Female gratification, sexual power, and safer sex: Female sexuality as an empowering resource among women in Rwanda. *Culture, Health, & Sexuality*, *16*(1), 1–13.

Smit, J., McFadyen, L., Zuma, K., & Preston-Whyte, E. (2002). Vaginal wetness: An underestimated problem experience by progestogen injectable contraceptive users in South Africa. *Social Science & Medicine*, *55*(9), 1511–1522.

Spitzack, C. (1990). *Confessing excess: Women and the politics of body reduction*. Albany, NY: State University of New York Press.

Streicher, L. (2015). 25 facts about Flibanserin (Addyi), the new "Viagra for women". *Everyday Health*. www.everydayhealth.com/columns/lauren-streicher-midlife-menopause-and-beyond/everything-you-always-wanted-to-know-about-addyi-aka-the-little-pink-pill-but-were-afraid-to-ask/

Stubbs, M. L., & Costos, D. (2004). Negative attitudes toward menstruation: Implications for disconnection within girls and between women. *Women & Therapy*, *27*(3–4), 37–54.

Sutton, K. S., Boyer, S. C., Goldfinger, C., Ezer, P., & Pukall, C. F. (2012). To lube or not to lube: Experiences and perceptions of lubricant use in women with and without dyspareunia. *Journal of Sexual Medicine*, *9*, 240–250.

Tanner, A. E., Zimet, G., Fortenberry, J. D., Reece, M., Graham, C., & Murray, M. (2009). Young women's use of a vaginal microbicide surrogate: The role of individual and contextual factors in acceptability and sexual pleasure. *Journal of Sex Research*, *46*(1), 15–23.

Tiefer, L., Hall, M., & Tavris, C. (2002). Beyond dysfunction: A new view of women's sexual problems. *Journal of Sex & Marital Therapy*, *28*(1), 225–232.

Vannier, S. A., & O'Sullivan, L. F. (2010). Sex without desire: Characteristics of occasions of sexual compliance in young adults' committed relationships. *Journal of Sex Research*, *47*(5), 429–439.

PART 2

Veering and queering

4

KILLJOY'S KASTLE AND THE HAUNTINGS OF QUEER/LESBIAN FEMINISM

In October 2013, artist and filmmakers Allyson Mitchell and Deirdre Logue designed and showcased in Toronto an interactive performance installation, Killjoy's Kastle. Exhibited again at the British Film Institute in 2014, with a subsequent showing in Los Angeles in October 2015, the project elicited a wide swath of responses ranging from celebration to contempt. The Kastle created, by all accounts, a fascinating, rebellious, absurd world in which the history of feminism (particularly lesbian feminism) took center stage.

The ad for the 2015 show (One Archives, 2015) described it as follows:

Lesbian Rule.
Forget the dead this Halloween.
Feel the pulsing throb of something larger than life in *KillJoy's Kastle*.

> Each Halloween radical evangelical groups build hell houses. These per-former-animated installations showcase a gruesome retribution for the sins of fornication, abortion, suicide, occultism, and—of course—same-sex relation-ships. This Halloween, Toronto based-artists **Deirdre Logue** and **Allyson Mitchell** reclaim this hellish scenario with their sex positive, trans inclusive, queer lesbian-feminist-fear-fighting celebration. Organized by One Archives in West Hollywood, *KillJoy's Kastle: A Lesbian Feminist Haunted House* is designed to pervert, not convert. This haunted house of freaky feminist skill sharing and paranormal consciousness-raising reanimates the archive of lesbian herstory with all its wonders and thorny complications. Expect horror.

> **Holey Hell House!**

> Dare to be scared by gender-queer apparitions, ball-busting butches, and never-married, happy-as-hell spinsters. Get down on riot ghouls and radical

vampiric grannies while channeling your inner consciousness hell-raiser. Each evening of nightmarishly non-assimilated lesbian mayhem will include multiple live performances from a spirited group of international and local weirdos.

Deep Lez becomes Creep Lez

Follow your demented women's studies tour guide through the glorious and grisly *KillJoy's Kastle*. Groups are welcome, especially the unruly kind. This ground-up, maximalist, not-to-be-missed haunted house—nailed, knit, and glued by a coven of dedicated feminists—provides a rare glimpse into this dystopic/utopic craftivist world-view.

Taking up the playful reversals and queer performativity of this exhibition, in this chapter I look at Killjoy's Kastle and its implications for thinking about queer theory and queer history, particularly as the history of feminism becomes increasingly appropriated, distorted, and rewritten to exclude that which does not represent feminism's more tame and palatable side. The Kastle, on the other hand, prioritizes play and humor as a form of resistance, but also the radical reimagining of storytelling, an embrace of women's madness, and the queering of the (frankly homophobic) "hell house" concept. In this chapter, I explore the utility of these tactics, and the notion of (quite literally in this case) *queer feminist hauntings*, that is, the way that queer identities and feminist narratives function as a hidden, silenced, shadowy, and even spooky entity. The chapter begins by looking at the academic readings of Killjoy's Kastle, followed by an analysis of play and humor as forms of rebellion, particularly as the Kastle highlights feminist comedy, the writings of Valerie Solanas, and the undermining of academia. I follow this with an analysis of queer hauntings, including finding the queer archive, how queer theory opens and shifts discourses of the "hell house" through this performance, and the ways that progressive and radical artists can appropriate and transform narratives of homophobia and misogyny by shifting the affective and emotional reactions we have to queer space.

A tour of Killjoy's Kastle

The experience of the Kastle begins before entering its doors, with an undead Valerie Solanas (author of the notoriously misandrist *SCUM Manifesto*, first self-published in 1967 and later published by Olympia Press in 1968) giving visitors their instructions. After entering the Marvelous Emasculator (a giant vagina dentata—a vagina with teeth), guests are guided through the Kastle by demented women's studies professors (or a disgruntled, bitter teaching assistant) in what one critic calls a "dystopic/utopic craftist worldview" designed by a "coven of dedicated feminists" (King, 2018, p. 15). Visitors pass the intersectional activist section of the house, boxing various giant tampons labeled with capitalism, colonialism, and transphobia. Signs in the Kastle point cheekily to "Beware the Sinking Pit of Identity Politics," "Paradigm Shift Ahead," "Giant Bearded Clam," "Cunt Breath," "Super Natural Pussy," and "Back Tickling & Hair Braiding Indoctrination Ahead." Next, they encounter "ghost vaginas." On one tour, Mitchell herself said:

> The problem is, the feminist stereotype of consciousness-raising has been reduced to this empty husk of the lone suburban housewife, gazing at her vagina with a mirror in her living room … Not that there's anything wrong with that, but let's do it collectively! *These* ghosts are reclaiming that empty stereotype in a sex-positive way.
>
> *(Cited in Yamato, 2015)*

Aiming for a fully immersive sensory experience, visitors then visit the Para-normal Consciousness Raisers section where they are asked to tune into the Smell of Bodily Presence; they then enter the Gender Studies Professor Dance Party with over-sized paper mâché books straight from the "canon" of gender studies texts. (Lesbians yell at guests, "You haven't READ THAT?" and shriek at others' ignorance.) Guests also visit a "blood-spattered bathroom in which courageous patrons are asked to help a sister empty her diva cup" along with the "Day-Glo lair of the Lesbian Feminist Internet Troll" (cited in Yamato, 2015). Mitchell says,

> By day, her politics are right on. By night, she's a fucking bitch patrolling the universe waiting for you to screw up, go to the wrong event, use the wrong words to describe your own experience … Don't get too close to her—she'll friend you, then she'll fuck you up!
>
> *(Cited in Yamato, 2015)*

Continuing on, visitors walk through the gender-ambiguous "hairy hole" where they are greeted by trans-masculine police officers who allow passage into the next space. (There's also a "Daddy Tank" where "deviant" butch women were once held away from others in jail—see Derrick, 2015). Visitors next head to the Graveyard of Dead Feminist Ideas (e.g., Little Frida's Coffee Shop, Lesbian Tide, Catch One Disco, Michigan Womyn's Music Festival), followed by the "domestic space" (with a nest of polyamorous vampiric gran-nies). Next up is the straw feminist hall of shame and its hall of portraits (e.g., Beyoncé, Liz Lemon, Sarah Palin), followed by the stitch witches room, where visitors learn about the complex relationship between the war on drugs and the prison industrial complex (complete with a sacrament for all guests).

Visitors end their trip in the Real Life Feminist Killjoy Processing Room and are meant to leave with more questions than answers. Guests sit down with "real life feminist killjoys" and talk with them about their feelings, followed by a final exit through the last hairy curtain. To actually leave, visitors work together to escape:

> Once you acquiesce and get to a certain layer of that immersion then you
> actually depend on the trust of your collective to get you out the other
> side because it's a labyrinth, because it's a haunted house; you won't
> know how to find your way alone. You need the collective to work that
> out with you—and you need to stick together.
>
> *(Mitchell, as quoted in King, 2018, p. 16)*

Visitors then visit Yee Old Feminist Gift Shop and wander out into the courtyard to the café of the Lesbian Zombie Folk Singers where they can listen to
music. In the courtyard:

> The two zombies openly bickered about their past relationship as lovers
> and proclaimed they had been resurrected together to perform as a form
> of purgatory after murdering each other when their personal and profes-
> sional relationships turned sour. Playing their own repertoire, as well as
> covers of lesbian folk classics, the zombies performed their anachronism
> self reflexively, making snide comments about current political affairs and
> comparing their experiences of the 1990s lesbian heyday "when it was
> possible to have a lesbian band" with current culture, which they seem to
> regard as a dystopic failure of their vision for a feminist future.
>
> *(Flavelle, 2017)*

Visitors also have a choice of bathrooms between Oppressed and Oppressor
("you choose").

Because the Kastle was situated outside in a public park (in Los Angeles) or in
a back alley (Toronto), it works against the pretenses of a "high-art" gallery space
and removes barriers between art and audience. It is, according to Mitchell,
decisively queer, lesbian, and feminist without being separatist or exclusionary; further, she argues that the Kastle works to make feminism more accessible (YouTube,
2015). Ultimately, Killjoy's Kastle features Mitchell and Logue's "sex-positive,
trans-inclusive, queer lesbian-feminist-fear-fighting celebration. Killjoy's Kastle:
A Lesbian Feminist Haunted House is designed to pervert, not convert" (King,
2018, p. 15). Logue concludes, "You will be harshly entertained" (Miranda, 2015).

The Kastle meets the tower

In a fitting tribute to Allyson Mitchell and Deirdre Logue, the response to Killjoy's Kastle has fused together popular critiques, infuriated open letters, celebratory art columns, and a handful of academic articles that have begun to analyze
the meaning of this unique and singular performance piece. (Mitchell and her
colleague, Cait McKinney, have just released a book about the Kastle as well,
see Mitchell & McKinney, 2019.) While the Kastle is designed as "agit-prop"
that teaches people about feminist history and feminist thought, it does so outside of the typical channels of teaching and learning, and, most importantly,

resists any claims to respectability and politeness. Mitchell has said of the Kastle's outsider status: "Right, but the Kastle isn't some sort of a public relations outreach project" (King, 2018, p. 16). It purposefully pushes back and subverts from the margins of both feminist/lesbian art and the women and gender studies canon; it is both playful and serious, frivolous and serious, trivial and intensely consequential. It draws from second-wave radical feminist traditions of using humor and satire to provide scathing social critique (e.g., Flo Kennedy's conceptualization of pro-Vietnam war propaganda as "Penta-gonorrhea," see Fahs, 2019).

The Kastle fits with Mitchell and Logue's longstanding interest in deconstructing the dichotomies and hierarchies of feminist and queer history. As artists, they have themselves prioritized the erasure of boundaries between the academic, the artistic, and the personal. In 2010, they cofounded and opened the FAG Feminist Art Gallery, described as a "political pot luck, free-schooling, backyard screening, axe grinding, directed reading, protest sign making, craft den, incantation, herbal tea and gluten-free muffin top artist talk sensation" (Logue, Mitchell, Cho, & Sea, 2017, p. 123). In this space, the artists worked to blur notions of home and work as well:

> We open our house a FAG to you and other visitors. You are welcome here. We are vulnerable to you. Like queer objects, we tend towards each other. Part of FAG's mission is to break down the divisions between public and private, home and social, gallery and studio.
>
> *(p. 123)*

With regard to the Kastle, the work has been hailed as singular, unique, bizarre, and at once hilarious and impactful (Derrick, 2015; King, 2018). The Kastle draws directly on Sara Ahmed's (2018) conception of the feminist killjoy:

> In my work I have explored, reclaimed, and affirmed the figure of the feminist killjoy, the one who gets in the way of happiness or who just gets in the way. The feminist killjoy is snappy: she is heard as shouting however she speaks, because of the point she makes, the words she uses, words like sexism, words like racism, just to make these points, use these words, is to be heard as shouting, abrasive, as if by opening your mouth you are breaking something. If pointing out racism and sexism is to cause unhappiness, we are quite willing to cause unhappiness. We become mouthy when they don't like what comes out of our mouths.

She goes on to write, in *The promise of happiness*, "To kill joy … is to open a life, to make room for life, to make room for possibility, for chance" (2010, p. 20).

In this sense, the Kastle embraces a kind of purposeful "too-muchness," a willful sense of overdoing it, a frankly over-the-top kind of abrasive shouting. It simultaneously opens up discursive space for new possibilities, one where feminism can be both explicitly angry and wholly funny. As scholar Moynan King (2018) argued,

The work is physically, intellectually, and ideologically immersive; labyrinthine, theoretical, and queer. The performance is not interactive; it is tactically exploratory, and explanatory, taking the spectator through a fantastical version of what Judith Butler termed the "site of collective contestation" that is a queer community.

(p. 16)

She goes on to say that Killjoy's Kastle draws upon Sara Ahmed's notion of "questioning of worlds" (p. 16) to theorize the unique ways that the audience is positioned as both spectator and inhabitant (King, 2018).

By using the Kastle to grapple with some of the "undead tropes from feminist herstories" (p. 56), Mitchell and Logue explore uneasy queer feelings that allow for disagreement, contention, and difference as much as a cohesive, unified feminist/queer story. In short, the Kastle makes space for a shared experience that allows for profoundly different subjectivities within feminism and queerness. Instead of reinforcing the viciousness of identity politic warfare, they playfully undermine it, showing instead the value of *building something new* that draws from the "perverse" histories of queer and feminist subjectivities. (Notably, they do not plan to re-stage the Kastle again, thereby encouraging it to itself become mythic, ghost-like, and alive in memory only—this too might mimic queer experience in the real world, as stories and histories of queerness feel displaced, forgotten, and untethered.)

The Kastle's relationship to queer affect may also stem from the direct rebellion that the Kastle has against Christian "hell houses." Originally conceived as tools for Christian fundamentalists to teach about morality, hell houses have morphed into fully theatrical fear-based performances of sin and punishment (Jackson, 2007). As Ann Pellegrini (2007) wrote,

Hell Houses are evangelical riffs on the haunted houses that dot the landscape of secular culture each Halloween. Some of these haunted houses are seasonal attractions mounted by for-profit amusement parks; others are low-tech fund-raisers run by local community groups. Where haunted houses promise to scare the bejeezus out of you, Hell Houses aim to scare you to Jesus. In a typical Hell House, demon tour guides take the audience through a series of bloody staged tableaux depicting sinners whose bad behavior—homosexuality, abortion, suicide, and, above all, rejection of Christ's saving grace—leads them straight to hell.

(p. 912)

Hell houses target the visitor's *feelings* and existential insecurities in order to scare them into religious fervor (Pellegrini, 2009). As such, Pellegrini (2007) calls hell houses "affectively rich worlds" (p. 912) that literally demonize LGBT identities (and any sexual appetites) and frame queerness as a reason for going to (an actual) hell.

Mitchell and Logue have described the piece as a direct reaction to the creation of "hell houses" by Evangelical Christians. Logue has said of Evangelical Christian Hell Houses that they "use space and theatricality and ramp it right up. They take theatre to its absolute extreme: Plexiglas floors with demons underneath, incredible diorama style scenarios playing out—it's very intense" (King, 2018, p. 16). The Kastle, while putting forth quite a different story, nevertheless draws from and exacerbates the visitor's *emotional* experience of the space; visitors are encouraged to feel the weightiness of the "undead" feminist figures, the numbness of the feminist zombie, the intensity of the sensory-immersive experience they have entered.

And, of course, this intense affect—good and bad—also appeared in the critical appraisals of the Kastle. The work has been lauded by feminist scholars and critics as walking that fine line between embracing and celebrating the killjoy while also embracing subversiveness and camp. As Lisa Derrick (2015) wrote:

> In the drive for political correctness, uptight killjoys have taken the transgressive and sexy fun out being queer, while glossing over the unpleasantries in a drive for moral supremacy. As a countermeasure, Killjoy's Kastle has resurrected the past—the good, the bad and the ugly—and laid it out in a high camp, super-smart, ultimately loving way.

Mitchell and Logue also enact, in practical terms, Mitchell's Deep Lez ideologies put forth in her 2009 "Deep Lez I Statement," which argues against a one-dimensional version of feminist/queer history and instead argues for multiple, competing, contradictory histories that collide in productive and messy ways. She wrote of these profound complexities:

> Deep Lez uses cafeteria-style mixings of craft, context, food, direct action and human connections to maintain radical dyke politics and resistant strategies. Part quilting bee, part public relations campaign, and part Molotov cocktail, Deep Lez seeks to map out the connections between the second position feminisms that have sustained radical lesbian politics and the current "third wave" feminisms that look to unpack many of the concepts upon which those radical politics have been developed. These recent feminisms have set forth a host of important critiques about radical lesbianisms as they have historically unfolded, and look to provide correctives in this regard. Unfortunately, this is often accomplished through the wholesale dismissal of a radical lesbian practice and identification. Deep Lez was coined to acknowledge the urgent need to develop inclusive liberatory feminisms while examining the strategic benefits of maintaining some components of a radical lesbian theory and practice. This project is carefully situated not to simply hold on to history, but rather to examine how we might cull what is useful from lesbian herstories to redefine contemporary urban lesbian (and queer) existence. In so

doing, "lesbian" is resurrected as a potential site of radical identification, rather than one of de-politicized apathy (or worse, shame).

(Mitchell, 2009)

In this sense, Mitchell has laid a framework for the success of the Kastle as an art piece. Scholar Genevieve Flavelle (2017) highlights the Kastle's successes thusly:

> The Haunted House attempted to resurrect "lesbian" as a potential site of radical identification, rather than one of de-politicized apathy or shame. Mitchell and Logue grappled with some of the harmful and problematic aspects of lesbian feminism that caused the movement to lose relevance while also exploring how dominant society actively maligns otherness to maintain supremacy.

She goes on to say, "Feminism as a social, political, and intellectual movement has been fraught with schisms, losses, infighting and *feelings*."

In tandem with this praise, some have openly criticized the complex representations of both feminism and lesbianism at the Kastle. While conservative *Toronto Sun* critic Joe Warmington slammed the Kastle for its use of public funding (Anonymous, 2013/2014), message boards went aflame with various critical perspectives. As Genevieve Flavelle (2017) wrote:

> I identified that the majority of the dialogue centered on critiques of trans misogyny, the maintenance of the structural whiteness of feminism, the consent of visitors, and the accountability of the artist. As artist Mary Tremonte aptly identifies in her discussion of the installation, "the barrage of criticism for the LFHH (Lesbian Feminist Haunted House) centered on representation and identity politics, an example of difference within difference; how multifaceted and various the identities of 'lesbian' and 'feminist' are, and how a diverse audience responded to the project's provocations."

Mitchell (2014) responded to these critiques with her own open letter, in which she refutes many of these critiques of her work:

> You claim that people left the Kastle questioning their own place in feminism. That is good and kind of the point. I am constantly questioning my own place in feminism. That's how it should be—not a secure, stagnant engagement … It seems like the critique you are trying to articulate is that the haunted house should have been more welcoming. A haunted house is meant to be intimidating. Art is meant to be critically engaged.

(p. 8)

She goes onto critique the implied narcissism of assuming that art should be easily digested and well-liked:

It's as though I baked you a cake for your birthday and you didn't like the flavor. You assume that my art is a product for your consumption, that it is something that should answer the questions you have about your "womanhood."

(p. 8)

She wrote in an earlier post that Killjoy's Kastle "is meant to be an apt and symbolic funeral for dead and dying lesbian feminist monsters as well as a place to cathartically face fears, self-critique, and contradictions" (Mitchell, 2013).

Play and humor as rebellion

Notably, Mitchell and Logue have embraced the difficulty of conceptualizing feminist humor amidst a "feminist killjoy" stance. Sara Ahmed said of this tension:

Sometimes being a feminist killjoy can feel like you are getting in the way of your own happiness; and if happiness means not noticing the injustices around us, so be it. But that's not the only way of telling a feminist story, because apprehending the world from a feminist point of view is apprehending more, not less. Living a feminist life helps to create a more complete picture because we try not to turn away from what compromises our happiness. Of course, sometimes it can be tiring being unhappy *about* so many things! But I find joy in the fullness of living a feminist life, though not only, and not always.

(Mehra, 2017)

Like the key tensions in Sara Ahmed's (2018) framing of the "feminist killjoy," the relationship between feminism as serious versus feminism as playful has haunted feminist art and writing for decades. With "undead" stereotypes of feminists as humorless shrew-like characters (Bailey, 1997), feminist art has often struggled to forge a path forward for playful, cheeky, subversive, and silly depictions of feminism without undermining its core critiques of the status quo.

Numerous scholars have tried to assert space for feminist comedy and feminist play as key elements of justice work. Whether espousing the value of feminist comedians Tina Fey (Lauzen, 2014), Phyllis Diller (Lavin, 2004), Amy Schumer (Goltz, 2015), and Lena Dunham (Woods, 2015), making space for feminist comedy work of Margaret Cho, Wanda Sykes, and Sarah Silverman as an intersectional art form (Mizejewski, 2014) or embracing the new and edgy in feminist stand-up (e.g., Ali Wong, Hannah Gadsby) and feminist television (e.g., *Broad City, Baroness Von Sketch Show*), attempts to make visible the subversive work of feminist comedians has begun. As Linda Mizejewski (2014) wrote of feminist comedians:

Women's comedy has become a primary site in mainstream pop culture where feminism speaks, talks back, and is contested … Overall, the political impetus of their work reflects the strategies, trends, and contradictions of the women's movement since the 1970s. That is, their work reflects feminism as a diverse set of discourses that range from "women's lib" to the queer-friendly politics that veer away from acknowledging "women" as a category at all.

(p. 6)

Feminist humor has also taken more satirical, absurdist, and sarcastic manifest-ations, evidenced most clearly in the work of Valerie Solanas (whom Mitchell and Logue include as a kind of greeter and instruction-provider to visitors at the Kastle). Feminists have accused Solanas of being many things: a man-hater, the embodiment of feminist rage, an emblem of queer/feminist outsider-ness, a "schizophrenic scream," a "bad meal that didn't go down well," a prescient socially-conscious ahead-of-her-time thinker, a case study of women's madness, and a brilliant writer (for the detailed version of Solanas's life and what other feminists thought of her, see Fahs, 2014). A less-discussed but, I think, hugely significant part of her persona was Solanas's insistence on humor as a tool of expressing rage, of satire as an alarming weapon of justice, of outrageousness as a form of seriousness. This blurring is most evident in reactions to Valerie Sola-nas that demand to know whether the Warhol shootings represented the *SCUM Manifesto* (1968) in practice, that is whether readers should take *SCUM* seriously or view it as satire (Fahs, 2008). (My typical reaction to this: It is both, simultaneously.)

Valerie Solanas symbolizes a key figure in feminist humor and feminist play in part because she understood that feminists should *make fun of themselves* and should never take their eye off of the tensions and contradictions within the feminist movement. Herself an embodiment of contradiction and paradox, Sola-nas had a bad temper laced with a deeply humorous style of expression. For example, in a 1977 interview with the *Village Voice*, Solanas said, "I go by an absolute standard," and when asked about shooting Andy Warhol, she replied, "I consider that a moral act. And I consider it immoral that I missed. I should have done target practice" (Fahs, 2014, p. 155). Solanas maintained a deep dis-trust toward organized social movements and, in particular, the goals and tactics of the women's liberation movement. She famously said of the women's liber-ation movement:

We're impatient. That's why. I'm not going to be around 100 years from now. I want a piece of a groovy world myself. That peaceful shit is for the birds. Marching, demonstrating. That's for little old ladies who aren't serious. SCUM is a criminal organization, not a civil disobedience lunch club. We'll operate under dark and as effectively as possible and get what we want as fast as possible.

(Fahs, 2014, p. 87)

In *SCUM Manifesto*, she wrote:

> SCUM will not picket, demonstrate, march, or strike to attempt to achieve its ends. Such tactics are for nice, genteel ladies who scrupulously take only such action as is guaranteed to be ineffective … If SCUM ever marches, it will be over the President's stupid, sickening face; if SCUM ever strikes, it will be in the dark with a six-inch blade.
>
> *(Solanas, 1996, p. 43)*

With particular contempt for feminists that she saw as riding her coattails, she wrote numerous angry letters that had an arguably humorous slant. (She had a habit of crossing out GOOD CORRECTION REDUCES CRIME from the prison letterhead and replacing it with ELIMINATING MEN REDUCES CRIME (Fahs, 2014, p. 170).) Ever an outsider, she busted up hippie communes by organizing women to fight back against doing the "shit work," and she threatened to throw acid in the faces of her enemies. Solanas also wrote numerous letters where she poked and prodded feminism itself. Solanas wrote in a 1977 letter, "*C.L.I.T. Papers* isn't the only totally worthless work produced by the Women's Bowel Movement (which constitutes a very large percentage, but not all of the women's movement) … Flush away one turd and the Bowel Movement's diminished by one. Bye. Bye" (Fahs, 2014, p. 290). Writer J. C. Pan (2014) has called Solanas's style "trasher feminism," the work of a disgruntled outsider. Drawing again from Ahmed (2017), one could also argue that Solanas was the feminist killjoy of her time, disallowing even the basic forms of solidarity and alliance that those in the feminist movement took pride in during the late 1960s and early 1970s.

In her use of humor, absurdity, and outrageousness to further her feminist claims, Valerie Solanas was not alone. Feminist and civil rights lawyer, Florynce "Flo" Kennedy also had a reputation as a person who publicly and shamelessly drew upon humor and outrageousness to make her points. She had a flamboyant and biting manner and garnished a reputation for hilarious actions and dry humor (along with a cowboy hat, pink sunglasses, and bold outfits). For example, when Flo toured with Gloria Steinem giving speeches on feminism, men in the audience sometimes stood up and demanded, "Are you lesbians?" Flo would respond—using an old phrase Ti-Grace Atkinson often used—that it depended. "Are you my alternative?" she would wryly ask (Fahs, 2018, p. 89). Kennedy also organized a "pee in" on the Harvard University steps to protest lack of women's restrooms on campus in Lowell Hall, saying of Harvard: "If you had to give the world an enema, you would put it in Harvard Yard. This has got to be the asshole of the world" (Grundhauser, 2016) and she famously rebuffed both the National Organization for Women and the early black feminist groups as full of talk and no action. (She once said of black feminists who met in her home: "I'm so sick and damn tired of hearing you bitches running around here, talking about you're going to form something. Form it! Call a meeting!") (Randolph, 2015, p. 206).

Notably, Killjoy's Kastle uses these tactics of absurdity and outrageousness not only to target individual examples of feminist thought and feminist theory, but to also simultaneously undermine the right wing (by poking fun at "hell houses") and academic versions of women's studies. The inclusion of the demented women's studies professor tour guide, for example, attacks the framing of feminism within the academy by undermining feminism's ivory tower connections. This stereotype of the "crazed" women's studies professor is both a form of self-immolation and good-spirited fun. It is a serious critique (women's studies has sharply distanced itself from its more radical activist roots) and a playful depiction (both Mitchell and Logue are deeply connected to "highbrow" feminist theory, for example). Most notably, their use of humor in Killjoy's Kastle plays upon the feminist stereotype of unhappiness ("killjoyness") both to reinforce this stereotype and to subvert it, and in doing so they effectively take aim at both lefty infighting and identity politics *and* right-wing, conservative discourses of homophobia, transphobia, and racism. That the Kastle was attacked more by other queer/feminist visitors than by right-wingers testifies again to the critical importance of their work, particularly as it sorts through the chaos and messiness of queer feminist politics and history. Humor and absurdity —coupled with performance and spectacle—might, I think, be the *only way* to accomplish such a Herculean task.

Queer hauntings?

This brings us to another crucial question: How do we document, act out, find, and perform queer history, particularly if such history mostly appears as frightening, scary apparitions? How is Killjoy's Kastle a kind of meditation on queer hauntings? And what, exactly, is haunting queer and feminist memory? This all sounds very academic, but I ask this with sincerity. Logue and Mitchell are working through a crucial problem in queer feminist lives— the *erasure of those lives*, the rendering of queerness to a fringe "haunting" presence, the permanent marginality of queerness. A number of scholars are starting to take this up with the notion of a queer asexual archive (Cerankowski & Milks, 2010; Przybylo & Cooper, 2014), asking us to consider: How do we find something that we never saw in the first place? In other words, how do we make an archive—a history—of queer feminist stories if those stories are mostly erased, forgotten, driven underground? How do we see something that's often rendered invisible?

Mark Clintberg and Jon Davies (2016) argued that Killjoy's Kastle, by taking up both the physical (e.g., architectural) and atmospheric aspects of the haunted house, along with its affective structures, has made theoretical space for examining queer affect (they define this as the "fraught or stigmatized feelings that often adhere to queer experience" (p. 56)) as a kind of haunting. Clintberg and Davies write:

The haunted house is only truly frightening when a visitor begins to doubt its representational quality, when they become uncertain as to whether it *represents* the haunted or actually *is* haunted. The critical edge enabled through its simulacral qualities gives the haunted house affective power and excitement … Haunted houses inherit and perform Gothic literature's fascination with acts of extreme violence, the spectral and the psychotic overlaid onto the domestic.

(p. 58)

Building onto this, they argue that haunted houses are not merely harmless surprises, but also a way to confirm the absurdity of the outside world, to frame reality as itself haunted. This assertion—that the absurdity within the haunted house actually pushes a reconsideration of the absurdity *outside* of the haunted house—helps us to understand the key queer interventions that Killjoy's Kastle inspires. I argue that the Kastle operates as a way to provoke extreme affect (e.g., laughter, repulsion, joy, fear) to capture something not only of queer art and representation, but of *queer experience itself.*

The Kastle works to simultaneously highlight the wide varieties of queer affects possible in a performative space, and to dislodge those affects from a space of "haunting" queer identity. In other words, affect itself lurks in the shadows of the haunted house, and the Kastle, by framing the more shameful or troubling or fight-picking aspects of feminist history at the fore of the performance, pushes viewers to acknowledge the "hauntings" of their own emotional relationship both to the house and to queerness more broadly. The condition of queer lives is one all-too-often constituted by marginalization, shame, and shadows. Clintberg and Davies (2016) appropriately draw connections between queer shame and the notion of queer haunting—that is, the material reality of living in a culture where one is pushed out, taught not *to be* gay. Citing Eve Kosofsky Sedgwick's (1991) work, Clintberg and Davies (2016) write, "[Sedgwick] proposes that the effeminate, proto-gay male child is the 'haunting abject' that inflects gay male adulthood with the shame of gender deviance" (p. 59). Queer childhood is a pulling inward, an erasure, a creation of blurred and fuzzy subjectivity that lurks in the background of adult life.

Perhaps most importantly, Clintberg and Davies (2016) hone in on the particular ways that queer hauntings might upend the expected emotional reactions we have to certain spaces; as Sedgwick (2003) says, "affects can be, and are, attached to things, people, ideas, sensations, relations, activities, institutions, and any number of other things, including other affects. Thus, one can be excited by anger, disgusted by shame, or surprised by joy" (p. 19). Clintberg and Davies extend this by arguing, "we are drawn to the potential for these projects to generate a sense of *excitement* around queer haunting, transforming the fearful and somber into the thrilling and even joyful" (p. 60).

In my reading of the Kastle and its power, its impact, and its potential legacy not only within the art world but within feminist history in general, one of its great contributions is this meditation on the scary apparitions that not only haunt feminism itself (for example, consciousness-raising, long-dead lesbian bars and music festivals, and so on) but also the ways that queerness itself is rendered as itself an apparition, *permanently on the margin, permanently in the shadows*. Mitchell and Logue ask, through humor, play, and absurdity— and through the various ways that emotions produce surprising and expected paradoxes—if hauntings themselves are always/already queer, and if so what that might mean for the finding and telling of queer feminist histories. How might we tell a story about something that haunts us, and what sorts of for- getting, archiving, and memories can we generate from something perman- ently on the edges? How are the ghosts of queer, lesbian feminism alive/ visible, and how are they dead/invisible? What does the story on the *inside* of the house tell us about the world outside of the house? And, finally, how might the feminist killjoy—the persistent complainer, embracing feminism's edges—be the exact thing we need to save these histories from total demolition?

References

Ahmed, S. (2010). *The promise of happiness*. Durham, NC: Duke University Press.

Ahmed, S. (2017). *Living a feminist life*. Durham, NC: Duke University Press.

Ahmed, S. (2018, March 27). Notes on feminist survival. *Feminist Killjoys*. https://feminist killjoys.com/.

Anonymous. (2013/2014). Art, austerity, and the production of fear. *Fuse Magazine, 37*, 11.

Bailey, C. (1997). Making waves and drawing lines: The politics of defining the vicissitudes of feminism. *Hypatia, 12*(3), 17–28.

Cerankowski, K. J., & Milks, M. (2010). New orientations: Asexuality and its implications for theory and practice. *Feminist Studies, 36*(3), 650–664.

Clintberg, M., & Davies, J. (2016). Haunted by queer affect: Geoffrey Farmer's *the intellec- tion of lady spider house* and Allyson Mitchell's *Killjoy's Kastle*. *Journal of Curatorial Studies, 5*(1), 56–75.

Derrick, L. (2015). Killjoy's Kastle: Sexiest, smartest haunted house ever! *Huffington Post*. www.huffingtonpost.com/lisa-derrick/killjoys-kastle-smartest-_b_8402546.html.

Fahs, B. (2008). The radical possibilities of Valerie Solanas. *Feminist Studies, 34*(3), 591–617.

Fahs, B. (2014). *Valerie Solanas: The defiant life of the woman who wrote SCUM (and shot Andy Warhol)*. New York: Feminist Press.

Fahs, B. (2018). *Firebrand feminism: The radical lives of Ti-Grace Atkinson, Kathie Sarachild, Rox- anne Dunbar-Ortiz, and Dana Densmore*. Seattle, WA: University of Washington Press.

Fahs, B. (2019). Reinvigorating the traditions of second-wave radical feminism: Humor and satire as political work. *Women's Reproductive Health*.

Flavelle, G. (2017). Affecting activist art: Inside Killjoy's Kastle, a lesbian feminist haunted house. *InVisible Culture, 27*. https://ivc.lib.rochester.edu/affecting-activist-art-inside- killjoys-kastle-a-lesbian-feminist-haunted-house/#fn-6594-46.

Goltz, D. B. (2015). Ironic performativity: Amy Schumer's big (white) balls. *Text and Per- formance Quarterly, 35*(4), 266–285.

Grundhauser, E. (2016). The great Harvard pee-in of 1973. *Atlas Obscura*. www .atlasobscura.com/articles/the-great-harvard-peein-of-1973.

Jackson, B. (2007). Jonathan Edwards goes to hell (house): Fear appeals in American Evangelism. *Rhetoric Review, 26*(1), 42–59.

King, M. (2018). Deep lez immersion: A conversation with *Killjoy's Kastle* creators Deirdre Logue and Allyson Mitchell. *Canadian Theatre Review, 173*(Winter), 15–20.

Lauzen, M. (2014). The funny business of being Tina Fey: Constructing a (feminist) comedy icon. *Feminist Media Studies, 14*(1), 106–117.

Lavin, S. (2004). *Women and comedy in solo performance: Phyllis Diller, Lily Tomlin and Roseanne.* New York: Routledge.

Logue, D., Mitchell, A., Cho, H., & Sea, M. (2017). #silence=violence. *Artjournal, 76* (3–4), 122–123.

Mehra, N. J. (2017, July 17). Sara Ahmed: Notes from a feminist killjoy. *Guernica Magazine.* www.guernicamag.com/sara-ahmed-the-personal-is-institutional/.

Miranda, C. A. (2015). Inside West Hollywood's feminist haunted house: Zombie folk singers and body-positive vampires. *Los Angeles Times.* www.latimes.com/entertainment/arts/miranda/la-et-cam-feminist-haunted-house-west-hollywood-20151014-column.html.

Mitchell, A. (2009). Deep Lez I statement. *No More Potlucks.* http://nomorepotlucks.org/site/deep-lez-i-statement/.

Mitchell, A. (2013). Killjoy's Kastle Facebook event page. www.facebook.com/events/166258290234212/.

Mitchell, A. (2014). Letters: Dear Jess Carroll. *C Magazine,* ARTbibliographies Modern (ABM). p. 8.

Mitchell, A., & McKinney, C. (Eds.) (2019). *Inside Killjoy's Kastle: Dykey ghosts, feminist monsters, and other lesbian hauntings.* Vancouver: UBC Press.

Mizejewski, L. (2014). *Pretty/funny: Women comedians and body politics.* Austin, TX: University of Texas Press.

One Archives at the USC Libraries. (2015). Killjoy's Kastle: A lesbian feminist haunted house. https://one.usc.edu/exhibition/killjoys-kastle-lesbian-feminist-haunted-house.

Pan, J. C. (2014). Trasher feminism: Valerie Solanas and her enemies. *Dissent.* www.dissentmagazine.org/article/trasher-feminism-valerie-solanas-and-her-enemies.

Pellegrini, A. (2007). "Signaling through the flames": Hell house performance and structures of religious feeling. *American Quarterly, 59*(3), 911–935.

Pellegrini, A. (2009). Feeling secular. *Women & Performance, 19*(2), 205–218.

Przybylo, E., & Cooper, D. (2014). Asexual resonances: Tracing a queerly asexual archive. *GLQ: A Journal of Lesbian and Gay Studies, 20*(3), 297–318.

Randolph, S. M. (2015). *Florynce "Flo" Kennedy: The life of a black feminist radical.* Chapel Hill, NC: University of North Carolina Press.

Sedgwick, E. K. (2003). Shame, theatricality, and queer performativity: Henry James's *the art of the novel.* In E. Sedgwick (Ed.), *Touching feeling: Affect, pedagogy, performativity* (pp. 35–65). Durham, NC: Duke University Press.

Solanas, V. (1968). *SCUM manifesto.* New York: Olympia Press.

Solanas, V. (1996). *SCUM manifesto.* San Francisco, CA: AK Press.

Woods, F. (2015). Girls talk: Authorship and authenticity in the reception of Lena Dunham's *girls. Critical Studies in Television, 10*(2), 37–54.

Yamato, J. (2015). Inside Killjoy's Kastle, the lesbian feminist house of horrors. *Daily Beast.* www.thedailybeast.com/inside-killjoys-kastle-the-lesbian-feminist-house-of-horrors.

YouTube. (2015). Killjoy's Kastle: A lesbian feminist haunted house. www.youtube.com/watch?v=a4S-OORBj9o.

5

THE POLITICS OF TURNING RAPE INTO "NONCONSENSUAL SEX"

Al Jazeera recently ran a piece that critically traced the obfuscation of rape language from (violent, highly politicized, and potentially stigmatizing) *rape* to (corporate and university approved) *nonconsensual sex*. Apparently, calling college men "rapists" harmed the public relations campaigns of universities, especially when it implicated the sons of the rich white mega-donor families that paid much of the tab for university operations. This calculated ploy to use *nonconsensual sex* instead of *rape* arrives at a crucial juncture in the politics of sexual assault on college campuses.

Widespread accusations of sexual assaults, administrative and bureaucratic careless-ness, and systematic failure to properly address rape and sexual harassment have reached fever pitch, not only on individual college campuses but also with the recent cultural consciousness-raising of #MeToo and radical feminist activism following the start of Donald Trump's presidency (Kearl, 2018; Tobias, 2018). This shift in language on campuses began before the occupation of the White House by a self-admitted "pussy grabber", at a time when feminists could rely on at least some public support for sexual assault awareness. In 2014, for example, then-President Barack Obama called for a new task force to ensure the confidentiality of rape reporting, a move cor-roborated by then-Vice President Joe Biden who stated publicly:

> Colleges and universities need to face the facts about sexual assault. No more turning a blind eye or pretending it doesn't exist. We need to give victims the support they need, like a confidential place to go, and we need to bring the perpetrators to justice.
>
> *(Steinhauer, 2014)*

However, while articles about the denial of rape on college campuses, the staggering statistics of university rapes, and the consistent lack of attention to and prosecution of rape cases for those who report these crimes proliferated during the end of the Obama presidency (Dick & Ziering, 2016; Kingkade, 2016; New York Public Radio, 2016), the 2016 election season saw a rise in the number of news reports that expressed worry about men being falsely accused of sexual assault (see Yoffe, 2017 and Wong, 2016 as key examples, see also Jackson, 2018). As the #MeToo movement has gathered strength, college campuses have scrambled to protect college men from being "derailed" (Yoffe, 2017), emphasizing *consent* and *nonconsent* rather than using the language of rape. College men could not *be rapists*; instead, they engaged in "nonconsensual sex."

Why get so picky about the language? Why might it matter that public discourse has attempted to wipe the word *rape* off the map in favor of a phrase generated in university boardrooms by public relations managers? Well, for starters, this language lets rapists off easily and does not hold them accountable to the violence they have committed. Further, many people do not classify rape as a "kind of sex." "Nonconsensual sex" is not comparable to vaginal sex or oral sex, nor is it a "position" or a "type" of sex. Rape is a crime of power and violence, most often enacted onto the bodies of women by the bodies of men (though men raping other men, and women raping women also disappears in mainstream conversations about rape despite that fact that this occurs not infrequently).

When I interviewed women across a wide range of demographics and ages about their sexual experiences in my book, *Performing sex* (Fahs, 2011), I found that women did *not* typically discuss rape in response to the question I asked about women's "worst sexual experiences." Instead, women discussed their experiences of rape, incest, and sexual abuse later on in the conversation when we talked about *violence*. Many women did not, and do not, actually categorize rape as about sex at all. It is, rather, something more akin to battery (what we now call "domestic violence" or "intimate partner violence," phrases that second-wave radical feminist activists cringe at), abuse, and assault. Calling rape *nonconsensual sex* is somewhat akin to calling someone shooting someone else on the street *homicidal dialogue*. You're not "having sex" if you are being raped; you are not "in dialogue" if you get shot in the head. There is nothing mutual about an act of violence; rape is the exertion of power by one person at another's expense.

Perhaps more important, however, are the experiences that these conversations about language mask or cover up. What we *do not* talk about are the staggering rates of "gray rape," or sexual experiences that lie in the middle ground between rape and non-rape. As a sex researcher and therapist, I am continually astounded by the number of women who describe having had coercive or pseudo-coercive experiences that they did not label as rape. These experiences include: having painful sex; agreeing to have sex while sick; feeling like sex is an obligation; exchanging blowjobs for rent money or a car payment; having a boyfriend force anal penetration; being asked by men to engage in sexual behaviors that were humiliating or degrading and not feeling like they could refuse; having "hard sex" or aggressive sex that physically harmed and discomfited them; having drunken sex and feeling used and/or regretful ... and that's just from a sample of a few dozen women. Add to that the slightly less coercive but still depressing facts that many women feel the need to fake orgasms in order to end a sexual encounter (and to support and maintain their partner's ego), that alarming numbers of women get off to rape fantasies, or that women endure so much bad sex for the sake of maintaining relationships, and the picture gets even bleaker (see Chapters 1 and 2).

The bottom line is this: We live in a culture that relies on caricatures and myths of sexual violence in order to sustain the violence that everyday women endure, and ordinary men perpetuate. The general public imagines that the "rape victim" needs to be a woman battered, at-knife-point, in-a-parking-lot in order to obscure the fact that women endure rape, sexual violence, coercion, disappointment, bad sex, and sexual extortion all-too-often in their romantic lives and in their short and long-term relationships. (This mythology also obscures the all-too-common reality that women endure sexual assault and abuse *within* their families, from childhood through to old age.) Or, better yet, this oft-depicted "rape victim" is scantily-clad, asking-for-it, and "deserves" to be raped. In turn, the "sex offender" and the "rapist" (which couldn't possibly be college men!) need to be the scary trench-coat-wearing greasy-haired sleazeball who preys on little girls and warrants neighborhood watches in order to obscure the fact that our culture socializes boys and men to engage in coercive, selfish, and sometimes violent sexual acts in order to validate their status as "real men." Sexual violence must be perpetrated by a "creepy" Other and not by loved ones, acquaintances, or ourselves, an inversion of reality that has long plagued feminist scholars who want people to understand a more accurate depiction of rape and sexual violence (Pryor & Hughes, 2013; Wesely & Gaarder, 2004).

Notably, *systemic levels of harassment and sexual violence* in nearly *every* profession only further accentuates the problem that epidemic rates of sexual violence have *always* been there, lurking under the surface. From sex researchers (Fahs, Plante, & McClelland, 2018), economists and scientists (NASEM, 2018), medical workers (Holroyd-Leduc & Straus, 2018; Jagsi, 2018), newsroom workers (Corcione, 2018), and throughout working-class professions and the military (Bell, Dardis, Vento, & Street, 2018), #MeToo is shifting the conversation from "oversexualization" of women to the actual material consequences of a culture that has so long denied its mistreatment of women (Gill & Orgad, 2018).

Normalizing, finding, and naming rape

What would it mean if we acknowledged that *normative* experiences of being a woman meant dealing with sexual violence and coercion and *normative masculinity* meant perpetuating violence against women and other men? It is, in fact, the *minority* of women who never experience sexual coercion of any sort; further, most women (and some men) fear men's violence and organize their understanding of public space around such fears (e.g., not walking alone at night; wanting protection from strong men; fear of alleys and parking lots) (Valentine, 1989). In fact, women's fear of crime in general relates to their fear of being raped (Mellgren & Ivert, 2018), and one of the main drivers of online harassment is the way that harassers play into women's fear of rape when targeting them, a fear that internet trolls exploit when harassing women (Sobieraj, 2018).

While corporations, universities, and the military (another institution with a serious rape problem, see O'Brien, Keith, & Shoemaker, 2015; White et al., 2018) sit around trying to "manage" the bad PR they're getting from sexual assault reports, women continue to endure a rape culture that enables a Yale fraternity (not coincidentally, George W. Bush's old fraternity) to chant the slogan, "NO MEANS YES, AND YES MEANS ANAL!" (Beyerstein, 2011). Rape and sexual violence are woven deeply into cultural norms of male bonding and men's way of relating to each other, particularly as women's bodies become vehicles for men's displays of aggression *in front of* other men (Pascoe, 2011). (One of the most dangerous things in the world is men's desire to impress other men, and to use sexualized violence against women as a means to do this.)

The caricatures of "rapist" and "rape victim" serve to normalize sexual violence and exclude incidents that should be reported as such. For example, many people resist the label *rape*, which makes it increasingly difficult to locate and track accurate rape statistics. Most rape statistic reporting significantly underestimates the actual prevalence of sexual violence, a fact exemplified with the explosion of the #MeToo movement (Wilson & Miller, 2016). In fact, 21–25% of women in the US have been sexually assaulted (Campbell & Wasco, 2005; Koss, Heise, & Russo, 1994), a proportion higher than in any other industrialized nation (e.g., 4 times higher than Germany, 12 times higher than England, and 20 times higher than Japan, see Rozee, 2005). Different subsets of women report especially high rates of rape and sexual assault, perhaps connected to their increased vulnerability based on class, race, and social status. Young women, those with sexual abuse histories, indigenous women, and those who attended colleges and drank heavily were especially at risk for sexual assault (Mohler-Kuo, Dowdall, Koss, & Wechsler, 2004; Parillo, Freeman, & Young, 2003; Tjaden & Thoennes, 2000). And, while 91% of those reporting rape were women, men committed 99% of reported rapes; further, 40% of rapes occurred in women's homes and the vast majority of rapes went unreported entirely (Tjaden & Thoennes, 2000).

These data become even more convoluted when we consider the reasons why women who have experienced rape do not *label* it as such. A recent meta-analysis of 5,917 women found that a full 60.4% of them had experienced unacknowledged (unlabeled) rape (Wilson & Miller, 2016). In other studies, approximately half of college women who described a rape experience did not label it as *rape* (Bondurant, 2001; Kahn, 2004; Koss, 1985; Orchowski, Untied, & Gidycz, 2013). Women more often labeled their experience as rape if they experienced a forceful assault by an acquaintance, they awoke to someone performing a nonconsensual sex act on them, or experienced assault as a child.

They labeled their experience as rape less often if they gave in to a whining or complaining boyfriend or husband, knew the perpetrator better and/or were assaulted by a boyfriend or husband, felt more self-blame, felt severely drunk or unable to resist, or if they felt forced to engage in oral or manual sex instead of penetrative penile-vaginal intercourse (Kahn, 2004; Littleton & Breitkopf, 2006; Orchowski, Untied, & Gidycz, 2013).

Notably, women also labeled their experiences as *rape* less often if they initially wanted to have sex more (Peterson & Muehlenhard, 2004), if their perception of what rape was differed from the events in which the rape occurred (Littleton, Rhatigan, & Axsom, 2007), or if they felt less stigma about the rape than other women (Littleton & Breitkopf, 2006). Women asked in a study to judge other women's experiences did not label rape if the victim had more previous sexual partners (Flowe, Ebbesen, & Putcha-Bhagavatula, 2007), which suggests that ideas about sexual stigma also inform women's judgments about other women's coercion experiences. That said, another study found that rape victims expressed more empathy toward other women who had been raped, suggesting inroads for solidarity between women (Osman, 2016).

Why does it matter if women label rape or not? Should we chalk this up to women feeling "empowered" to avoid a stigmatized label? The data on these questions are also important to consider, as naming or labeling rape can impact women's well-being. While naming rape did not correlate with a higher or lower likelihood of recovering from rape (McMullin & White, 2006), labeling rape correlated with higher incidences of health complaints (Conoscenti & McNally, 2006).

That said, many women who label or report rape meet with disbelief and hostility from those they disclose to, all of which can harm women and suppress disclosure of sexual violence (Heath, Lynch, Fritch, & Wong, 2013; Orchowski & Gidycz, 2015). Marital rape, for example, is extraordinarily high, with studies showing that 10–14% of all married women in the US have been raped by their husbands (Martin, Taft, & Resick, 2007). Marital rape was not officially illegal in all 50 US states until 1993 (Yllö & Torres, 2016). In marriages where rape occurred, women reported higher rates of other kinds of violence and more marital dissatisfaction compared to other women, including depression, PTSD, gynecological problems, and negative physical health symptoms (Martin, Taft, & Resick, 2007). Rape and coercive sex also present a host of challenges to mental health and well-being, including PTSD, anxiety and depression, sexual disorders, personality disorders, avoidant coping, and risky sexual behaviors (e.g., lack of condom use, using drugs and alcohol during sex) (Campbell, Sefl, & Ahrens, 2004; Clarke, Rizvi, & Resick, 2008; Faravelli, Giugni, Salvatori, & Ricca, 2004; Littleton & Breitkopf, 2006; Ullman, Townsend, Filipas, & Starzynski, 2007; Wolitzky-Taylor et al., 2008).

The cultural lexicon of rape

I had a conversation with a patient of mine recently that spoke volumes to the problems of living in a rape culture that no longer wants to use the dirty word *rape.* She told me that she and her best friend (both 19-years-old) frequently endured sex with their boyfriends that involved drug use, painful and coerced anal sex, utter boredom, and transmission of a sexually-transmitted infection. When I asked her if she ever felt pleasure during sex, or ever *wanted to feel* pleasure, she said, point blank, "I thought sex was only supposed to be pleasurable for the guys, right?" This anecdote reveals the crisis of imagining what is possible for girls and women in a culture that routinizes sexual violence and lack of entitlement to pleasure as normative practices. What happens if women's sense of sexual possibility has been molded *only* to imagine men's sexual needs? What does such a viewpoint do to understanding consent and coercion?

Feminists have long argued that the way people speak about sex matters, and that rape is situated between an array of cultural tensions about gender, power, desire, objectification, masculinity, and mythologies of "deservingness" and "entitlement" to sex (Gavey, 2013; Ringrose & Renold, 2014). In other words, we cannot divorce rape from the context in which we socialize people to think about sexuality on the whole, a consideration that raises new questions about culpability, complicity, and responsibility for the staggering voicelessness women often feel regarding sexual violence. Using language to assert power is one such way that women might imagine distancing themselves from the horrors of *everyday sexual violence* (that is, the mundaneness of sexual coercion). More importantly, the various public relations rewordings that occur for rape these days—"nonconsensual sex" as a key example—imply a frank unwillingness to directly address the problem of rape (and the assorted forms of sexual violence, coercion, and aggression around rape) as systemic and appallingly common.

How, then, might we speak about sexual violence differently? The cultural madness of our time is encapsulated in these very dilemmas around the handling of sexual violence. *For example, if sexual violence becomes so normal that women can no longer recognize it as an aberration, how then can women feel outraged, mistreated, or seek justice about their experiences with sexual coercion?* Understanding something as *unjust* requires, at the very least, a sense that it *should not happen.* Perhaps part of our cultural pathology is the frank unwillingness to collectively feel outrage about sexual violence, which then inspires various forms of resistance to spring up (e.g., Pussy Grabs Back, #MeToo). In this split—between normative ways of ignoring and failing to recognize sexual violence as important, alongside the forms of resistance which make visible sexual violence—lies the recipe for a culture that fails women. By overtaxing women to seek their own justice, cultivate outrage, and work around formal mechanisms for the punishment of rape, we cannot then act surprised when women stop seeing rape and all forms of sexual violence as an anomaly. Instead, women may start to normalize rape, sexual coercion, and sexual violence as a routine or even mundane part of their lives, facilitated in large part by cultural blindspots, politicized language that fears directly targeting men as rapists, and an overwhelming unwillingness to account for the cultural pathologies of masculinity, dominance, and destruction.

References

Bell, M. E., Dardis, C. M., Vento, S. A., & Street, A. E. (2018). Victims of sexual harassment and assault in the military: Understanding risks and promoting recovery. *Military Psychology*, *30*(3), 219–228.

Beyerstein, L. (2011). "No means yes, yes means anal" frat banned from Yale. *Big Think*. https://bigthink.com/focal-point/no-means-yes-yes-means-anal-frat-banned-from-yale.

Bondurant, B. (2001). University women's acknowledgment of rape. *Violence against Women*, *7*(3), 294–314.

Campbell, R., Sefl, T., & Ahrens, C. E. (2004). The impact of rape on women's sexual health risk behaviors. *Health Psychology*, *23*(1), 67–74.

Campbell, R., & Wasco, S. M. (2005). Understanding rape and sexual assault: 20 years of progress and future directions. *Journal of Interpersonal Violence*, *20*(1), 127–131.

Clarke, S. B., Rizvi, S. L., & Resick, P. A. (2008). Borderline personality characteristics and treatment outcome in cognitive-behavioral treatments for PTSD in female rape victims. *Behavior Therapy*, *39*(1), 72–78.

Conoscenti, L. M., & McNally, R. J. (2006). Health complaints in acknowledged and unacknowledged rape victims. *Journal of Anxiety Disorders*, *20*(3), 372–379.

Corcione, D. (2018). The shitty media men list is the# MeToo of toxic newsrooms: A failure to protect non-male freelance workers. *Feminist Media Studies*, *18*(3), 500–502.

Dick, K., & Ziering, A. (2016). Those who deny that campus sexual assault is dire must misread the numbers. *The Guardian*. www.theguardian.com/commentisfree/2016/feb/12/campus-sexual-assault-statistics-kirby-dick-amy-ziering.

Fahs, B. (2011). *Performing sex: The making and unmaking of women's erotic lives*. Albany, NY: State University of New York Press.

Fahs, B., Plante, R. F., & McClelland, S. I. (2018). Working at the crossroads of pleasure and danger: Feminist perspectives on doing critical sexuality studies. *Sexualities*, *21*(4), 503–519.

Faravelli, C., Giugni, A., Salvatori, S., & Ricca, V. (2004). Psychopathology after rape. *American Journal of Psychiatry*, *161*(8), 1483–1485.

Flowe, H. D., Ebbesen, E. B., & Putcha-Bhagavatula, A. (2007). Rape shield laws and sexual behavior evidence: Effects of consent level and women's sexual history on rape allegations. *Law and Human Behavior*, *31*(2), 159–175.

Gavey, N. (2013). *Just sex? The cultural scaffolding of rape*. New York: Routledge.

Gill, R., & Orgad, S. (2018). The shifting terrain of sex and power: From the "sexualization of culture" to# MeToo. *Sexualities*, *21*(8), 1313–1324.

Heath, N. M., Lynch, S. M., Fritch, A. M., & Wong, M. M. (2013). Rape myth acceptance impacts the reporting of rape to the police: A study of incarcerated women. *Violence against Women*, *19*(9), 1065–1078.

Holroyd-Leduc, J. M., & Straus, S. E. (2018). #MeToo and the medical profession. *CMAJ*, *190*(33), E972–E973.

Jackson, A. (2018). American colleges have a massive rape problem, and there's no clear solution in sight. *Business Insider*. www.businessinsider.com/colleges-rape-problem-title-iv-2018-4.

Jagsi, R. (2018). Sexual harassment in medicine—# MeToo. *New England Journal of Medicine*, *378*(3), 209–211.

Kahn, A. S. (2004). 2003 Carolyn Sherif award address: What college women do and do not experience as rape. *Psychology of Women Quarterly*, *28*(1), 9–15.

Kearl, H. (2018). The facts behind the #MeToo movement: A national study on sexual harassment and assault (executive summary). *Center for Victim Research Repository*. https://ncvc.dspacedirect.org/handle/20.500.11990/790.

Kingkade, T. (2016). There's no more denying campus rape is a problem. This study proves it. *Huffington Post*. www.huffingtonpost.com/entry/college-sexual-assault-study_us_569e928be4b0cd99679b9ada.

Koss, M. P. (1985). The hidden rape victim: Personality, attitudinal, and situational characteristics. *Psychology of Women Quarterly, 9*(2), 193–212.

Koss, M. P., Heise, L., & Russo, N. C. (1994). The global health burden of rape. *Psychology of Women Quarterly, 18*(4), 509–537.

Littleton, H. L., & Breitkopf, C. R. (2006). Coping with the experience of rape. *Psychology of Women Quarterly, 30*(1), 106–116.

Littleton, H. L., Rhatigan, D. L., & Axsom, D. (2007). Unacknowledged rape: How much do we know about the hidden rape victim? *Journal of Aggression, Maltreatment, & Trauma, 14*(4), 57–74.

Martin, E. K., Taft, C. T., & Resick, P. A. (2007). A review of marital rape. *Aggression and Violent Behavior, 12*(3), 329–347.

McMullin, D., & White, J. W. (2006). Long-term effects of labeling a rape experience. *Psychology of Women Quarterly, 30*(1), 96–105.

Mellgren, C., & Ivert, A. K. (2018). Is women's fear of crime fear of sexual assault? A test of the shadow of sexual assault hypothesis in a sample of Swedish university students. *Violence against Women, 25*(5), 511–527.

Mohler-Kuo, M., Dowdall, G. W., Koss, M. P., & Wechsler, H. (2004). Correlates of rape while intoxicated in a national sample of college women. *Journal of Studies on Alcohol, 65*(1), 37–45.

National Academies of Sciences, Engineering, and Medicine (NASEM). (2018). *Sexual harassment of women: Climate, culture, and consequences in academic sciences, engineering, and medicine.* Washington, DC: National Academies Press.

New York Public Radio. (2016). Why rape is so prevalent on American college campuses. www.wnyc.org/story/justice-denied-college-rape-victims/

O'Brien, C., Keith, J., & Shoemaker, L. (2015). Don't tell: Military culture and male rape. *Psychological Services, 12*(4), 357–365.

Orchowski, L. M., & Gidycz, C. A. (2015). Psychological consequences associated with positive and negative responses to disclosure of sexual assault among college women: A prospective study. *Violence against Women, 21*(7), 803–823.

Orchowski, L. M., Untied, A. S., & Gidycz, C. A. (2013). Factors associated with college women's labeling of sexual victimization. *Violence and Victims, 28*(6), 940–958.

Osman, S. L. (2016). Predicting rape victim empathy based on rape victimization and acknowledgment labeling. *Violence against Women, 22*(7), 767–779.

Parillo, K. M., Freeman, R. C., & Young, P. (2003). Association between child sexual abuse and sexual revictimization in adulthood among women sex partners of injection drug users. *Violence and Victims, 18*(4), 473–484.

Pascoe, C. J. (2011). *Dude, you're a fag: Masculinity and sexuality in high school.* Berkeley, CA: University of California Press.

Peterson, Z. D., & Muehlenhard, C. L. (2004). Was it rape? The function of women's rape myth acceptance and definitions of sex in labeling their own experiences. *Sex Roles, 51* (3–4), 129–144.

Pryor, D. W., & Hughes, M. R. (2013). Fear of rape among college women: A social psychological analysis. *Violence and Victims, 28*(3), 443–465.

Ringrose, J., & Renold, E. (2014). "F** k rape!" exploring affective intensities in a feminist research assemblage. *Qualitative Inquiry, 20*(6), 772–780.

Rozee, P. D. (2005). Rape resistance: Successes and challenges. In A. Barnes (Ed.), *The handbook of women, psychology, and the law* (pp. 265–279). Hoboken, NJ: John Wiley & Sons.

Sobieraj, S. (2018). Bitch, slut, skank, cunt: Patterned resistance to women's visibility in digital publics. *Information, Communication & Society, 21*(11), 1700–1714.

Steinhauer, J. (2014). White House to press colleges to do more to combat rape. *New York Times*. www.nytimes.com/2014/04/29/us/tougher-battle-on-sex-assault-on-campus-urged.html.

Tjaden, P., & Thoennes, N. (2000). Prevalence and consequences of male-to-female and female-to-male intimate partner violence as measured by the National Violence against Women Survey. *Violence against Women, 6*(2), 142–161.

Tobias, S. (2018). *Faces of feminism: An activist's reflections on the women's movement.* New York: Routledge.

Ullman, S. E., Townsend, S. M., Filipas, H. H., & Starzynski, L. L. (2007). Structural models of the relations of assault severity, social support, avoidance coping, self-blame, and PTSD among sexual assault survivors. *Psychology of Women Quarterly, 31*(1), 23–37.

Valentine, G. (1989). The geographies of women's fear. *Area, 21*(4), 385–390.

Wesely, J. K., & Gaarder, E. (2004). The gendered "nature" of the urban outdoors: Women negotiating fear of violence. *Gender & Society, 18*(5), 645–663.

White, K. L., Harris, J. A., Bryan, A. O., Reynolds, M., Fuessel-Herrmann, D., & Bryan, C. J. (2018). Military sexual trauma and suicidal behavior among National Guard personnel. *Comprehensive Psychiatry, 87*, 1–6.

Wilson, L. C., & Miller, K. E. (2016). Meta-analysis of the prevalence of unacknowledged rape. *Trauma, Violence, & Abuse, 17*(2), 149–159.

Wolitzky-Taylor, K. B., Ruggiero, K. J., Danielson, C. K., Resnick, H. S., Hanson, R. F., Smith, D. W., … Kilpatrick, D. G. (2008). Prevalence and correlates of dating violence in a national sample of adolescents. *Journal of the American Academy of Child and Adolescent Psychiatry, 47*(7), 755–762.

Wong, A. (2016). Why the prevalence of campus sexual assault is so hard to quantify. *The Atlantic*. www.theatlantic.com/education/archive/2016/01/why-the-prevalence-of-campus-sexual-assault-is-so-hard-to-quantify/427002/.

Yllö, K., & Torres, M. G. (Eds.). (2016). *Marital rape: Consent, marriage, and social change in global context.* New York: Oxford University Press.

Yoffe, E. (2017). The uncomfortable truth about campus rape policy. *The Atlantic*. www.theatlantic.com/education/archive/2017/09/the-uncomfortable-truth-about-campus-rape-policy/538974/.

6

GENITAL ANXIETIES

Using critical sexuality studies to examine women's attitudes about the vulva and vagina

Women's feelings about their vulvas and vaginas often reveal intense underlying anxiety about normality, adherence to social rules, and avoidance of being "gross," "disgusting," or abject (that is, lowdown, vile, repulsive). Sociologist Paula England (2010) has argued that the gender revolution is stalled because, although women have made immense progress in the public sphere (e.g., work, economics, owning property), the private sphere continues to present women with many opportunities for disempowerment, particularly in relation to sexuality, the body, and domestic tasks. For example, women routinely describe their bodies in negative ways; they criticize their own appearance and internalize feelings of inadequacy and distress about many aspects of their bodies (e.g., weight gain, body shape, skin color, genital appearance). In this chapter, I ask why, in an age so often characterized by women's empowerment and freedom, do women continue to feel so much distress about their bodies? Further, how might women's genitals come to symbolize some of the most insidious aspects of negative body image and body distress?

Women are faced with a plethora of challenges in today's society when they assess the "normality" and "appropriateness" of their bodies. For example, though women's genitals are often made invisible and erased by mainstream media, schools, public health, religion, and art (i.e., we rarely see diverse images of vulvas, and we almost never publicly discuss the vulva or vagina openly, even on college campuses), women are nevertheless tasked with *knowing* and *imagining* their genitals in relationship to clear cultural norms and practices. Though schools do not teach students about masturbation, the location of the clitoris, the cycles of discharge that occur with menstruation, and the health benefits of pubic hair, women and girls are nevertheless supposed to "just know" these things. Girls have very few sources to draw upon for imagining a positive relationship to their genitals, particularly in light of clear cultural norms and differential valuation of phallic (penis) vs. yonic (vagina) imagery. As one example, most people cannot accurately draw a vulva (i.e., produce an accurate drawing of a woman's clitoris, urethra, vagina, and anus), though most people can depict a man's testicles, penis, and anus with remarkable accuracy.

Representations of the vulva and vagina—particularly accurate ones—appear only intermittently in popular culture. Phallic imagery permeates the public land-scapes of many major cities throughout the world, particularly in the US (e.g., the Washington Monument epitomizes an obsession with phallic imagery in US archi-tecture). Films that show a vulva, or that even imply interacting with a vulva, are rated by the Motion Picture Association of America (MPAA) board more severely (that is, given an R or NC-17 rating) than those that show a penis (or interaction with a penis) (Leone, 2002). The famed art activist group, the Guerrilla Girls (1989), found that over 85% of nudes in the Metropolitan Museum of Art were women but women artists made up a mere fraction (5%) of the total artists repre-sented in the Met's collection. These facts are not inconsequential; women's atti-tudes toward the vulva and vagina often reveal distress, anxiety, shame, and worry, which then translates into a perceived need to "manage" their vulvas and vaginas in ever-more intense ways (Braun & Wilkinson, 2001; Fahs, 2014b).

In this chapter, I look carefully at five different symptoms of genital anxieties for women, which together paint a portrait of the ways in which women are concerned to various degrees about how their genitals fit within certain socio-cultural norms. I draw upon critical sexuality studies (Fahs & McClelland, 2016), which posits that power and privilege impact the way that the sexualized body is experienced and enacted in daily life to argue that women's genital distress (or the various traces and moments of distress they may feel) stems from broader stories of how patriarchy, sexism, racism, classism, and homophobia bleed into women's most private and intimate experiences of their bodies. I first examine women's experiences with sex during menstruation, followed by a brief analysis of the existing research on genital self-image and shame, including the quest for the "designer vagina," pubic hair discourses, and women's feelings about oral sex. I conclude by describing some of the ways in which people have engaged in activism to combat these cultural messages of negativity and to reframe the vulva and the vagina as a site of agency, embodiment, pleasure, and resistance.

Sex during menstruation

Menstruation represents one of the key areas that women consistently feel distressed about in relation to their genitals and their bodies, in part because of the negative discourses about menstruation (Mansfield & Stubbs, 2007). Historically, menstru-ation was considered taboo and in need of management and containment, as men-strual blood indicated disease, and reflected social taboos about decency and shame, spiritual corruption, and even outright contamination (Delaney, Lupton, & Toth, 1998; Read, 2008). The construction of menstruation as "failed reproduction" or frankly abject (Kerkham, 2003; Martin, 2001; Rosewarne, 2012) is more normative than its more celebrated form in some African cultures where menstruating women are seen as powerful and revered (Brain, 1988). Women in the US learn to imagine their menstrual cycles as sources of distress, something to suppress, or as debilitating and abnormal, particularly in comparison to men's bodily processes (Chrisler, Rose, Dutch, Sklarsky, & Grant, 2006; Johnston-Robledo, Barnack, & Wares, 2006). Girls learn that menstruation should be kept secret and that periods are associated with fear, disgust, and shame (Burrows & Johnson, 2005; Erchull, Chrisler, Gorman, & Johnston-Robledo, 2002), a trend that continues throughout women's adult lives. This collectively leads to a framework where menstruation is, at best, distressing, and at worst, debilitating; menstrual blood, then, becomes associated with something negative or "gross" rather than healthy or normal.

Attitudes toward sex during menstruation reveal similar trends in women's negative feelings about their menstrual cycles. One study of college women showed that fewer than one-half of them had engaged in menstrual sex and that those who did were typically younger, in committed relationships, more mature, and less disgusted by menstrual sex (Allen & Goldberg, 2009). Two studies show that women had sharply contrasting views on menstrual sex; many claimed that they would never do it (Allen & Goldberg, 2009; Fahs, 2011). That said, some women reported that menstrual sex made them feel closer to their partners, relieved menstrual cramps, or contributed to feeling less disgusted by their bodies (Fahs, 2011; Hensel, Fortenberry, & Orr, 2007; Rempel & Baumgartner, 2003). My work shows that women with negative attitudes toward menstrual sex often emphasized the discomfort and the physical labor required to clean "messes," negative self-perception, overt partner discomfort, and the emotional labor necessary to manage their partner's disgust. Women who felt positively about menstrual sex described having experienced physical and emotional pleasure from sex during menstruation and a mentioned desire to rebel against anti-menstrual attitudes in the culture at large (Fahs, 2011). This suggests that the same experience (i.e., having sex during menstruation) can elicit a range of emotional responses, though women's perceived need to manage their partners' feelings and contain their "messy" bodies most prominently appeared in women's narratives about menstrual sex.

Genital self-image and shame

Questions about women's feelings about genital self-image (i.e., how women feel about their vulvas and vaginas) often elicit feelings of shame and distress, which imply that women do not routinely feel positive about their genitals. This negativity has arisen in part from a cultural context that teaches women to see their bodies as a series of components—breasts, legs, butt, eyes, stomach, and so on—rather than a cohesive whole. Women learn to imagine their bodies as a collection of individual parts, and the genitals comprise one such part to manage, control, and contain (Aubrey, 2010; Kilbourne, 1999). It is interesting that many body image researchers neglect to ask questions about women's attitudes toward their genitals, which suggests that most body image researchers also invisibilize vulvas and vaginas (Grabe, Ward, & Hyde, 2008). Nevertheless, results of several studies that specifically addressed genital self-image suggest that women struggle with a negative vaginal self-image (Berman, Berman, Miles, Pollets, & Powell, 2003; Herbenick, Schick, Reece, Sanders, & Fortenberry, 2010). Women who reported more negative genital self-imagine included those who felt more self-conscious during sex, those with lower self-esteem, and those with less sexual satisfaction and lower sexual desire (Berman et al., 2003; Schick, Calabrese, Rima, & Zucker, 2010). Further, women's feelings about their genitals were far more negative than men's feelings about their own genitals, as most women described their genital attitudes as frankly negative or, at best, moderately positive (Reinholtz & Muehlenhard, 1995). A variety of scales have recently been developed to assess genital attitudes, though some feminists worry that this will only lead to more pharmaceutical or surgical intrusions as the medical field attempts to capitalize on women's sense of distress or inferiority (Tiefer, Hall, & Tavris, 2002).

In my work, I (Fahs, 2014b) found that women attach a variety of meanings to their genitals when asked to describe their feelings about their vaginas: "dirty" or "gross," in need of maintenance, unknown or frustrating, unnatural, comparative, ambivalent, or affirmative. For example, women described their vaginas as "dirty" when they menstruated, often stating that menstruation helps to "clean out" their vaginas; other women described their genitals as "nasty." Some women thought that their vaginas needed "maintenance" in the form of grooming (e.g., removing pubic hair, cleaning, washing), whereas others felt anxious about their genitals not working "properly" or about not being able to find their g-spot. Women also described their genitals as unnatural (e.g., they look "weird" or do not compare favorably to other women's genitals). This comparison came up when women imagined other women's genitals, compared their genitals to images in pornography, or believed their genitals were the "wrong" color. Finally, some women described ambivalence and conflict about the vagina (e.g., fighting back against something their mothers taught them) or, on occasion, expressed affirmative and positive feelings about their genitals (e.g., seeing them as healthy, fighting back against men's descriptions of vaginas as "gross").

Designer vaginas

Connected to genital self-image, the recent push for women to seek "designer vaginas" (e.g., perfectly symmetrical and pink inner labia, a "tight" vagina, attractive and hairless outer labia) has led women to feel even more self-conscious about their vulvas and vaginas (Braun & Tiefer, 2009; Rodrigues, 2012). Recently, compared to earlier decades, women have reported an increase in persistent negative identifications with their genitals, seeing them as inadequate, dirty, misshapen, or gross (Berman & Windecker, 2008). The New View Campaign—a grassroots group of feminist scholar/activists that works against the medicalization of sex—has argued that the push toward designer vaginas has led women to imagine a much more narrow idea about what "good vaginas" look like (Braun, 2010) and thus to an increase in female genital cosmetic surgery (FGCS), as doctors push the notion of abnormal genitals and many women feel the need to maintain, perfect, trim, and cut their genitals to make them more normative (Herzig, 2009; Tiefer, 2008).

Virginia Braun and Sue Wilkinson (2001) identified seven common aspects of vaginal negativity found in popular culture, including writings about women's bodies. These included the vagina as inferior to the penis, absent, a passive receptacle for the penis, sexually inadequate, disgusting, vulnerable and abused, and dangerous. They noted: "The vagina is, among other things, the toothed and dangerous vagina dentata; the (symbolic) absence of the penis; the core of womanhood; and a symbol of reproduction" (p. 17). The paradox of hearing messages from the media that women should not discuss or celebrate their vaginas while also learning that there is a cultural obsession with women's sexuality is one of the central contributors to genital anxieties (Braun, 1999; Ensler, 1998). Further, there is a dangerous solipsistic logic in medical (and pharmaceutical) companies capitalizing on women's genital anxieties and selling them surgical or medical interventions to "cure" these anxieties, when those very companies contributed to the anxiety in the first place. In short, they are "fixing" a problem they created a market for, something the New View Campaign has fought against since its inception in 2000.

Pubic hair discourses

Body hair also represents a site of intense anxiety, particularly as it relates to gender, race, class, sexuality, and broader norms of "respectability." Clear ideas about power and privilege intersect with ideas about grooming, cleanliness, and proper femininity (Fahs, 2012, 2013, 2014a; Fahs & Delgado, 2011; Terry & Braun, 2013). Related to this, researchers have begun to examine the frequency of pubic hair removal as compared to "letting it grow" (DeMaria & Berenson, 2013; Herbenick et al., 2010; Riddell, Varto, & Hodgson, 2010), though these studies often frame pubic hair removal more as a behavior rather than a set of beliefs about one's genitals. As a bit of history, women's pubic hair removal stopped in the late nineteenth century and restarted in the 1980s (Ramsey, Sweeney, Fraser, & Oades, 2009), with a dramatic increase in pubic hair removal in the past decade. Younger and partnered women, White women, and women with more sexual partners remove pubic hair more often than other groups (DeMaria & Berenson, 2013; Herbenick, Hensel, Smith, Schick, & Reece, 2013; Herbenick et al., 2010). One study showed that 50% of women removed pubic hair along their bikini line, and 30% removed all pubic hair (Riddell et al., 2010). Although both men and women now experience pressure to remove pubic hair, women have reported stronger pressure to remove their pubic hair and said that they experience far less choice and flexibility than men do (Terry & Braun, 2013). US women have also reported a belief that pubic hair removal is becoming increasingly compulsory (Herzig, 2015).

When asked why they remove their pubic hair, women reported that doing so represents choice, privacy, physical attractiveness, and cleanliness, and they said that it improved their sex lives (Braun, Tricklebank, & Clarke, 2013). Pubic hair removal is also associated with women's use of genital creams and vaginal "hygiene" products (Herbenick et al., 2013). Further, women who removed their pubic hair more often described more self-surveillance and self-objectification than women who did not remove it (Smolak & Murnen, 2011). Adolescent girls have also reported feeling that they had "too much" pubic hair most of the time and that they felt pressured by family and friends to remove pubic hair, particularly if they were sexually active (Bercaw-Pratt et al., 2012). These norms of pubic hair removal are also communicated by mainstream pornography, which typically depicts hairless genitals as the "industry standard" for beauty (Cokal, 2007). Hairless vulvas appear as pervasively "normal" in pornography, particularly in the past decade (Rodrigues, 2012; Schick, Rima, & Calabrese, 2011). The quest for hairless genitals has also created some new dangers, as pubic hair removal has been shown to increase some sexually-transmitted infections (Desruelles, Cunningham, & Dubois, 2013) and grooming-related cases of folliculitis, abscesses, lacerations, allergic reactions to waxing burns, and vulvar and vaginal infections (Hoffman, 2016). Genital anxieties, of course, minimize these risks by focusing on sociocultural norms rather than on the health risks of hair removal.

In my work on pubic hair removal (Fahs, 2013, 2014a, 2014b), I found that women overwhelmingly imagined pubic hair growth in relation to their partners' feelings, particularly with regard to asking partners' "permission" (something men rarely report wanting or needing from their female partners). For example, women worried about pubic hair as "disgusting" or deterring for sexual activities like oral sex or vaginal sex, and they expressed the fear that pubic hair is contaminating, problematic, or makes them feel unclean. These findings point to the ways that women's fears and anxieties do not connect to reality, as pubic hair actually protects women from infection and keeps them cleaner than they would be if they did not have pubic hair. Further, women imagined pubic hair removal as a way to feel inoffensive, contained, and well-groomed, particularly as they see more and more images of hairless genitals in pornography and popular culture at large. These socially-constructed ideas about pubic hair point to the ways that women may feel controlled and disciplined by the broader patriarchal culture; even more important, these messages often become internalized uncritically, as most women say that hair is "just gross" or "dirty" without recognizing where those narratives come from.

Feelings about oral sex

Women also express strong feelings of ambivalence about receiving oral sex. While no qualitative studies have examined lesbian women's experiences with oral sex with other women, quantitative data from a British study suggests that bisexual women were more likely to have had oral sex with men than with women (95% versus 53.5%) (Mercer et al., 2007). Studies of heterosexual women consistently show that they give oral sex more often than they receive it

(Chambers, 2007) and that they feel an overwhelmingly responsibility to give oral sex to men even when they do not receive it in return or feel undeserving of receiving it (Jozkowski & Peterson, 2013). Further, a cross-sectional study showed that fewer young women in 2010 labeled oral sex as *sex* than did so in 1991 (Hans, Gillen, & Akande, 2010). These findings suggest that women's experiences of cunnilingus may attach directly both to the sense that *giving* oral sex to a partner may feel compulsory even though *receiving* oral sex feels less expected or assumed. Women's reluctance to receiving oral sex may also connect to feeling self-conscious about their genitals or believing that their vulvas and vaginas are "dirty" or "gross."

The context in which women feel more comfortable receiving oral sex also points to the complexities of whether and when women feel confident, safe, and attractive during oral sex. Those in committed relationships feel more comfortable receiving oral sex and receive it more often than do those not in such relationships (Backstrom, Armstrong, & Puentes, 2012; Chambers, 2007). Sexual assertiveness, agency, and skill are also connected to receiving oral sex (Fava & Bay-Cheng, 2012). Related to this, younger women and women who do not feel love for their partners have reported more negative emotions connected to receiving oral sex (Malacad & Hess, 2010).

My work on women's experiences with oral sex suggests that women often feel compelled to give oral sex to partners (particularly if they have male partners) but that receiving oral sex is far less assumed or expected. Women in my studies reported feelings of genital shame and embarrassment, concern about "offending" their partners with their genitals' taste and smell, lack of knowledge about how to make oral sex feel good, and worry about not having an orgasm quickly enough. These each suggest that performance standards and normative pressures on women during oral sex may impede their ability to enjoy receiving cunnilingus. The emotion work required in managing their bodies and watching closely for partner discomfort or distress also sharply contrasted with women's reports of their male partners' experiences when the women performed fellatio, as men were more undistracted and focused on themselves (Fahs, In progress-b).

Vulva/vagina activism

Activists' efforts to fight back against the shaming of women's bodies (particularly the vulva and vagina) have played a key role in creating new narratives in opposition to genital anxieties. Much like menstrual activism, which argues that positive views of women's bodies can facilitate solidarity between women and raise critical consciousness about body shaming (Bobel, 2006; Fahs, 2016), activism that focuses on the vagina has also called attention to the widespread and largely unacknowledged shaming of women's vaginas and the necessity of resistance. For example, the New View Campaign launched a public demonstration in New York City in 2008 to protest unnecessary female genital cosmetic surgeries by having women dressed as giant vulvas protest in front of cosmetic surgeons' offices (New View

Campaign, 2008). Sex therapists have begun to address vaginal negativity by helping clients to positively reframe negative feelings about the vagina and to engage in vaginal art (Garbi, 1997), and some artists and playwrights have worked to construct the vagina as attractive rather than unknown or shameful (for example, Eve Ensler's *Vagina monologues* play) (Ensler, 1998; Frueh, 2003). Feminists have also worked to fight back against depictions of "good vaginas" as hairless, girlish, symmetrical, and fake, and have instead framed genital diversity as a key part of body acceptance and positivity (Braun & Tiefer, 2009; Ensler, 1998; Liebert, Leve, & Hui, 2011). Student activists have also imagined new ways of celebrating the vulva and the vagina, confronted patriarchal attitudes about women's bodies, called attention to misinformation about vaginas, and made room for the vagina in mainstream public consciousness. For example, they have gone "undercover" at genital cosmetic surgeons' offices; asked people to draw a clitoris, vulva, and vagina; campaigned for women to engage in more masturbation; questioned people's attitudes toward pubic hair; worked for more and better sex education; and expanded the cultural lexicon of the vagina to include more positive words and adjectives (Fahs, In progress-a).

Critical sexuality studies (Fahs & McClelland, 2016) reminds us that the workings of power and privilege must be examined whenever we study sexuality and the body. We must study not only what is said, but also what is *not* said or what is obscured or silenced. Further, in order to understand women's relationships to their bodies, researchers cannot simply offer statements of hope ("we should celebrate genital diversity") without also understanding the numerous, intricate, intimate ways that women experience a loss of pleasure or a sense of anxiety about their bodies. An understanding of the contexts of disempowerment and distress helps feminists to set priorities for future research, activism, and clinical interventions. In this chapter, I have offered some examples of the ways that genital anxieties may enter women's personal or sexual lives via sex during menstruation, genital shame, the quest for designer vaginas, pubic hair removal (or not), and feelings about receiving oral sex. Each of these reveals the ways that patriarchal narratives of women's vaginas as "dirty," different from men's genitals, messy or leaky, or otherwise "abnormal," permeate beliefs, attitudes, and feelings about women's genitals. Ultimately, although the challenge of lessening genital anxieties remain rather daunting, the hopeful lessons of individual and collective resistance, both within and outside of the academy, remind us that sociocultural norms can and do change and that we have an obligation to continue a sustained sense of opposition to that which diminishes, silences, violates, or devalues women and women's bodies.

References

Allen, K. R., & Goldberg, A. E. (2009). Sexual activity during menstruation: A qualitative study. *Journal of Sex Research, 46*, 535–545.

Aubrey, J. S. (2010). Looking good versus feeling good: An investigation of media frames of health advice and their effects on women's body-related self-perceptions. *Sex Roles, 63*, 50–63.

Backstrom, L., Armstrong, E. A., & Puentes, J. (2012). Women's negotiations of cunnilingus in college hookups and relationships. *Journal of Sex Research, 49*(1), 1–12.

Bercaw-Pratt, J. L., Santos, X. M., Sanchez, J., Ayensu-Coker, L., Nebgen, D. R., & Dietrich, J. E. (2012). The incidence, attitudes, and practices of the removal of pubic hair as a body modification. *Journal of Pediatric & Adolescent Gynecology, 25*, 12–14.

Berman, L. A., Berman, J., Miles, M., Pollets, D., & Powell, J. A. (2003). Genital self-image as a component of sexual health: Relationship between genital self-image, female sexual function, and quality of life measures. *Journal of Sex & Marital Therapy, 29*, 11–21.

Berman, L. A., & Windecker, M. A. (2008). The relationship between women's genital self-image and female sexual function: A national survey. *Current Sexual Health Reports, 5*, 199–207.

Bobel, C. (2006). "Our revolution has style": Contemporary menstrual product activists "doing feminism" in the third wave. *Sex Roles, 54*, 331–345.

Brain, J. L. (1988). Male menstruation in history and anthropology. *Journal of Psychohistory, 15*, 311–323.

Braun, V. (1999). Breaking a taboo? Talking (and laughing) about the vagina. *Feminism & Psychology, 9*, 367–372.

Braun, V. (2010). Female genital cosmetic surgery: A critical review of current knowledge and contemporary debates. *Journal of Women's Health, 19*, 1393–1407.

Braun, V., & Tiefer, L. (2009). The "designer vagina" and the pathologisation of female genital diversity: Interventions for change. *Radical Psychology, 8.* URL:www .radicalpsychology.org/vol8-1/brauntiefer.html.

Braun, V., Tricklebank, G., & Clarke, V. (2013). "It shouldn't stick out from your bikini at the beach": Meaning, gender, and the hairy/hairless body. *Psychology of Women Quarterly, 37*, 478–493.

Braun, V., & Wilkinson, S. (2001). Socio-cultural representations of the vagina. *Journal of Reproductive & Infant Psychology, 19*, 17–32.

Burrows, A., & Johnson, S. (2005). Girls' experiences of menarche and menstruation. *Journal of Reproductive and Infant Psychology, 23*, 235–249.

Chambers, W. C. (2007). Oral sex: Varied behaviors and perceptions in a college population. *Journal of Sex Research, 44*(1), 28–42.

Chrisler, J. C., Rose, J. G., Dutch, S. E., Sklarsky, K. G., & Grant, M. C. (2006). The PMS illusion: Social cognition maintains social construction. *Sex Roles, 54*, 371–376.

Cokal, S. (2007). Clean porn: The visual aesthetics of hygiene, hot sex, and hair removal. In A. C. Hall, & M. J. Bishop (Eds.), *Pop-porn: Pornography in American culture* (pp. 137–154). Westport, CT: Praeger.

Delaney, J., Lupton, M. J., & Toth, E. (1998). *The curse: A cultural history of menstruation.* Chicago, IL: University of Illinois Press.

DeMaria, A. L., & Berenson, A. B. (2013). Prevalence and correlates of pubic hair grooming among low-income Hispanic, Black, and White women. *Body Image, 10*, 226–231.

Desruelles, F., Cunningham, S. A., & Dubois, D. (2013). Pubic hair removal: A risk factor for "minor" STI such as molluscum contagiosum?. *Sexually Transmitted Infections, 89*, 216.

England, P. (2010). The gender revolution: Uneven and stalled. *Gender & Society, 24*, 149–166.

Ensler, E. (1998). *The vagina monologues.* New York: Villard.

Erchull, M. J., Chrisler, J. C., Gorman, J. A., & Johnston-Robledo, I. (2002). Education and advertising: A content analysis of commercially produced booklets about menstruation. *Journal of Early Adolescence, 22*, 455–474.

Fahs, B. (2011). Sex during menstruation: Race, sexual identity, and women's qualitative accounts of pleasure and disgust. *Feminism & Psychology, 21*, 155–178.

Fahs, B. (2012). Breaking body hair boundaries: Classroom exercises for challenging social constructions of the body and sexuality. *Feminism & Psychology*, *22*, 482–506.

Fahs, B. (2013). Shaving it all off: Examining social norms of body hair among college men in a women's studies course. *Women's Studies*, *42*, 559–577.

Fahs, B. (2014a). Perilous patches and pitstaches: Imagined versus lived experiences of women's body hair growth. *Psychology of Women Quarterly*, *38*, 167–180.

Fahs, B. (2014b). Genital panics: Constructing the vagina in women's qualitative narratives about pubic hair, menstrual sex, and vaginal self-image. *Body Image*, *11*, 210–218.

Fahs, B. (2016). *Out for blood: Essays on menstruation and resistance.* Albany, NY: State University of New York Press.

Fahs, B. (in progress-a). *A new generation of vagina activists.*

Fahs, B. (in progress-b). *Jobs and joys: Women describe giving and (sometimes) getting oral sex.*

Fahs, B., & Delgado, D. A. (2011). The specter of excess: Race, class, and gender in women's body hair narratives. In C. Bobel, & S. Kwan (Eds.), *Embodied resistance: Breaking the rules, challenging the norms* (pp. 13–25). Nashville, TN: Vanderbilt University Press.

Fahs, B., & McClelland, S. I. (2016). When sex and power collide: An argument for critical sexuality studies. *Annual Review of Sex Research*, *53*, 392–416.

Fava, N. M., & Bay-Cheng, L. Y. (2012). Young women's adolescent experiences of oral sex: Relation of age of initiation to sexual motivation, sexual coercion, and psychological functioning. *Journal of Adolescence*, *35*, 1191–1201.

Frueh, J. (2003). Vaginal aesthetics. *Hypatia*, *18*, 137–158.

Garbi, Z. (1997). Female genital self-image. *Sexuality and Disability*, *15*, 17–18.

Girls, G. (1989). Do women have to be naked to get into the Met. Museum? *Tate Museum.* www.tate.org.uk/art/artworks/guerrilla-girls-do-women-have-to-be-naked-to-get-into-the-met-museum-p78793.

Grabe, S., Ward, L. M., & Hyde, J. S. (2008). The role of the media in body image concerns among women: A meta-analysis of experimental and correlational studies. *Psychological Bulletin*, *134*, 460–476.

Hans, J. D., Gillen, M., & Akande, K. (2010). Sex redefined: The reclassification of oral-genital contact. *Perspectives on Sexual and Reproductive Health*, *42*(2), 74–78.

Hensel, D. J., Fortenberry, J. D., & Orr, D. P. (2007). Situational and relational factors associated with coitus during vaginal bleeding among adolescent women. *Journal of Sex Research*, *44*, 269–277.

Herbenick, D., Hensel, D. J., Smith, N. K., Schick, V., & Reece, M. (2013). Pubic hair removal and sexual behavior: Findings from a prospective daily diary study of sexually active women in the United States. *Journal of Sexual Medicine*, *10*, 678–685.

Herbenick, D., Schick, V., Reece, M., Sanders, S., & Fortenberry, D. (2010). Pubic hair removal among women in the United States: Prevalence, methods, and characteristics. *Journal of Sexual Medicine*, *7*, 3322–3330.

Herzig, R. (2009). The political economy of choice: Genital modification and the global cosmetic services industry. *Australian Feminist Studies*, *24*, 251–263.

Herzig, R. M. (2015). *Plucked: A history of hair removal.* New York: New York University Press.

Hoffman, J. (2016). Most women prefer to go bare, citing hygiene (and baffling doctors). *New York Times.* http://well.blogs.nytimes.com/2016/06/29/most-women-prefer-to-go-bare-citing-hygiene-and-baffling-doctors/?_r=0.

Johnston-Robledo, I., Barnack, J., & Wares, S. (2006). "Kiss your period good-bye": Menstrual suppression in the popular press. *Sex Roles*, *54*, 353–360.

Jozkowski, K. N., & Peterson, Z. D. (2013). College students and sexual consent: Unique insights. *Journal of Sex Research*, *50*, 517–523.

Kerkham, P. (2003). Menstruation—The gap in the text? *Psychoanalytic Psychotherapy*, *17*, 279–299.

Kilbourne, J. (1999). *Can't buy my love: How advertising changes the way we think and feel.* New York: Touchstone.

Leone, R. (2002). Contemplating ratings: An examination of what the MPAA considers "too far for R" and why. *Journal of Communication*, *52*, 938–954.

Liebert, R., Leve, M., & Hui, A. (2011). The politics and possibilities of activism in contemporary feminist psychologies. *Psychology of Women Quarterly*, *35*, 697–704.

Malacad, B. L., & Hess, G. C. (2010). Oral sex: Behaviors and feelings of Canadian young women and implications for sex education. *European Journal of Contraception and Reproductive Health Care*, *15*, 177–185.

Mansfield, P. K., & Stubbs, M. L. (2007). The menstrual cycle: Feminist scholarship from the Society for Menstrual Cycle Research. *Women & Health*, *46*, 1–5.

Martin, E. (2001). *The woman in the body: A cultural analysis of reproduction.* Boston, MA: Beacon Press.

Mercer, C. H., Bailey, J. V., Johnson, A. M., Erens, B., Wellings, K., Fenton, K. A., & Copas, A. J. (2007). Women who report having sex with women: British national probability data on prevalence, sexual behaviors, and health outcomes. *American Journal of Public Health*, *97*, 1126–1133.

New View Campaign. (2008). Female genital cosmetic surgery (FGCS) activism. www .newviewcampaign.org/fgcs.asp

Ramsey, S., Sweeney, C., Fraser, M., & Oades, G. (2009). Pubic hair and sexuality: A review. *Journal of Sexual Medicine*, *6*, 2102–2110.

Read, S. (2008). Thy righteousness is but a menstrual clout: Sanitary practices and prejudice in early modern England. *Early Modern Women*, *3*, 1–25.

Reinholtz, R. K., & Muehlenhard, C. L. (1995). Genital perceptions and sexual activity in a college population. *Journal of Sex Research*, *32*, 155–165.

Rempel, J. K., & Baumgartner, B. (2003). The relationship between attitudes toward menstruation and sexual attitudes, desires, and behaviors in women. *Archives of Sexual Behavior*, *32*, 155–163.

Riddell, L., Varto, H., & Hodgson, Z. (2010). Smooth talking: The phenomenon of pubic hair removal in women. *Canadian Journal of Human Sexuality*, *19*(3), 121–130.

Rodrigues, S. (2012). From vaginal exception to exceptional vagina: The biopolitics of female genital cosmetic surgery. *Sexualities*, *15*, 778–794.

Rosewarne, L. (2012). *Periods in pop culture: Menstruation in film and television.* New York: Lexington Books.

Schick, V. R., Calabrese, S. K., Rima, B. N., & Zucker, A. N. (2010). Genital appearance dissatisfaction: Implications for women's genital image self-consciousness, sexual esteem, sexual satisfaction, and sexual risk. *Psychology of Women Quarterly*, *34*, 394–404.

Schick, V. R., Rima, B. N., & Calabrese, S. K. (2011). Evulvalution: The portrayal of women's external genitalia and physique across time and the current Barbie doll ideals. *Journal of Sex Research*, *48*, 74–81.

Smolak, L., & Murnen, S. K. (2011). Gender, self-objectification, and pubic hair removal. *Sex Roles*, *65*, 506–517.

Terry, G., & Braun, V. (2013). To let hair be, or not to let hair be? Gender and body hair removal practices in Aotearoa/New Zealand. *Body Image*, *10*, 599–606.

Tiefer, L. (2008). Female genital cosmetic surgery: Freakish or inevitable? Analysis from medical marketing, bioethics, and feminist theory. *Feminism & Psychology*, *18*, 466–479.

Tiefer, L., Hall, M., & Tavris, C. (2002). Beyond dysfunction: A new view of women's sexual problems. *Journal of Sex & Marital Therapy*, *28*(1), 225–232.

PART 3

On the couch

7

COMPULSORY PENETRATION?

A sex therapy romp

In the courses I teach on sexuality at my university, I challenge students in the first few weeks of class to catalog (privately) which experiences they "count" as a sexual encounter. On the surface, this is a seemingly simple task: count up your sexual partners based on your sexual history. At a deeper level, however, I am asking them to assess how they decide which encounters "count" as sex and which do not. The criteria for "what counts as sex" varies dramatically, with some students counting all genital contact with anyone, while others count only penetrative sex. Some count oral sex as sex, while others don't. A few count kissing and touching as sex, while most students don't. Several students emphasize the importance of orgasm (especially for men and male partners), while most do not expect to orgasm during every encounter. Some count experiences with rape and sexual trauma as sex, and others see those as violence (or otherwise erase them from their sexual history). When I ask them to verbalize their thoughts on this topic, a lengthy discussion about the centrality of the phallus inevitably emerges. Why, when sex so clearly has such diverse expressions and interpretations, do people so adamantly return to the importance of the penis and penetrative sex in deciding what counts as "real sex"? Has penetration become a compulsory part of how people define sex? And if so, how does this obscure not only queer sexualities but also other avenues to pleasure?

Unfortunately, this emphasis on penetrative sex and the phallus has paramount importance in defining so much about the sex people have. As sexual scripting theory reiterates, the stories we tell about sex and sexuality follow predictable, socially-constructed narratives that guide how people see the "normal" and "abnormal" (Plante, 2007). For example, sexual scripts often dictate that sex starts with kissing and touching and ends with (male) orgasm. Scripts about the specific "set-design" of sex also appear—should people have sex with the lights on or lights off? Naked or partially clothed? On a bed or outside in the back-yard? Attending to these interpersonal dynamics and the ways that messages and stories about sex are transmitted between partners, and between people and the culture they live in, requires an awareness that sexual scripts inform how people have sex.

First introduced by Simon and Gagnon (1986), sexual scripting theory argues that much of how people have sex occurs in relation to dominant cultural scripts rather than biological impulses. Following up on this, Jackson and Scott (2010) have long argued that the dominant discursive accounts of sex (for example, what "counts" as sex, and how people "should" have sex) do not adequately account for interactions between people and how those interactions draw from sexual scripting theory. Explorations of how people internalize scripts around penetrative sex as *required* have been called the "coital imperative" (McPhillips, Braun, & Gavey, 2001).

Many aspects of sexuality derive from diverse social scripts, and this can create a rather chaotic feel to how people understand sexuality. For example, Lisa Jean Moore (2007) argued in her book, *Sperm Counts*, that the social scripts and cultural stories around sperm are so diverse and differently understood that sperm can mean nearly anything to anyone:

> The bombardment of images, news stories, and scientific rhetoric about semen can sometimes seem overwhelming. Semen can be represented as engendered, malleable, agentic, emotive, instructive, sacred, profane, entertaining, contro-versial, empowering, dirty, clean, normal, abnormal, potent, impotent, power-ful, incriminating, anthropomorphic, uniform, polymorphic, and deterministic. Even though semen is diversely, even contradictorily, represented in the pre-ceding list of terms, the meanings of semen are deployed, on the whole, to reinforce a sense of virile masculinity.
>
> *(p. 8)*

At the same time, other scripts are becoming increasingly narrow. For example, the scripts of pornography emphasize an even more narrow idea about what sex looks like, sounds like, and (in theory) feels like. As scholar Robert Jensen (2007) points out, "contemporary pornography predominantly reflects the male sexual imagination rooted in a dominant conception of masculinity: sex as control, con-quest, domination, and the acquisition of pleasure by the taking of women" (p. 98). The scripts of pornography are, in Jensen's view, particularly narrow and, as such, quite destructive in their portrayal of women as objects for "use" by (mostly) men. Gail Dines (2010), too, has critiqued the intensely rigid and mis-ogynistic scripts found in pornography by arguing that pornography puts forth dangerously narrow scripts about race, masculinity, power, dominance, and hier-archy, and that pornography has straight-jacketed people's sexual imaginations and disallowed for sexual creativity. She writes of how the scripts of porn have infected women's sexual lives even if they do not themselves consume pornography:

> Most college-aged women I speak with have never seen gonzo [a type of porn where the performers are filming and performing the sex acts], but their sexuality is increasingly shaped by it as the men they partner with want to play out porn sex on their bodies. Whether their sexual partners pressure them into anal sex, want to ejaculate on their face, or use porn as a sex aid, these women are on the frontiers of the porn culture.
>
> *(p. xii)*

Beyond pornography, American culture at large also emphasizes phallic power and phallic imagery at every turn. As Michelle Gohr (2018) points out, people in the US feel surrounded by phallic imagery, from Kanamara Matsuri in Japan to the xenomorph in Ridley Scott's *Alien* franchise. Whether through historical structures that replicate the phallus (e.g., Washington Monument) or the ubiquitous circulation of "dick pics" among teens and 20-somethings, phallic imagery is an abundant part of everyday life. And, more importantly, yonic (or vaginal) imagery is mostly unrecognized, minimized, obscured, and forgotten. Gohr writes:

> Within these contexts of fabricated reality, women are positioned as agents upon which heteronormative masculinity must be performed using newly available technologies as modes of spread … The absurdity of these assumptions can only be laid bare through an imagined reversal; the mere idea of unwanted "vulva pics" circulated similarly and spread as an assumed mode of dominance seems funny or strange.
>
> *(p. 192)*

No wonder, then, that the emphasis on the penis and erections dominates conversations in sex therapy. Many couples enter therapy and describe sexual difficulties centered on "erectile dysfunction" or, at the very least, inconsistent (or, by their perception, inadequate) relationships to erections. This chapter features three case studies with heterosexual married couples in sex therapy where erections formed a central role in their perceived distress. I look at how the erection functions as a symbol of masculinity, power, and sexual success, and how reducing the importance of the erection had positive outcomes for the couple. I conclude with implications for de-centralizing the erection and re-scripting their sexual lives to allow for more diverse expressions of sex beyond "compulsory penetration."

A brief history of sex therapy

At its inception, sex therapy took a highly biological (and, at times, even evolutionary) approach to how to treat sexual problems, often leaning toward a strongly heterosexist idea about "good" and "healthy" sexuality. Along with assumptions about sexuality that situated traditional gender roles as central— including beliefs that "normal sex" existed at all—sex therapy most often served as a way to *return* the (heterosexual) couple to "normal" functioning. This often meant a dogged emphasis on penetration, complete with a wide variety of problematic treatments like vasodilation (widening the vaginal canal to allow for penetration, often by inserting devices into the vagina that get increasingly large over time) (Barnes, 1998; Canavan & Heckman, 2000). Dilation of the vagina using either pharmacological or physical vasodilators has continued as a first-line treatment for vaginismus, a disorder where the vagina tightens up involuntarily and therefore does not allow penetration of any kind (including the insertion of tampons in the more extreme cases) (Furman, Becker, & IsHak, 2017). Additionally, other treatments for sexual dysfunction include hormone manipulation (including those off-label treatments not recommended by the FDA) (Davis & Braunstein, 2012), a wide variety of pharmacological interventions to induce erections (for a criticism of their overuse, see Virag, 2005), and estrogen replacement therapies (Bachman & Leiblum, 2004).

Notably, sex therapy as a treatment modality did not emerge until long into the twentieth century, in part because nineteenth-century beliefs about sexuality did not frame sexuality as something that occurred across the lifespan. In the nineteenth century, older adults (especially older women) were rendered asexual and therefore without the need for medical intervention to lengthen their sex lives into old age. In the twentieth century, a greater interest in sexuality for older adults led to a push for more medical interventions (Leiblum, 2006). Further, many sex therapists have argued in the last 30 years that men and women's sexualities *should* be treated differently, as women report different types of complaints than men. Most prominently, women typically report sexual problems related to feelings and desire (particularly related to the perceived lack of emotional connection with partners) while men report sexual problems related to performance (particularly erectile performance) (Leiblum, 2006; Schmitt, 2003). This gender divide has led to an ever-increasing focus on men's erectile needs rather than a focus on sexual connection, emotionality, mutuality, and bonding.

With regard to men's erections, traditional sex therapy has emphasized pharmaceutical interventions to medically-induce more consistent (and harder) erections (for a critique of this, see Gavey, 2007). First approved in 1998, Viagra attracted a media frenzy that ultimately functioned to normalize the medicalization of sex; this dangerous shift in sexuality politics reinforced sex as biological rather than social (Tiefer, 2006). Laura Mamo and Jennifer Fishman (2001) have argued that Viagra worked to reinforce dominant hegemonic scripts about both masculinity and men's sexuality, particularly the idea that hard penises were intimately linked to potent masculinity. Viagra essentially worked to unite capitalistic scripts of "buying things" (e.g., pills) to reinforce traditional gender roles, alongside the cultural reinforcement of erections as the ultimate symbol of "successful" and "powerful" sexuality. Fundamentally, these drugs emphasize that erection problems have biological origins rather than social ones, and that drug treatments can stand in for the more difficult work of assessing what else may contribute to men's erectile functioning. Viagra also functions as a way to defy normative processes of aging, emphasizing that men's erections *should* stay the same across the life-span (Marshall, 2006).

Feminist critiques of sex therapy treatments have worked to counter these narratives of treating sex as a biological entity that could (or should) be treated with drugs, devices, and penetration-at-all-costs interventions. Peggy Kleinplatz (2012) argued that an overly medicalized approach to sexuality undermines the social and relational dimensions of sex and shifts attention away from the dynamic social processes of sexuality. Similarly, Leonore Tiefer has famously argued against pharmacological treatments for sexual dysfunction, stating that the social and relational aspects of sexuality are of paramount importance when understanding women's so-called sexual "problems" (Kaschak & Tiefer, 2014; Tiefer, 2010; Tiefer, Laan, & Basson, 2015). Tiefer helped to found the New View, a group dedicated to fighting against the medicalization of sex and sexuality. The New View, for example, argued that sexual problems often had roots in the *social circumstances* of people's lives. Women might report lack of desire for sex not because they had sexual dysfunction but because they felt fatigued from work and/or child-rearing, angry or disappointed at their partners, disconnected from their bodies, or resentful about their jobs. They may also not desire sex because such fluctuations in desire are, in fact, quite normal. People do not typically maintain an equal or level interest in sex throughout their lives, particularly as they cope with hormonal fluctuations, menopause, health issues, weight loss or weight gain, childbirth and breastfeeding, and other bodily changes and fluctuations.

Further, many things classified as "sexual problems" were, according to the New View, not problems at all. When an oft-cited study claimed that 43.1% of women had "sexual dysfunction" (Shifren, Monz, Russo, Segreti, & Johannes, 2008), media outlets and scholarly papers often failed to address the far more important detail in that study: *women themselves did not perceive many of those things as a problem.* In fact, 43.1% reported "sexual problems" of any kind, while only 22.2% of those women reported any personal distress about that sexual problem. In short, how women's distress was measured, and the assumptions made about that distress, often has layers of sexism, heterosexism, and misogyny built into both the research and its dissemination into more colloquial domains. For example, while the medical establishment might see vaginal dryness as a "sexual dysfunction" that needs treatment, women themselves might not. Or, while researchers might classify low interest in sex as problematic, many women find that they feel satisfied with low frequency, high-quality sex (Fahs & Swank, 2011).

Feminists have also critiqued the ways that the medical field sees erections. Leonore Tiefer argued, in her classic book, *Sex is not a natural act and other essays* (2004),

> We're also inundated with the idea that sex is just biology and can be "fixed" by medicine. That causes a kind of fragmentation in people's thinking. If your focus is on a particular body part as the source of the

problem, it prevents you from seeing sex as an act that involves your entire emotional, sensual, intellectual makeup—your whole self.

(p. 94)

Even prior to the advent of Viagra, Tiefer (1994) also found that women whose husbands wanted erectile implants and injections had highly diverse responses to these types of interventions. While some women supported the use of these interventions (particularly for women wanting to get pregnant), many expressed frustration that their husbands felt so driven toward erections rather than non-penetrative activities and emotional connection. One study found that a majority of women wanted to move away from a coital imperative after their husbands got diagnosed with cancer (Ussher, Perz, & Gilbert, 2014). Some women even worried that their own sexual enjoyment might be endangered by penile injections and implants (Tiefer, 1994).

Leonore Tiefer has directed especially astute critiques toward the whole trend of medicalizing sexual problems, writing in her later work, "Medicalization perpetuates a phallocentric construction of men's sexuality that literally and symbolically perpetuates women's sexual subordination through silencing and invisibility and thus operates to preserve men's power" (Tiefer, 2004, p. 196). She further argued that medicalization is an insidious process that relies on turning social norms into clinical standards and then developing drugs and medical interventions based on those "clinical standards," which only perpetuates more medicalization of sex. She wrote:

The problem is that the very existence of standards of normality breeds negative psychological consequences for those who deviate—that is known as the "social control" function of norms. And once norms become clinical standards, it's very difficult to identify those psychological problems that might not exist if social conformity weren't so important.

(Tiefer, 2004, p. 11)

Other feminist critiques of our cultural obsession with erections—and our relative lack of attention to the social aspects of sexuality—have also emerged in recent years. For example, Wood, Koch, and Mansfield (2006) argued for five major problems of the biomedical model for female sexual desire, including an overuse of the male model as standard, the use of a linear model of sexual response, biological reductionism, depoliticization, and medicalization of variation. Other feminist critics have argued that Viagra attaches sexuality to the idea of "functioning" rather than social exchange, and Viagra reinforces the idea of a universal body that can be "normal" or "pathological" (Potts, Grace, Gavey, & Vares, 2004). Khan and colleagues (2008) also convincingly argue that, when men's superiority and power over women are proclaimed as "normal" and "natural," men's erections become the vehicle for proving sexual power. Sustained critiques of these modes of thinking and their associated practices are needed to prevent an over-emphasis on erections as symbols of male dominance.

Related to this, Peggy Kleinplatz (2004) has argued that the discourse of erections within sex therapy discourses has too often mimicked the language and imagery of machines in disrepair, and has created rigid erections that ignore the couple and the processes of desire. She also argues that clinicians and psychologists too often ignore the problems of Viagra related to reductionism, desensitization, alienation, fragmentation, and mechanization. Ultimately, erections should comprise only a small part of sexual life but, because they have become scripted as having ultimate importance for men's experiences of sex, they have taken on new discourses that give erections primacy over other aspects of sexual and social life.

Compulsory heterosexuality, compulsory sexuality, compulsory penetration?

The notion that aspects of sexuality move from optional to compulsory has a long history in feminist theory over the years. In 1980, feminist poet and activist Adrienne Rich wrote a now-classic essay called, "Compulsory heterosexuality and the lesbian existence" where she argued that heterosexuality and homosexuality did not exist as two possible choices for sexual identity, but rather, as a choice between something entirely compulsory (forced, coerced, mandated) and something denigrated and invisibilized. She wrote, "Heterosexuality has been both forcibly and subliminally imposed upon women. Yet everywhere women have resisted it, often at the cost of physical torture, imprisonment, psychosurgery, social ostracism, and extreme poverty" (Rich, 1980, p. 653). Building on this, I argued in a 2009 essay that bisexuality seemed to take on compulsory dimensions among young women, particularly as both heterosexual women and sexual minority women felt pressured from heterosexual men to engage in kissing or sexual activities in front of heterosexual men in order to titillate them and enhance their pleasure at watching women "hook up" (Fahs, 2009).

Recently, feminist scholars Ela Przybylo and Danielle Cooper (2014) compellingly argued, in their essay about the erasure of asexuality from both the queer archive and the public landscape of sexuality, that sex itself was compulsory. That is, without the recognition of asexuality, people assume that *all people are sexual* and that *all people should be sexual*. They wrote:

> But [asexuality] is less that queerness should be expanded or revised to include asexuality than that queerness should be reworked and rethought from asexual perspectives … whenever sexuality is at the heart of literary, historical, and theoretical analysis, so is *asexuality*. While entirely neglected as a sexual identity and cultural trope, both historically and contemporarily, asexuality *can* be found in history, in literature, and in the everyday.
>
> *(pp. 298, 303)*

Ela Przybylo (2011) has also argued that people exist in "sexusociety" where expectations of mandatory sexuality are rampant:

> The 'sexual world' is for asexuals very much akin to what patriarchy is for feminists and heteronormativity for LGBTQ populations, in the sense that it constitutes the oppressive force against which some sort of organizing and rebellion must take place.
>
> *(p. 446)*

Other scholars have also begun to debate the concept of compulsory sexuality—that belief that all people are sexual—as something that marginalizes all kinds of non-sexualities, asexualities, or alternatively imagined sexualities (Cerankowski & Milks, 2014; Gupta, 2015). These new arguments in the sexuality literature encourage a more serious consideration of how and why sexual scripts have become so narrow, and what we miss (particularly about queer, asexual, and marginalized perspectives) when we perpetuate these narrow sexual scripts.

In this chapter, I build on these widespread rigid notions of compulsory sexuality to also wonder whether penetration has become compulsory within the framework of compulsory sexuality. In other words, the sexual scripting of heterosexual sex is so rigid and centered on men's bodies that penetration has become a requirement rather than an option for hetrosex. As the following case studies suggest, such a narrow script for sexuality disadvantages couples where men have inconsistent erections, and unduly puts stress on their sense of "normal" sex and "good" sexual performance.

Three case studies

The following three case studies that come from my practice as a clinical psych-ologist—each quite different from one another in terms of presenting problems—all share an emphasis on distress about erections, beliefs that better erectile functioning will automatically help their relationship with their partners, and an insistence that therapy should focus on "restoring" erections. I provide here brief sketches about the details of their presenting problems, treatment, and reso-lution to their sexual issues.[1]

Armando and Celine (fertility)

Armando, a 47-year-old Latino, and Celine, a 38-year-old Latina, came to ther-apy as a married couple to get help with their sexual problems. For the last seven years, the couple had been trying (unsuccessfully) to conceive a child. Celine had undergone years of fertility treatments, including several rounds of IVF that had produced a small number of embryos, none of which ever resulted in a pregnancy. Both of them expressed that they wanted desperately to become parents, and both believed that having a biological child was an essential part of their future. They had not yet considered other options like adoption. The couple sought help not only for coping with the fertility issues they had but also with ongoing issues that Armando had with his erectile functioning. Armando reported that he had a very difficult time getting or maintaining erections in recent years, and that he felt sure that some kind of medical problem could explain this. He recently had a physical workup to rule out medical problems and, while the doctors found no medical reason for his issues, he nevertheless remained convinced that the doctors had missed something. Celine agreed that their sex life had become consumed with Armando obsessing about his erections and worrying about his ability to have penetrative intercourse.

When describing their sexual relationship, Armando said that most of their sexual encounters involved (in his words) "the normal stuff." He said that he really enjoyed having sex with Celine but that his thoughts became highly anxious when he worried about having an erection. He thought that he would disappoint Celine or that she would become sexually frustrated if they could not have penetrative intercourse. He also believed that he would be "weird" or "abnormal" if they did not have penetrative intercourse according to a highly predictable script. Celine described the mechanics of their sexual interactions as "always the same," with "a few minutes of foreplay, followed by Armando obsessing over his erections." Celine felt distant and withdrawn when she felt that Armando was thinking about his erections instead of their connection; conversely, Armando worried that Celine's disappointment about his erections would overwhelm him and that it would "make things worse." The two had entered into a synergistic cycle where Celine's annoyance and disappointment about Armando worrying about his erections was misconstrued by Armando as actual disappointment about the erections themselves. What Celine wanted was the feeling of intimacy and connection; what Armando wanted was to not disappoint Celine.

The treatment began by emphasizing the importance of clear communication about their desires. Celine tried to openly talk to Armando about how she believed that sex meant connection and time together. Armando said that he wanted to "show her how he could perform." This led to a series of conversations where Celine described their best sexual encounters, ones where they spent a lot of time cuddling and touching rather than having penetrative intercourse. She eventually admitted that she could "take or leave" intercourse and that she "did not care whether I ever have sex that way again." This came as a shock to Armando, who had until then imagined penetrative intercourse as the "only way to be normal." He said that he associated his masculinity with erections and that not having consistent erections felt threatening and disappointing to him (he believed it made him "less of a man").

When we worked to make erections less of the center point of their sex life, Celine reported feeling much happier. I had asked them to purposefully avoid penetrative sex for a time, instead of focusing on the other aspects of sex that felt pleasurable or filled with the possibility of connection. Armando struggled with this, saying that he felt like he was "not really having sex." Celine said that she could tell that Armando was still obsessing over his erections, and she worried that he would "never see outside of himself and see me instead." Over time, however, Armando started to believe Celine that his erections did not matter to her. He relaxed and felt calmer and learned to focus on using his fingers and mouth instead of his penis during sex. He also started to see the ways that Celine was even *more* pleased with sex when penetration did not occur (much to his surprise). The de-emphasis on erections and penetration eventually led to far more consistency with being able to have erections. When Armando stopped focusing on his perceived deficiencies, he could more easily connect to his body, which led to more ease with erections.

By the end of therapy, the couple could also work on how their issues with sex connected with their disappointment and trauma around infertility. Armando made the links that his obsession with disappointing Celine really connected to larger issues about feeling like he "failed" to get her pregnant. Conversely, Celine better understood the ways that feeling physically and emotionally connected seemed crucial for her well-being, especially given that she chronically felt like she "failed" to get pregnant and "failed" to become a mother. Like many therapies that initially focus on sexuality, the issues raised during sex connected in deep ways to their other conflicts and struggles in their relationship more broadly. (Six months after the termination of therapy, the couple contacted me to tell me that they had finally conceived via IVF and surrogacy.)

James and Alice (health issues)

James, a 62-year-old African-American man, and Alice, a 56-year-old bi-racial (African-American/white) woman, entered therapy after 10 years of marriage to talk about issues they had with sexuality. Alice had recently undergone a cancer treatment that required her to wear a colostomy bag at all times. She reported that she was feeling better, and the doctors gave her a good prognosis for the cancer, but that her life had "completely changed" by having to wear the bag on the outside of her body. James, who described a "wonderful marriage" with her, said that he had been struggling for many years with erectile dysfunction but that it had recently gotten worse. While Alice believed this happened because James was "disgusted" with her, James said that he more felt worried about Alice's health and had a hard time divorcing his fears about her dying from cancer from their sexual interactions. He said that he "could not stop thinking about her death" and that sex had suffered as a result.

The couple described a harrowing couple of years dealing with Alice's cancer diagnosis and treatment. She had found out about the cancer three years prior and had had repeated rounds of chemotherapy and several surgeries. This had meant that the past three years were dominated by fears about Alice's health and constant surgery and recovery. The most recent surgery had removed a large section of Alice's colon and required her to wear a colostomy bag. The couple had learned how to cope with the technical aspects of these health problems—which pills to take, how to care for Alice after chemo treatments, how to change the bag, and so on—but they had not talked much about other aspects of their life. Their sex life, in particular, had understandably been a low priority.

James reported that he had developed a set of beliefs about sex that did not seem entirely rational but that he "could not be certain what was real anymore." He worried, for example, that penetrative intercourse would harm Alice physically and that it would derail her cancer treatment. Even though Alice told James that she enjoyed having penetrative intercourse, in part because it made her feel "normal" and healthy, James could not see past his fears that sex was destructive to Alice. He imagined his erections as "painful" to her and that any sort of expression of desire or lust was "insensitive." Alice, on the other hand, said that she struggled with her body image and felt ugly and unattractive, particularly now that she had the colostomy bag. She recounted how she used to weigh a healthy amount and have attractive skin and hair. She missed feeling "feminine, like before."

The treatment focused on imagining that, while penetrative intercourse appealed to Alice, the couple might benefit from de-emphasizing penetration right now. James had been struggling to maintain erections, and his anxiety had increased to the point that even thinking about having penetrative sex caused him to panic. He said that he did enjoy being alone together and interacting with Alice sexually as long as he did not worry about hurting her or exacerbating her health issues any further. Alice said that she would enjoy "just being sexual" and ultimately decided it did not matter that much how they accomplished that. She said that she "wanted to be normal" but also worked on expanding her ideas about what "normal sex" might look like. We also talked a lot about how couples had sex in all kinds of different ways that accommodated their body sizes and shapes, or even their physical limitations or difficulties.

James and Alice found, to their surprise, that when they worked on their sex life in these ways—by de-emphasizing penetration and erections and focusing instead on closeness and other modes of sexual affection and interaction—they also felt more motivated to interact more romantically with each other. For example, James started planning more date nights, and they made an effort to find clothes that made Alice feel more comfortable or even sexy. They also said that their sexual interactions felt far more emotional and intense and that they had bonded in a new way. Because their relationship had such strong foundations in the first place, reimagining their sexuality came easier to them than they anticipated. As with Armando and Celine, the work on sexuality also opened up some important conversations around James's fear of mortality and his fear of Alice suddenly dying. We talked about attachment, James's troubled childhood history of being abandoned, and Alice's desire for James to remarry if she did eventually die before him. The therapy ended when the couple decided that sex had become a "non-issue" and that James really enjoyed "giving to Alice." They also had re-introduced penetrative intercourse "on occasion" but did not feel as strongly that this was the only form of sexual expression that was normal or pleasurable to them any longer.

Chris and Suzanna (sexual desire)

Chris, a 33-year-old white man, and Suzanna, a 32-year-old white woman, sought therapy after being married for 18 months. During the intake appointment, Chris reported that he and Suzanna had problems with sex and that he "could not get it up" like he wanted to. He angrily blamed Suzanna for this, saying that she "was just not into it" like he thought she would be (referring to penetrative sex). He said that when they were dating, they had sex "all the time" and that he never had any difficulty with erections, but that since they were married a year and a half ago, he consistently struggled with his erections. He wanted to come to therapy so that a therapist could "fix her" (referring to Suzanna) because he thought she had "low desire."

Chris displayed signs of visible anxiety, tapping his toes, looking away, and sometimes anxiously leaving the room to "go for a walk" during the initial sessions. He had a difficult time expressing his feelings or imagining a story for why their sex life had derailed. Suzanna, on the other hand, said that she felt unhappy about how their marriage was going and that she had been "duped" about Chris. She described a series of things that had contributed to her waning interest in sex, including Chris's frequent drinking, which had become far worse since they got married. She wondered whether he had a drinking problem before their marriage as well and worried that he hid it from her. She also said that Chris had problems with deception in general, and that she had caught him online gambling "at all hours." Suzanna felt that Chris "did not really want to be married" and that he blamed her for everything that was going wrong.

The treatment began by focusing on their marital problems and the general lack of trust that they had in each other. We talked about boundaries and their comfort level with things like drinking, gambling, and spending time with friends. We also processed their feelings about marriage, particularly the space between what they imagined marriage would be and what it actually turned out to be. Additionally, we talked about what had attracted them to each other in the first place, and we talked about their vision for a "good sex life." This latter point had yielded two highly conflicting notions of what they wanted from sex. Chris wanted an abundant amount of sex and imagined sex as penetrative intercourse along with "lots of spicy things." He clarified that that meant Suzanna would have an interest in bondage and dominance, anal sex, and role playing. Suzanna said that she had imagined a good sex life as one where she "felt wanted" and that she believed that sex "a few times per week" would satisfy her completely. She also said that she did not feel very interested in "spicy" sex but that she wanted both of them to feel a lot of desire for each other.

Chris attached different meaning to sex than did Suzanna, particularly when he described how he felt angry at Suzanna when he had erection problems. He admitted that marriage felt to him like giving up on his freedom, especially his freedom to have a lot of sex with different women. He felt that it was "worth the sacrifice" when Suzanna wanted to have sex more frequently, but that he was now "paying the price" by not having access to other sexual partners. Suzanna, hurt by these admissions, said that she did not feel attracted to him when she did not trust him, and that she worried about him comparing her to other women. These fractures in their marriage, and their differing perceptions of the root of the problem, led to a series of discussions about what it would take to repair their sex life and their marriage. Chris believed that Suzanna needed to "get fixed" in order to want him again, and Suzanna felt that she needed to trust Chris and feel secure around him in order to want to have sex.

During the course of treatment, Chris described a slew of other things he had hidden from Suzanna, including that he watched a sizable amount of pornography (often "spicy" as he described it) and that he also struggled with erection problems during masturbation. This allowed us to more openly discuss the ways that Chris himself was struggling with masculinity, power, and sexuality both on his own and with Suzanna, and how Suzanna was not responsible for making him feel desired. He also talked about his (rather negative) views of women in general, including ex-girlfriends who had cheated on him in high school, and a rocky relationship with his mother, whom he perceived as chronically disapproving of his choices. When we talked more directly about erections, he described a belief that "sex is a time when men get to be men." By this, he meant that sex represented an avenue toward having power and control, something he generally lacked in most areas of his life. He held down a job successfully but had lost quite a lot of money gambling; similarly, he felt paranoid that his friends were using him for money.

The therapy moved from a couple's treatment of sexual problems to instead an individual therapy for Chris that focused on his issues with trust, power, control, masculinity, and marriage. His erection problems improved (but never fully resolved) when he focused on the ways that marriage made him feel vulnerable ("like I can never be alone again") and attached ("I want to be married, but I don't want to feel trapped") in ways that felt both good and bad. That said, he still struggled to revise his beliefs that Suzanna (and wives in general) should sexually service and please their husbands. During our occasional couple's sessions, Suzanna talked about how these beliefs clashed with her ideas of herself as an independent and autonomous person. Their marital problems continued to persist, even though both had more insight into the things they had overlooked in each other prior to getting married. They described that sex "sometimes felt satisfying" but that they "were two different people." Ultimately, the treatment ended when Chris lost so much money gambling on horseracing that he could no longer afford sessions.

Conclusion: beyond erections

As these case studies show, the importance of de-emphasizing erections in sex therapy is crucial not only for men's relationship to their own ideas about sexual performance but also for the happiness and well-being of their partners. The intensely gendered dynamics of prioritizing erectile functioning over other kinds of intimacies and sexual exchanges (e.g., non-intercourse-focused, non-genital touching, working on closeness and connectedness, sexual play, etc.) severely undermines sexual satisfaction and joy for both partners. Couples who can work together to see the erection as less meaningful or central to a healthy and robust sexual life end up, ironically, struggling less with erectile problems. By removing erections as the focus, this allows for different kinds of sexual expression and sexual connection to emerge that is often more emotive and egalitarian.

In terms of sexual scripting, though penetration often feels compulsory, there are real rewards for de-prioritizing penetrative sex for those struggling with erections. As these cases show, such a shift might benefit everyone, as women can put more emphasis on clitoral pleasure (and more orgasms) while men can learn to be less self-focused and more other-focused. Men can also learn that erections do not symbolize their sexual power (or, more disturbingly, dominance) and that more emphasis on mutuality serves their needs too. This kind of reworking of the sexual scripts that over-emphasize penetrative intercourse requires a deeper reworking of what sex is and what sex is for. One of the main reasons that couples want to have penetrative sex is because it makes them feel "normal"; pushing back against their ideas of "normal sex" and allowing for more diverse forms of sexual play, touching, connection, and intimacy allows them to take some of the performance pressures off of both partners while also (hypothetically, anyway) allowing for them to stay sexual together later in life (when erections will inevitably become more difficult and inconsistent).

These cases also convincingly argue for a shift from thinking about sex as an *individual* experience—that is, something where the individual considers his/her own functioning, desires, and needs—and instead as a more *couples* experience. In making such a shift, men can worry less about erections and more about mutuality, partner satisfaction, and communication. Further, the more neglected aspects of sexual scripts like creativity, compromise, and flexibility can come more fully into focus, as couples work to imagine sexual narratives as more open, broad, fluid, and co-constructed.

Note

1 Note that I have changed all names and identifying information, and I have assigned pseudonyms. In accordance with the Institutional Review Board at my institution, all of these clients consented to have their case materials used for research purposes.

References

Bachman, G., & Leiblum, S. R. (2004). The impact of hormones on menopausal sexuality: A literature review. *Menopause, 11*, 120–130.

Barnes, T. (1998). The female partner in the treatment of erectile dysfunction: What is her position? *Sexual and Marital Therapy, 13*(3), 233–240.

Canavan, T. P., & Heckman, C. D. (2000). Dyspareunia in women: Breaking the silence is the first step toward treatment. *Postgraduate Medicine, 108*(2), 149–166.

Cerankowski, K. J., & Milks, M. (Eds.). (2014). *Asexualities: Feminist and queer perspectives.* New York: Routledge.

Davis, S. R., & Braunstein, G. D. (2012). Efficacy and safety of testosterone in the management of hypoactive sexual desire disorder in postmenopausal women. *The Journal of Sexual Medicine, 9*(4), 1134–1148.

Dines, G. (2010). *Pornland: How porn has hijacked our sexuality.* Boston, MA: Beacon Press.

Fahs, B. (2009). Compulsory bisexuality? The challenges of modern sexual fluidity. *Journal of Bisexuality, 9*(3–4), 431–449.

Fahs, B., & Swank, E. (2011). Social identities as predictors of women's sexual satisfaction and sexual activity. *Archives of Sexual Behavior, 40*(5), 903–914.

Furman, K. A., Becker, B., & IsHak, W. W. (2017). Introduction to sexual medicine. In W. IsHak (Ed.), *The textbook of clinical sexual medicine* (pp. 3–15). New York: Springer.

Gavey, N. (2007). Viagra and the coital imperative. In S. Seidman, N. Fischer, & C. Meeks (Eds.), *Handbook of the new sexuality studies* (pp. 127–132). London: Routledge.

Gohr, M. (2018). Cult of the penis: Male fragility and phallic frenzy. In B. Fahs, A. Mann, E. Swank, & S. Stage (Eds.), *Transforming contagion: Risky contacts among bodies, disciplines, and nations* (pp. 160–172). New Brunswick, NJ: Rutgers University Press.

Gupta, K. (2015). Compulsory sexuality: Evaluating an emerging concept. *Signs: Journal of Women in Culture and Society, 41*(1), 131–154.

Jackson, S., & Scott, S. (2010). *Theorizing sexuality.* New York: Open University Press.

Jensen, R. (2007). *Getting off: Pornography and the end of masculinity.* Brooklyn, NY: South End Press.

Kaschak, E., & Tiefer, L. (2014). *A new view of women's sexual problems.* New York: Routledge.

Khan, S. I., Hudson-Rodd, N., Saggers, S., Bhuivan, M. I., Bhuiva, A., Karim, S. A., & Rauyajin, O. (2008). Phallus performance and power: A crisis of masculinity. *Sexual and Relationship Therapy, 23*(1), 37–49.

tKleinplatz, P. J. (2004). Beyond sexual mechanics and hydraulics: Humanizing the discourse surrounding erectile dysfunctions. *Journal of Humanistic Psychology, 44*(2), 215–242.

Kleinplatz, P. J. (2012). *New directions in sex therapy: Innovations and alternatives.* New York: Routledge.

Leiblum, S. R. (2006). Sex therapy today: Current issues and future perspectives. In S. R. Leiblum (Ed.), *Principles and practice of sex therapy, fourth edition* (pp. 3–22). New York: Guilford Press.

Mamo, L., & Fishman, J. R. (2001). Potency in all the right places: Viagra as a technology of the gendered body. *Body & Society, 7*(4), 13–35.

Marshall, B. L. (2006). The new virility: Viagra, male aging and sexual function. *Sexualities, 9*(3), 345–362.

McPhillips, K., Braun, V., & Gavey, N. (2001). Defining (hetero) sex: How imperative is the "coital imperative"? *Women's Studies International Forum, 24*(2), 229–240.

Moore, L. J. (2007). *Sperm counts: Overcome by man's most precious fluid.* New York: New York University Press.

Plante, R. F. (2007). In search of sexual subjectivities: Exploring the sociological construction of sexual selves. In M. S. Kimmel (Ed.), *The sexual self: The construction of sexual scripts* (pp. 31–48). Nashville, TN: Vanderbilt University Press.

Potts, A., Grace, V., Gavey, N., & Vares, T. (2004). Viagra stories': Challenging "erectile dysfunction." *Social Science & Medicine, 59*(3), 489–499.

Przybylo, E. (2011). Crisis and safety: The asexual in sexusociety. *Sexualities, 14*(4), 444–461.

Przybylo, E., & Cooper, D. (2014). Asexual resonances: Tracing a queerly asexual archive. *GLQ: A Journal of Lesbian and Gay Studies, 20*(3), 297–318.

Rich, A. (1980). Compulsory heterosexuality and the lesbian existence. *Signs, 5*(4), 631–660.

Schmitt, D. (2003). Universal sex differences in the desire for sexual variety: Tests from 52 nations, 6 continents, and 13 islands. *Journal of Personality and Social Psychology, 85*(1), 85–101.

Shifren, J. L., Monz, B. U., Russo, P. A., Segreti, A., & Johannes, C. B. (2008). Sexual problems and distress in United States women: Prevalence and correlates. *Obstetrics & Gynecology, 112*(5), 970–978.

Simon, W., & Gagnon, J. H. (1986). Sexual scripts: Permanence and change. *Archives of Sexual Behavior, 15*(2), 97–120.

Tiefer, L. (1994). The medicalization of impotence: Normalizing phallocentrism. *Gender & Society, 8*(3), 363–377.

Tiefer, L. (2004). *Sex is not a natural act and other essays.* Boulder, CO: Westview Press.

Tiefer, L. (2006). The Viagra phenomenon. *Sexualities, 9*(3), 273–294.

Tiefer, L. (2010). Still resisting after all these years: An update on sexuo-medicalization and on the New View Campaign to challenge the medicalization of women's sexuality. *Sexual and Relationship Therapy, 25*(2), 189–196.

Tiefer, L., Laan, E., & Basson, R. (2015). Missed opportunities in the patient-focused drug development public meeting and scientific workshop on female sexual dysfunction held at the FDA, October 2014. *The Journal of Sex Research, 52*(6), 601–603.

Ussher, J. M., Perz, J., & Gilbert, E. (2014). Women's sexuality after cancer: A qualitative analysis of sexual changes and renegotiation. *Women & Therapy, 37*(3–4), 205–221.

Virag, R. (2005). Comments from Ronald Virag on intracavernous injections: 25 years later. *Journal of Sexual Medicine, 2*, 289–290.

Wood, J. M., Koch, P. B., & Mansfield, P. K. (2006). Women's sexual desire: A feminist critique. *Journal of Sex Research, 43*(3), 236–244.

8

ARE WOMEN PEOPLE?

The lusty and chaotic world of sex addiction

While plenty of recent attention has been paid to the widespread problems of sexual assault, sexual harassment, and workplace abuse—particularly with the ascendency of Time's Up (Buckley, 2018; Time's Up, 2018) and #MeToo (NPR, 2018; Pincus-Roth, 2017) in 2017 and 2018—far less public attention has been directed toward the systemic roots of these problems. Though broad and blanket phrases like "toxic masculinity" and "sexual entitlement" have appeared in the public eye, the problem of how men interpret their relationships to women is still under-examined in mass media and public discourse. While the media has directed attention toward certain men outed as predators or sexual harassers, this undersells the normality of imbalanced gender relations and the pervasive problems of how sexuality links up with power and privilege.

In this chapter, I looked closely at three case studies with men in treatment for long-term sex addiction and compulsive sexual behavior. After reviewing a brief and controversial history of sex addiction and some of the clinical implications for treatment of sex addiction, I turn to three case studies that showcase the diverse range of sex addiction: sex addiction with prostitutes, porn addiction, and sex addiction through dating apps. I examine the ways that these clients imagine women, and how feminist therapy interventions work not only to help with their compulsive behaviors but also to reshape their views of women's sexual subjectivities. I also make links between cultural misogyny and the ways that sex addiction manifests in these men's attitudes and beliefs about women.

History of sex addiction

Scholars, researchers, and clinicians continue to debate the frameworks for understanding sex addiction and compulsive sexual behavior, defined currently as a proposed disorder called "hypersexual disorder." The American Psychological Association defines this as "distress about a pattern of repeated sexual relationships involving a succession of lovers who are experienced by the individual only as things to be used" (Kafka, 2010). Questions about whether sex addiction even constitutes a real disorder or problem continue to saturate both the psychological and popular literature, particularly in the wake of the Harvey Weinstein scandal and the increased attention to sexual "rehabilitation" (Carey, 2017). On the one hand, sex addiction has gained traction in recent years as a treatable problem, particularly when individual psychotherapy is coupled with Sex Addicts Anonymous (SAA) programs to work on the addiction through a 12-step model (Goodman, 1992; Schneider, 2004). Sex addiction now has a journal (*Sexual Addiction & Compulsivity*) and commonly appears as a topic at conferences for mental health professionals (Wahesh, Likis-Werle, & Moro, 2017). Many academics, professionals, and policymakers have noted that addiction models are applicable to sex (Ley, Prause, & Finn, 2014; Reay, Attwood, & Gooder, 2013; Voros, 2009), though an increasing number of scholars express concern about applying the addiction model to frequent sex and pornography viewing (Giugliano, 2009; Hall, 2014; Ley, 2012; Reid & Kafka, 2014). Many sex-positive advocates and activists worry that even the mere labeling of "sex addiction" could unnecessarily pathologize different or "deviant" sexual behavior, and it could lead to a hyper-normalization of only *certain kinds of* sexuality (Irvine, 1995; Reay, Attwood, & Gooder, 2013; Thomas, 2013).

For example, in late 2017, the Center for Positive Sexuality (CPS), The Alternative Sexualities Health Research Alliance (TASHRA), and the National Coalition for Sexual Freedom (NCSF) issued a joint position statement detailing their concerns about the label of "sex addiction" as applied to individuals who engage in frequent sex and/or those who frequently view pornography. The statement expresses concern with a diagnosis of sex addiction based on several problems in the existing frameworks: the American Psychological Association does not recognize sex addiction as a mental disorder; there is an overreliance on correlational data and a general lack of methodological rigor when studying sex addiction; religious and moral beliefs strongly impact perceptions of sex addiction; and research is subject to immense sociocultural bias (CPS, TASHRA, & NCSF, 2017).

In a subsequent email, NCSF wrote:

> There are many factors that could lead someone to engage in various sexual practices and or pornography viewing, and current assessments for the concepts of sex and porn addiction lack scientific rigor and validity. Furthermore, important cultural factors are not considered within a sex/ porn addiction model. This position statement also reports that the addiction model assumes that using sex or pornography as a coping mechanism is necessarily problematic, and maybe this is due to an overly conservative or religious view of sexuality, rather than a recognition that this may

actually be maladaptive. In fact, as pointed out, studies show that diverse sexuality may actually be considered a positive means of coping.

(NCSF, 2017)

Despite these concerns, sex addiction continues to expand as an increasingly relevant and urgent problem inside and outside of clinical settings. For example, a growing number of men identify pornography viewing as destructive to their lives, time-consuming, and problematic for their interpersonal relationships and views toward women (Grubbs, Volk, Exline, & Pargament, 2015); many men (and some women) associate increased pornography use with depression, anxiety, and stress (Levin, Lillis, & Hayes, 2012). That said, the line between "addicted" pornography use and "non-addicted" use is blurry (Griffiths, 2012); one study found that religiosity was a robust predictor of people's perceptions of *addiction* to pornography (Grubbs, Exline, Pargament, Hook, & Carlisle, 2015), suggesting that how people self-identify addictive behavior compared to problematic, destructive, excessive, or normal pornography consumption might be mediated by their associations between sex and morality.

In fact, the American Psychological Association did consider both internet addictive disorder and hypersexual disorder for the *Diagnostic and Statistical Manual of Mental Disorders, 5th edition* but ultimately left it out (Rosenberg, Carnes, & O'Connor, 2014). Some researchers have expressed concern that, while distress about pornography viewing is relatively widespread, the notion of addiction may map onto moral panics about sexuality instead of actual addictive processes (Dunn, Seaburne-May, & Gatter, 2012). That said, others have insisted that a variety of therapies (e.g., group, individual) can effectively treat behaviors that have been called sexual addiction (Nerenberg, 2000; Phillips, Hajela, & Hilton, 2015) even if therapists sometimes feel undertrained in how to use effective treatment modalities for sex addiction (Short, Wetterneck, Bistricky, Shutter, & Chase, 2016).

Regardless of how clinicians classify the behavior, links between men's sexually obsessive and misogynistic behaviors and their distress are clear. We do know that many men worry about their pornography consumption (Manning, 2006; Tylka, 2015) and that a significant percentage of men—15–20% in a recent global study—report paying for sex from prostitutes (ProCon, 2011). Men who paid for sex more often reported raping women in the past and engaging in sexual aggression (Farley, Golding, Matthews, Malamuth, & Jarrett, 2017); paying for sex was also associated with rape myth acceptance, attraction to violent sexuality, and less frequent condom use compared to other men (Monto & Dulka, 2009). Further, Sex Addicts Anonymous groups now have chapters in all 50 US states, and continually expands to accommodate more and more people seeking to recover from compulsive sexual activities, including groups that extend beyond men's groups (e.g., women-only and LGBT groups) (SAA, 2018). And, of course, increasing numbers of patients seek treatment from therapists for sex-related problems that fit into an addiction model (e.g., compulsively seeking out destructive sexual experiences, losing time and money to sex, experiencing interpersonal distress, losing jobs/friendships/marriages because of sex, compulsively lying about sex, taking extreme risks related to seeking out sex, etc.).

Clinical treatments of sex addiction

Sex addiction treatments focus broadly on biological, moral, and social models, each triggering a variety of critical reactions about their effectiveness and impact (Hall, 2011, 2014). Assessment of sex addiction has grown, with dozens of instruments that rely on self-report checklists and clinician rating scales to assess problematic sexual behavior (Hook, Hook, Davis, Worthington, & Penberthy, 2010). Most existing treatments of sex addiction focus either on medications to treat compulsive behaviors, such as naltrexone therapy (Bostwick & Bucci, 2008) or SSRI treatments at times combined with antiandrogenic treatments (Rosenberg, Carnes, & O'Connor, 2014; Stein et al., 1992). Treatments also focus on approaches that target cognitions, such as mentalization-based therapy (Berry & Berry, 2013), virtual treatment exposure (Cismaru Inescu, Andrianne, & Triffaux, 2013), emotionally focused therapy (Love, Moore, & Stanish, 2016), art therapy (Wilson, 1998), meditation awareness (Van Gordon, Shonin, & Griffiths, 2016), and classic Cognitive Behavioral Therapy (CBT) (Shepherd, 2010).

An increasing number of books and articles also outline protocols for treating couples where one partner has engaged in sex addicted behavior, recognizing the deleterious impacts on marriages and couples' lives (Cohn, 2013; Turner, 2009). One challenge with couples' therapies is that sex addiction and infidelity often coincide, making it difficult to determine how to distinguish between an internet infidelity scenario, a sex addiction facilitated by the internet, and an internet addiction (Jones & Hertlein, 2012). Further, most sex addiction treatment programs for couples situate men as addicts and women as their (faithful) partners. New attention to sex "coaddiction" (Manley, 1999)—where both partners are addicted—and sex addiction problems in women, are emerging (Dhuffar & Griffiths, 2016; McKeague, 2014).

Another challenge in treatment for sex addiction is that clinicians themselves have strong biases about "moral" sexual behavior. Many mental health professionals avoid discussing sexuality with clients and some conservative therapists turn away clients who have multiple sexual partners, practice polyamory, or identify as gay, lesbian, or bisexual (Miller & Byers, 2012). Further, therapists who discuss sexual issues often focus on sexual problems rather than positive aspects of sexuality (Heiden-Rootes, Brimhall, Jankowski, & Reddick, 2017; Urry & Chur-Hansen, 2018). One study found that therapists assessed women cheating on their partners more negatively than men cheating on their partners, suggesting that therapists may have built-in biases about what they recognize as problematic sexual behavior (Reddick, Heiden-Rootes, & Brimhall, 2017).

Feminist therapy for sex addicts?

Frequently missing in these various treatments used for sex addiction and compulsive sexual behavior, however, is an explicitly feminist therapeutic approach. This approach emphasizes the importance of gender and power alongside the recognition that sex addicted behaviors, while perhaps producing important chemical changes in the brain, also relate to core beliefs about women, power, and sexuality. For example, gender socialization, anger (or even hatred) toward women, beliefs that women "owe" men sex, feelings about their masculinity, relationships to money and work, beliefs about sexual entitlement and sexual service (and much more) all connect deeply to the treatment of sex addiction in men.

Feminist therapy—that is, therapy that focuses on understanding and reimagining these deeply-held beliefs about gender and power—is an important tool for working with men who feel addicted to sex and pornography. Other studies have shown that feminist therapy with men can be quite effective in changing maladaptive attitudes and beliefs about women (Conlin, 2017; Wolf, Williams, Darby, Herald, & Schultz, 2018). In the following three cases, I outline the ways that misogyny, sexual entitlement, issues of toxic masculinity, and maladaptive ways of relating to women all contributed to their sex-addicted behaviors and thoughts. While each of these cases differs in its approach to treatment, all relied on a feminist therapy orientation and all targeted underlying core beliefs about gender and power.

Case 1: Jesus

Jesus, a 56-year-old Latino man, began therapy because of a long-term problem with soliciting sex from female prostitutes, sometimes as often as five times per week. Married with three teenage children, Jesus ran his own construction business and had, as a result of his problems with prostitutes, spent much of the family's money on his sexual pursuits. He also reported a host of other problems: severe anxiety, profound levels of depression with occasional feelings of suicidality, problems in his marriage (his wife felt that sex was an obligation and nothing more), trouble staying afloat financially, and difficulties with chronic lying and deception. Jesus wanted help getting his "life back together" and figuring out why he continued to engage in this behavior.

During the early parts of our three-year work together, Jesus did not recognize his behavior as addictive or compulsive. Instead, he worried that it might be "genetic" given that his uncle had previously been arrested for soliciting underage girls for sex. He worried that he inherited his uncle's inclinations toward problematic sexual behavior—not toward children or young girls, in Jesus's case, but toward women in their 20s. He also felt that his depression and anxiety had a "root cause" he had not yet discovered and was especially drawn toward the idea that he would "find out" that he had a serious medical condition that caused his sexual problems. He fantasized about a number of different causes to his sex issues: a thyroid dysfunction, a medication that had strange side effects, a bad reaction to using drugs years ago, and poisonous food additives in his diet.

Early on in the treatment, I asked him to attend a Sex Addicts Anonymous meeting to assist in the treatment. He attended meetings with an almost compulsive level of interest, going to three or four of them per week and attending telephonic and internet-based meetings. He said that he found the meetings soothing and comforting but did not see himself wanting to be fully "sober" (as SAA calls it). He still sought out prostitutes and had only been sober for a maximum of 30 days before acting out again. He said that he often used sex to reward himself for "being good," and that he also used sex to comfort himself when had had a difficult week at work, or when he got into a fight with his wife.

Jesus's encounters with female prostitutes were always the same: a quick blowjob or an encounter that involved forceful insertive anal sex. He described these encounters as satisfying because he felt "in charge" and could "make women do what I want." He also felt like having an orgasm was a "drug-like hit" and that he felt frantic until he ejaculated, followed by crushing and often suicidal-feeling-levels of depression and shame. This cycle of feeling lustful and then seeking out prostitutes, followed by low mood, self-loathing, and self-hatred were often followed up with other negative behaviors like compulsive eating, compulsive gambling, and reckless behavior while driving. While he did not use drugs and alcohol often, he worried that he would "never be able to stop using sex to deal with life."

As a child, Jesus and his sister had coped with severe physical and emotional abuse from his father, often while his mother did not intervene or protect them. He felt simultaneously terrified of masculinity and its associations with power abuses, physical violence, and anger, while also feeling tremendous resentment toward his mother (and all women) for treating him poorly and not protecting him. He constantly talked about wishing that his wife would "save him" from his depression. He felt angry at his mother for "not caring enough" about him, and he sometimes resented therapy for "not helping him enough." These links to seeing women as failed protectors and failed saviors—and not seeing his own complicity and responsibility for his problems—led to persistent negative feelings toward women. He acted these feelings out with the various prostitutes that he saw.

Part of our treatment pushed Jesus to see these prostitutes as people, particularly given that he vaguely dissociated while interacting with them. Jesus often could not remember what the rooms looked like where he had sex with prostitutes, or what the women looked like in person. He could not remember many details of what they would say or do. When he started to consciously work to "see" these things more clearly, and to imagine the prostitutes as people with subjective lives and feelings, he felt increasing levels of horror with his own behavior. We had a particularly engaging session where he recounted his shock at how dirty the floors and rugs were in a room where he was having sex, and how he had not noticed that she had cigarette burn marks on her arms. He said that it was difficult to imagine these women as people—as fully human—because then he could not "use" them in the same way.

Ultimately, it took the loss of his marriage and his children finding out about his problems with sex to get Jesus to take his sobriety more seriously. He hit "bottom" and was then able to work his way toward longer and longer periods of sobriety. His work with the 12-step program combined with our work doing feminist-oriented sex addiction therapy resulted in Jesus refocusing on treating his depression and anxiety rather than relying on sex with prostitutes as a way to compulsively act out his anger toward women.

Case 2: Virgil

Virgil, a 76-year-old white married man, entered therapy after his couple's therapist referred him for treatment following a highly contentious and relatively unsuccessful series of couple's sessions to address his problems with pornography. His wife had complained that his excessive pornography usage had caused problems in their marriage, while Virgil felt that pornography was his "only escape" from his dreary and boring retirement. He described watching pornography every day, often compulsively, and having little interest in anything else. He had recently (three years ago) retired from his position as an architect at a local company and said that since his retirement he had fallen into a deep depression and felt aimless and unimportant. Pornography, he said, offered him a way to feel successful again.

A devout Christian, Virgil had been married for 51 years and had six grown children, all of whom he was relatively distant from. He described ongoing problems with his marriage that stemmed back to the very beginning, including "close calls" with infidelity, near-constant fighting, different values about child-rearing, and problems with sexuality. He believed he could never please his wife and that she did not enjoy sex or want sex (and that she never had enjoyed sex or wanted sex). He described daily problems with feeling irritated with his wife, fighting with her over trivial matters, and feeling "cut down" by her. At times, his anger and resentment toward her became so intense that he fantasized about her getting cancer. Because of his religious beliefs, he would not consider divorce or separation and felt it was his duty to "ensure" the marriage.

Virgil had started using pornography in his teenage years, progressing through the decades from photographs, magazines, pornography in movie theaters, VHS tapes, and, finally, pornography on the internet. Given the ease and widespread availability of porn now, he said that his problems with pornography had only intensified in the last few years, especially following retirement. He sought treatment to help him cope with feeling over-whelmed by his marriage, and he wanted to explore other ways to cope aside from pornography. Virgil also felt that he was not certain he wanted to stop using porn and was uncertain as to whether this constituted a "problem" or not. He was highly anxious about the idea of going "cold turkey" with his pornography usage.

The treatment focused first on exploring the meaning of pornography as a coping skill. We worked on the triggers for when he used porn, how he felt before and after watching porn, and how he compulsively felt like he needed to watch porn in order to soothe negative feelings he had toward his wife. We then talked in more detail about the fantasy world created in pornography, one where, as he said, "the women are always eager to please the men and the men don't need to work for approval." He started to piece together how the images he watched gave him an alternative (albeit unrealistic) story to latch onto about women and their roles with men. He liked how they were "always ready for sex," how easily they were "pleased with the men," and how they never "acted like they were disappointed." He contrasted this fantasy world to his own experiences with sexuality where he felt like his wife rejected him, trea-ted sex as a chore, and overwhelmingly was displeased with their sex life.

Like many treatments with men struggling with sexual compulsions, Virgil also had a murky profile in terms of whether he was "addicted" to pornog-raphy or not. He clearly used pornography in ways that caused him distress, disrupted his marriage, and compulsively served as a form of coping; that said, whether this usage constituted full-blown addiction was debatable. Nevertheless, the treatment focused, like other sex addiction treatments, on the importance of not substituting the fantasy world of sex and pornog-raphy for the actual experience of being married. Virgil, for instance, only saw his wife as an obstacle to his personal happiness; much of our work in treatment focused on him seeing his wife as fully human, complete with positive characteristics, needs that he could meet, and an (irreplaceable) his-tory of witnessing each others' lives for many decades.

By the end of the treatment, Virgil was more in touch with what he liked about his wife, and more apt to use multiple coping skills to deal with his depression and loneliness (e.g., reading novels, spending more time at the Elks club, and so on). He also was able to more critically examine the problems of wishing for the world created for him by pornography, articulating to me that he saw it more as "silly" and less as "intoxicating." While he still used porn on occasion, he cut back substantially in how much he felt he needed to watch it. Further, Virgil became far more cooperative with the treatment in general, coming to sessions on time and without canceling, and working on improving his existing marriage, particularly given that he refused to consider divorce, sep-aration, or dating anyone else. Ultimately, he reported more acceptance of the conditions of his marriage, and more awareness of how pornography had served as a substitute for his need to feel powerful, successful, and "in charge."

Case 3: Jason

Jason, a 32-year-old single white male, entered therapy to help him cope with a recent breakup from his girlfriend of ten years. Jason reported that he had a serious problem with compulsively using dating apps to have one-night-stands with women, all while lying to his then-girlfriend about his fidelity. He described these encounters as exhilarating and said he that he enjoyed "getting away with it" and "not getting caught." His then-girlfriend had eventually discovered for sure that he was cheating after she looked through his phone while he was in the shower. After discovering some of his activities, she had promptly declared that she was leaving and had packed her things the next day. Jason described that he felt empty and lonely, and that he worried that he might have a problem with sex addiction.

During the course of treatment, Jason simultaneously processed his grief about losing his long-term relationship, and he worked through why he felt so compelled to cheat on her "hundreds of times per year." He gave elaborate descriptions of how he orchestrated the cheating, arranged to meet different women and have sex with them, gave minimal information about himself, and typically never communicated with any of these women again after the one-time encounters. He also described intense contempt for the women he cheated with, saying that they were "stupid bitches" and "disgusting whores." He described his girlfriend in opposite terms, saying that she was "perfect," "pure," and "always there for him." He said that he could not believe he had intentionally hurt her this many times and that he felt "sick" with himself for that.

During the course of treatment, Jason described a history of intense risk-taking, including a period of his early-20s when he was involved in selling drugs and stealing cars. He had gone to prison for grand theft auto for a time and had recently gotten back on his feet financially after losing large sums of money. He reported that he started cheating on his girlfriend "almost instantly" when they started dating after he got out of prison. His interest in risk-taking had seemingly transferred from high-stakes auto-theft to high-stakes infidelity.

As treatment progressed, Jason reported that after the breakup he had an abrupt lack of interest in using dating apps for one-night stands, or in any kind of sexual risk-taking. He had started casually dating two different women (who did not know about each other) and had expressed that he liked keeping secrets from each of them, though he also "felt guilty." We worked on the ways that his sexual compulsions—particularly around risky secret-keeping—were being used to mask his insecurity, depression, and feelings about his father (who also had a criminal history). Jason also admitted that he did not know how to respect women whom he had sex with, or how to see women being sexual as acceptable or "moral." He admitted to believing that sexual women were "whores" and girlfriends were "angels." His dichotomous and problematic way of seeing women as not fully human—not capable of being *both* sexual and faithful, or interested in sex and interested in relationships—had warped his sense of how to go about seeking out women on dating apps.

Eventually, Jason started a 12-step program in tandem with our work together on his problems with chronic infidelity and sexual risk-taking. He saw himself in the stories of the other men in the program and finally admitted that he had a problem with sex that felt overwhelming and beyond what he could simply change on his own. While our work in therapy focused on his views of women and his relationship to feelings of risk-taking, his work in SAA focused on the ways that he used sex to cope with feelings about his own power and masculinity. He told me that he saw in other men his own hatred of women, and his belief that women should serve his needs. His intense anger and jealousy that arose after he found out that his ex-girlfriend had started dating someone new provoked a series of discussions about how he felt entitled to women's caretaking and resentful that she was "giving that to someone else." Ultimately, we worked on different ways of imagining his relationship to women—not as caretakers or virgin/whores, but as complex and autonomous.

Conclusion: what can sex addicts teach us about misogyny?

While much of the emphasis on sex addiction in the existing literature focuses on whether clinicians should label compulsive sexual behavior as an *addiction*—and I agree that that debate is compelling and worthy of more exploration—I also argue here that sex addicts can teach us much about misogyny. Given what we know about internet pornography (e.g., that men report increasing levels of distress about it, and that it links up with reports of depression, anxiety, and stress), and what we know about men who solicit prostitutes (e.g., they hold more negative views of women and more often have histories of rape), a closer look at sex addicts can also shed some light on the relationship between *distress* and *sexual behavior* as it relates to misogyny.

These three case studies illustrate the various ways that seeing women with more nuance—as fully-realized humans—helps men to better understand and regulate their compulsive sexual behavior. For men who compulsively seek out sex with women (or pornography), they often believe fundamentally that women should be available for their sexual needs and that women should serve them sexually. These beliefs often obscure women's sexual subjectivities—that is, women's perceptions, views, inner lives. Women's sexual subjectivities seem to get erased when men behave in compulsive sexual ways, perhaps in part because compulsive sexual behavior connects so deeply to internalized shame, lower empathy toward women, blaming women for sexual violence, and higher narcissism (Reid, Temko, Moghaddam, & Fong, 2014; Shimberg, Josephs, & Grace, 2016; Willis, Birthrong, King, Nelson-Gray, & Latzman, 2017).

The necessity of chipping away at deeply-held beliefs about women's (traditional) roles, or challenging men to imagine the women they're having sex with (or masturbating to) as not merely "performers" or "characters," pushes a more holistic view of sex as about *humans*. Rather than maintaining indifferent, narcissistic, and often hostile relationships with women, a feminist-oriented therapy with men emphasizes instead the following: a) exploitation breeds exploitation; that is, the more that men imagine they are exploiting women, the more shame and sadness they will feel about the sex they are having; b) women have sexual subjectivities (and subjectivities in general) that need to be considered in order to not treat them as receptacles for men's sexual "needs"; c) masculinity gets configured such that power, aggression, and dominance are valued over mutuality, consent, and playfulness; this leads to problematic dynamics when men become compulsive about seeking out "powerful" and "dominant" interactions during sex with prostitutes or one-night-stands; and d) sex addicts can benefit from feminist therapy even though they would never label the therapy as such; for example, seeing women as people benefits them by allowing them to recognize the humanness of their sexual interactions. A shift in focus away from the validity of sex addiction as a construct—and toward the very real problems of how men imagine, interact with, and relate to women—will better serves men who want to act less compulsively around sex, just as it also serves broader feminist goals of men imagining women as more fully human.

References

Berry, M. D., & Berry, P. D. (2013). Mentalization-based therapy for sexual addiction: Foundations for a clinical model. *Sexual and Relationship Therapy*, *29*(2), 245–260.

Bostwick, J. M., & Bucci, J. A. (2008). Internet sex addiction treated with naltrexone. *Mayo Clinic Proceedings*, *83*(2), 226–230.

Buckley, C. (2018, January 1). Powerful Hollywood women unveil anti-harassment action plan. *The New York Times*. www.nytimes.com/2018/01/01/movies/times-up-hollywood-women-sexual-harassment.html.

Carey, B. (2017, November 27). Therapy for sexual misconduct? It's mostly unproven. *New York Times*. www.nytimes.com/2017/11/27/health/sexual-harassment-addiction-treatment.html.

Center for Positive Sexuality (CPS), The Alternative Sexualities Health Research Alliance (TASHRA), & The National Coalition for Sexual Freedom (NCSF). (2017). Addiction to sex and/or pornography: A position statement from the Center for Positive Sexuality (CPS), The Alternative Sexualities Health Research Alliance (TASHRA), and the National Coalition for Sexual Freedom (NCSF). *Journal of Positive Sexuality*, *3*(3), 40–43.

Cismaru Inescu, A., Andrianne, R., & Triffaux, J. (2013). Virtual reality as a complementary therapy to sexual addiction treatment. *International Journal of Advanced Computer Science*, *3*(7), 1–5.

Cohn, R. (2013). Calming the tempest, bridging the gorge: Healing in couples ruptured by "sex addiction." *Sexual and Relationship Therapy*, *29*(1), 76–86.

Conlin, S. E. (2017). Feminist therapy: A brief integrative review of theory, empirical support, and call for new directions. *Women's Studies International Forum, 62*, 78–82.

Dhuffar, M., & Griffiths, M. (2016). Barriers to female sex addiction treatment in the UK. *Journal of Behavioral Addictions, 5*(4), 562–567.

Dunn, N., Seaburne-May, M., & Gatter, P. (2012). Internet sex addiction: A license to lust? *Advances in Psychiatric Treatment, 18*(4), 270–277.

Farley, M., Golding, J. M., Matthews, E. S., Malamuth, N. M., & Jarrett, L. (2017). Comparing sex buyers with men who do not buy sex: New data on prostitution and trafficking. *Journal of Interpersonal Violence, 32*(23), 3601–3625.

Giugliano, J. R. (2009). Sexual addiction: Diagnostic problems. *International Journal of Mental Health and Addiction, 7*, 283–294.

Goodman, A. (1992). Sexual addiction: Designation and treatment. *Journal of Sex & Marital Therapy, 18*(4), 303–314.

Griffiths, M. D. (2012). Internet sex addiction: A review of empirical research. *Addiction Research & Theory, 20*(2), 111–124.

Grubbs, J. B., Exline, J. J., Pargament, K. I., Hook, J. N., & Carlisle, R. D. (2015). Transgression as addiction: Religiosity and moral disapproval as predictors of perceived addiction to pornography. *Archives of Sexual Behavior, 44*(1), 125–136.

Grubbs, J. B., Volk, F., Exline, J. J., & Pargament, K. I. (2015). Internet pornography use: Perceived addiction, psychological distress, and the validation of a brief measure. *Journal of Sex & Marital Therapy, 41*(1), 83–106.

Hall, P. (2011). A biopsychosocial view of sex addiction. *Sexual and Relationship Therapy, 26*(3), 217–228.

Hall, P. (2014). Sex addiction—An extraordinarily contentious problem. *Sexual and Relationship Therapy, 29*, 68–75.

Heiden-Rootes, K. M., Brimhall, A. S., Jankowski, P. J., & Reddick, G. T. (2017). Differentiation of self and clinicians' perceptions of client sexual behavior as "problematic". *Contemporary Family Therapy, 39*(3), 207–219.

Hook, J. N., Hook, J. P., Davis, D. E., Worthington, E. L., & Penberthy, J. K. (2010). Measuring sexual addiction and compulsivity: A critical review of instruments. *Journal of Sex & Marital Therapy, 36*(3), 227–260.

Irvine, J. M. (1995). Reinventing perversion: Sex addiction and cultural anxieties. *Journal of the History of Sexuality, 5*(3), 429–450.

Jones, K., & Hertlein, K. (2012). Four key dimensions for distinguishing internet infidelity from internet and sex addiction: Concepts and clinical application. *The American Journal of Family Therapy, 40*(2), 115–125.

Kafka, M. P. (2010). Hypersexual disorder: A proposed diagnosis for DSM-V. *Archives of Sexual Behavior, 39*(2), 377–400.

Levin, M. E., Lillis, J., & Hayes, S. C. (2012). When is online pornography viewing problematic among college males? Examining the moderating role of experiential avoidance. *Sexual Addiction & Compulsivity, 19*(3), 168–180.

Ley, D. (2012). *The myth of sex addiction.* Lanham, MD: Rowman & Littlefield.

Ley, D., Prause, N., & Finn, P. (2014). The emperor has no clothes: A review of the "pornography addiction" model. *Current Sexual Health Report, 6*, 94–105.

Love, H. A., Moore, R. M., & Stanish, N. A. (2016). Emotionally focused therapy for couples recovering from sexual addiction. *Sexual and Relationship Therapy, 31*(2), 176–189.

Manley, G. (1999). Treating chronic sexual dysfunction in couples recovering from sex addiction and sex coaddiction. *Sexual Addiction & Compulsivity, 6*(2), 111–124.

Manning, J. C. (2006). The impact of internet pornography on marriage and the family: A review of the research. *Sexual Addiction & Compulsivity*, *13*(2–3), 131–165.

McKeague, E. L. (2014). Differentiating the female sex addict: A literature review focused on themes of gender difference used to inform recommendations for treating women with sex addiction. *Sexual Addiction & Compulsivity*, *21*(3), 203–225.

Miller, S. A., & Byers, E. S. (2012). Practicing psychologists' sexual intervention self-efficacy and willingness to treat sexual issues. *Archives of Sexual Behavior*, *41*(4), 1041–1050.

Monto, M. A., & Dulka, J. (2009). Conceiving of sex as a commodity: A study of arrested customers of female street prostitutes. *Western Criminology Review*, *10*(1), 1–14.

National Coalition for Sexual Freedom (NCSF). (2017, November 8). Addiction to sex and/or pornography. Email to listserv.

Nerenberg, A. (2000). The value of group psychotherapy for sexual addicts in a residential setting. *Sexual Addiction & Compulsivity*, *7*(3), 197–209.

NPR. (2018). Why #MeToo happened in 2017. *NPR News*. www.npr.org/2018/02/07/583910310/why-metoo-happened-in-2017.

Phillips, B., Hajela, R., & Hilton, D. L., Jr. (2015). Sex addiction as a disease: Evidence for assessment, diagnosis, and response to critics. *Sexual Addiction & Compulsivity*, *22*(2), 167–192.

Pincus-Roth, Z. (2017, December 6). The year in #MeToo: Read *The Post's* stories about the movement. *The Washington Post*. www.washingtonpost.com/news/soloish/wp/2017/12/06/the-year-in-metoo-read-the-posts-stories-about-the-movement/?utm_term=.47679e9ed9cc.

ProCon. (2011, January 6). Percentage of men (by country) who paid for sex at least once: The Johns chart. *ProCon.Org*. https://prostitution.procon.org/view.resource.php?resourceID=004119.

Reay, B., Attwood, N., & Gooder, C. (2013). Inventing sex: The short history of sex addiction. *Sexuality & Culture*, *17*(1), 1–19.

Reddick, G., Heiden-Rootes, K. M., & Brimhall, A. (2017). Therapists' assessments in treating "sex addiction" and their relationship to clients' gender, relationship status, and exclusivity status. *Journal of Marital and Family Therapy*, *43*(3), 537–553.

Reid, R. C., & Kafka, M. (2014). Controversies about hypersexual disorder and DSM-V. *Current Sexual Health Report*, *6*, 259–264.

Reid, R. C., Temko, J., Moghaddam, J. F., & Fong, T. W. (2014). Shame, rumination, and self-compassion in men assessed for hypersexual disorder. *Journal of Psychiatric Practice*, *20*(4), 260–268.

Rosenberg, K., Carnes, P., & O'Connor, S. (2014). Evaluation and treatment of sex addiction. *Journal of Sex & Marital Therapy*, *40*(2), 77–91.

Schneider, J. P. (2004). Sexual addiction & compulsivity: Twenty years of the field, ten years of the journal. *Sexual Addiction & Compulsivity*, *11*(1–2), 3–5.

Sex Addicts Anonymous. (2018). Meetings in the United States. *SAA*. https://saa-recovery.org/meetings/united-states/

Shepherd, L. (2010). Cognitive behavior therapy for sexually addictive behavior. *Clinical Case Studies*, *9*(1), 18–27.

Shimberg, J., Josephs, L., & Grace, L. (2016). Empathy as a mediator of attitudes toward infidelity among college students. *Journal of Sex & Marital Therapy*, *42*(4), 353–368.

Short, M. B., Wetterneck, C. T., Bistricky, S. L., Shutter, T., & Chase, T. E. (2016). Clinicians' beliefs, observations, and treatment effectiveness regarding clients' sexual addiction and internet pornography use. *Community Mental Health Journal*, *52*(8), 1070–1081.

Stein, D. J., Hollander, E., Anthony, D. T., Schneier, F. R., Fallon, B. A., Liebowitz, M. R., & Klein, D. F. (1992). Serotonergic medications for sexual obsessions, sexual addictions, and paraphilias. *The Journal of Clinical Psychiatry*, *53*(8), 267–271.

Thomas, J. N. (2013). Outsourcing moral authority: The internet secularization of Evangelicals' anti-pornography narratives. *Journal for the Scientific Study of Religion*, *52*, 457–475.

Time's Up Now Legal Defense Fund. (2018). Our letter of solidarity. www.timesupnow.com.

Turner, M. (2009). Uncovering and treating sex addiction in couple's therapy. *Journal of Family Psychotherapy*, *20*(2–3), 283–302.

Tylka, T. L. (2015). No harm in looking, right? Men's pornography consumption, body image, and well-being. *Psychology of Men & Masculinity*, *16*(1), 97–107.

Urry, K., & Chur-Hansen, A. (2018). Who decides when people can have sex? Australian mental health clinicians' perceptions of sexuality and autonomy. *Journal of Health Psychology*. doi: 10.1177/1359105318790026.

Van Gordon, W., Shonin, E., & Griffiths, M. (2016). Meditation awareness training for the treatment of sex addiction: A Case Study. *Journal of Behavioral Addictions*, *5*(2), 363–372.

Voros, F. (2009). The invention of addiction to pornography. *Sexologies*, *18*, 243–246.

Wahesh, E., Likis-Werle, S. E., & Moro, R. R. (2017). Addictions content published in counseling journals: A 10-year content analysis to inform research and practice. *Professional Counselor*, *7*(1), 89–103.

Willis, M., Birthrong, A., King, J. S., Nelson-Gray, R. O., & Latzman, R. D. (2017). Are infidelity tolerance and rape myth acceptance related constructs? An association moderated by psychopathy and narcissism. *Personality and Individual Differences*, *117*, 230–235.

Wilson, M. (1998). Portrait of a sex addict. *Sexual Addiction & Compulsivity*, *5*(4), 231–250.

Wolf, J., Williams, E. N., Darby, M., Herald, J., & Schultz, C. (2018). Just for women? Feminist multicultural therapy with male clients. *Sex Roles*, *78*(5–6), 439–450.

9

THERAPY WITHOUT BODIES, OR WHY FLESHINESS MATTERS

When formally learning how to do psychotherapy in graduate school, I learned much about modalities of psychotherapy, theoretical orientations, ethical issues that may arise when doing therapy, and strategies for managing transference and countertransference. As a notable absence in my training, I learned very little about how to think about the body in the therapy room, even though the body plays a major role in how therapists and patients interact with each other. For example, what does it mean when patients "read" various identities onto you based on your body? How does it impact the therapy if patients mention their menstrual status, urinary incontinence, chronic pain, or their history of mastectomy? Is the body a nuisance (something to avoid and ignore) or a source of knowledge and meaning-making?

In this essay, I look at the corporeal, material, fleshy body—that is, the body not as an abstraction but as a concrete entity—in the therapy room, particularly how the body figures centrally in many conversations between patients and therapists. I do this in order to examine the materiality of the body and its impact on the therapy relationship for both patients and practitioners. I structure this essay by looking at three major areas where the corporeal body appears in the therapy room: Leaky bodies (e.g., incontinence, menstruation, breastfeeding, runny nose); Identity-marked bodies (e.g., marital/child status, gender, race, clothing and class status); and Gendered bodies (e.g., fatness, breasts, trans/cis identity, hair, make-up). I conclude by drawing parallels with qualitative research and teaching in order to specifically look at how the body functions differently in the therapy room than in other similar spaces that feminist psychologists might encounter.

The body in the therapy room

Feminist theories of the body have a long legacy of helping people to think more deeply and critically about the body and its social and political meanings. Rather than a "blank slate" or an absence, the body as framed in feminist theory is a container for many different cultural and social stories. For example, Mary Douglas (2003) argued that the concepts of purity and pollution often frame women's bodies as "dirty" and in need of management. A wide variety of feminist social scientists and theorists have argued that women often contend with their bodies being marked as abject, disgusting, gross, or unclean in comparison to men's bodies (Grosz, 1994; Irigaray, 1997; Kristeva, 1982; Martin, 2001; Miller-Young, 2014). These tensions then translate for women into a near-constant state of self-monitoring, awareness of the body, and efforts/attempts to minimize their body's "offensive" qualities, whether through grooming, self-consciousness, self-loathing, eating disorders, or poor body image (Bordo, 2004; Braun, Tricklebank, & Clarke, 2013; Chrisler, 2011; Fahs, 2017). Scholars studying menstruation and breastfeeding have noted that women's leaky bodies figure centrally in how women understand shame and disgust about their bodies, and how bodies interface with broader institutional practices of disciplining and controlling bodies marked as "Other" (Chrisler, 2011; Scott & Mostyn, 2003; Shildrick, 2015).

Given that women are now the majority of practitioners in the field of clinical psychology, and that feminist therapy represents a robust subspecialty of psychotherapy modalities, I find it surprising that psychologists have largely neglected to theorize and understand the role of the corporeal body in the therapy room. While some graduate training programs teach about body language, biases, and stereotypes based on identities read/written onto the body (Burnes, Singh, & Witherspoon, 2017; Hall, Harrigan, & Rosenthal, 1995), students learn very little about body diversity and the corporeal body in the therapy room. Further, while some researchers have theorized about working on or with the body in psychotherapy (F. S. Anderson, 2013; Totton, 2014; White, 2014), or imagining the body as *revealing* aspects of patients' psyches (Caldwell, 1996; Miller, 2000), the material qualities of the patient and therapist's *mundane bodies* are largely absent from clinical literatures (as two notable exceptions, see Levinson & Parritt, 2006; Orbach, 2004). In other words, how might we reframe the body not as a *part of the therapy* but as a core part of the (largely unspoken) story in the room that unwittingly informs the therapeutic work?

The blind spot around the fleshy, material, corporeal body does not seem accidental; feminists have long theorized that, on a cultural level, women are assigned to their bodies, while men are assigned to their minds, and that the body is therefore degraded in comparison to the mind (Price & Shildrick, 2017). The overwhelming lack of attention to the body, then, may indicate that psychologists treat the body as secondary, or of far less importance, to the cognitive and cerebral constructions of the body. (Even in body psychotherapy, the body of the *client* is emphasized rather than being something embodied *by* the therapist.) In this chapter, I argue that therapists can learn much from looking closely at how the mundane body enters the therapy room in conversation, dialogue, and physicality for both therapist and patient.

Leaky bodies

The leaky body—that is, the gendered body that is viscous and has permeable boundaries (Shildrick, 2015)—shows up consistently in the therapy room, particularly when women discuss times when they feel, or have felt, shame, disgust, and self-loathing. For example, one of my patients, Marta[1] (mid-30s, Latina, Heterosexual), complained about urinary incontinence during intercourse with her husband, noting that it caused her more distress than an upcoming surgery. She described feeling that she could not control her body, that her husband might find her "gross," and that she wanted to fix it immediately. Another patient, Suzy (mid-20s, White, Queer), who enjoyed weight-lifting and frequent exercise, recalled a time when she bled through her workout pants during her recent period. The event caused her to feel intense shame in a space typically marked as sharply masculine, particularly given that weightlifting felt to her like a form of rebellion against gender stereotypes of women as weak and frail. These examples reveal the ways that stories of the leaky body—and taking seriously the corporeal experiences of the leaky body—represent important threads in the larger therapy stories. For Marta, the leaky body represented her anxiety about sexuality, accepting her body during sex, and broader issues about feeling out of control in other ways for her body. For Suzy, the leaky body symbolized the ways that she lost her sense of empowerment in male-dominated spaces, a theme that ran through other parts of my work with her.

The leaky body has also appeared in the room itself, in that both my body and my patient's bodies have at times leaked in noticeable and important ways. For example, when I had first begun learning how to do psychotherapy as a graduate student, I would at times try to continue seeing patients despite being sick with a cold. This meant that I spent far too much time worrying about managing my leaky body (e.g., runny nose) than focusing on their complaints. Figuring out how to tactfully blow my nose, cough, or manage the sweatiness or fatigue of a sickness overwhelmed my ability to work effectively as a therapist; as such, I now routinely cancel sessions if I feel sick. As another example of how the leaky body enters the room, a patient of mine who had recently had a baby, Lena (late-30s, Asian-American, Heterosexual), had a major breast leak during a session. She appeared quite flustered by this and expressed emphatic apologies for "disrupting" our session time with her body, again revealing that patients often think of their bodies as "unprofessional," "inconvenient," and problematic even when completely reasonable and normal things happen to their bodies. Patients have also left menstrual stains on my couch, or have coughed hard enough to noticeably fart, both of which have produced feelings of shame or horror. In these examples, leaky bodies move from abstract to concrete, from imagined to real and in-the-room.

My patients have also described their leaky bodies as troubling to them in their daily lives as well. A female-to-male trans patient, Pax (mid-20s, African-American, Trans and Queer) described that he started his period unexpectedly after not menstruating for over a year. Because this happened at work and he had no supplies with him and was not yet "out" to his coworkers, he panicked and felt terrified that people would discover him trying to manage the blood in the men's bathroom. This event tied in with his general fear of not passing as male and his ambivalent feelings about his menstrual cycle. Another patient, Lila (White, early-30s, Heterosexual), had her husband bring their newborn baby to her job so that she could breastfeed the baby during her lunch break at work. When her boss found out about this arrangement and chastised her about this at a staff meeting, she left the room crying. For Lila, this event not only symbolized the difficulty of feeling (and appearing) professional at work, but also of the overwhelming conflicts she had about trying to manage extreme fatigue, raising a newborn baby with her unemployed husband, and juggling her work and home obligations and responsibilities. In these stories, the leaky body becomes a basis for examining and exploring deeper issues about shame, disgust, conflicting roles, and fear of others' rejection and disapproval. By taking seriously the stories of the leaky body, therapists can better understand how people connect the experiences of their bodies to broader themes of distress and anxiety.

Identity-marked bodies

Psychotherapy also evokes patient's feelings about similarities and differences between themselves and their therapists. Research on race and gender matching in therapy speaks to the importance of taking seriously the ways that bodies are read and marked according to social identities, particularly salient identities that carry with them social scripts about power, hierarchy, and access to resources. While research does not consistently show that race matching between therapist and patient improves treatment longevity (Cabral & Smith, 2011; Shin et al., 2005; Sterling, Gottheil, Weinstein, & Serota, 2001), gender matching was consistently found to increase the therapeutic alliance and improve symptoms (Bhati, 2014; Kuusisto & Artkoski, 2013; Lambert, 2016; Wintersteen, Mensinger, Diamond, & Kenkel, 2005).

In line with this research, I have found that the marking of gender and race in the room—and the naming of it—occurs with regularity in psychotherapy. Beliefs about what women can and cannot understand as therapists serve as one example of this line of conversation. Male patients have said various comments like: "You wouldn't understand this because you're a woman" in relation to car-repairs they had done over the weekend or male-bonding-time they had with their male friends. Men in therapy have also assumed various things about me because of my gender: "I'll bet you're a great mom" or "You know how women are—so emotional!" Gender stereotyping of the patient toward the therapist can lead to fruitful discussions about their assumptions about women more broadly (see Chapter 8) and the girls and women in their lives (e.g., mothers, daughters, wives, coworkers, etc.).

Race, too, enters the therapy room frequently, as patients read racial difference or similarity onto me as their white therapist. Patients of color will at times comment that I am different from them and that I do not understand certain customs or practices that a same-race therapist would understand. For example, a patient named Arturo (early 40s, Latino, Heterosexual) talked about his stress at having to finance his daughters quinceanera party, noting that it would cost upwards of $3,000 to pay for the event on his minimum-wage salary. He expressed frustration that I "did not get it" about why it was a priority to him, even while I assured him that I understood the value of rituals and celebrations. A teenage patient of mine, Jeremiah (early-teens, African-American, Heterosexual) expressed anger at the Charlottesville events of 2017 and the visibility of white supremacy, noting that white kids at school were now "debating" white supremacy as a valid set of viewpoints. He hesitated when describing this and said, pointedly, "no offense." These examples point to how the body is racialized in therapy, and difference becomes marked in visible and tangible ways.

More commonly, white patients seem to imagine that I will agree with their views because I appear white, even when I vocally express disagreement. Years ago, a white patient, Angela (late-40s, White, Heterosexual) expressed irritation that the movie *Annie* was being remade with a black actress, and implied that I would also be angry about this. When I expressed that I was not and thought it would provide a compelling reinterpretation of the original film, she became irritated with me. As another example, during political campaigns, patients talk frequently about their political beliefs and the anger or excitement they may feel about certain candidates. White patients more often assume that I support or would agree with their racist beliefs than I would with patients of color. For example, during the two Obama elections, white patients at times expressed anger at the idea of a black president, and when I responded (as I typically do) that I "could not go there with them," they became uncomfortable, angry, or silent about it. The uncomfortable marking of race in the therapy room, and the assumptions that patients have about race, are a reminder of how the body and its identities are interpreted by both patient and therapist.

While race and gender represent the most salient examples of identity marking in the therapy office, other less-often discussed identities are also being marked during therapy. For example, a therapist's pregnancy can trigger intense feelings in patients about loss, jealousy, anger, and being displaced, in addition to patient's feelings about parental status changes and what that means for the therapeutic work (Korol, 1995; McCluskey, 2016). Patients have also expressed intense reactions to therapists diagnosed with serious illnesses (Simon, 1990). Perceptions of therapists' availability or accessibility are written into these interactions. In my own work, patients have often commented upon or noticed the presence or absence of a wedding ring, often drawing conclusions about my family life based on whether I have a ring or not. The assumption that I can only understand families with children if I have children, or that I can only understand marriage as a married person, underlies much of the discussion that occurs about my wedding ring status. One of my patients, Lupe (late-40s, Latina, Heterosexual), noticed when I switched from not wearing a ring on my left hand to when I started wearing one, and she admitted to feeling "more comfortable" when I started wearing a ring on my left hand. While I did not confirm or deny my marital status, this belief led to interesting discussions about her feelings of safety, security, and connection with me as a therapist based on how much she felt I could understand family life.

Social class and financial status also show up in the therapy room, often in circumvented ways. I typically park my car in the same spot each day, and many patients know what my car looks like based on the hours that I work. Until a few years ago, I drove a (very) old 1996 Toyota Camry to work, a fact that some patients responded to with concern ("Why do you drive such an old car if you're a doctor?") while others reacted with feelings of solidarity ("I feel like I can relate to you because you drive an old car too"). When I got a new car, a few of the working-class patients who had appreciated that I drove an old car expressed disappointment about the new car. One patient, James (early-60s, White, Heterosexual), commented that "It must be nice" to buy a new car and that I must be "rolling in the money." We used this as a springboard to think about his feelings about his impending retirement and the belief that others were better off than him, even though he had saved plenty of money and would retire comfortably quite soon.

Social class has also shown up in how patients imagine their clothing and my clothing in relation to one another. I typically dress quite similarly each day—in comfortable black slacks and a soft semi-professional-looking shirt, along with down-to-earth black sandals—and this has been commented upon by patients in the past. One patient, Annie (late-60s, White, Heterosexual), expressed that she thought I should "wear more color" and that I must not have done this because I wanted to "hide myself." (This was a classic example of projection and again led to fruitful discussions about her feelings about aging and sexuality.) Another patient, Jenny (late-20s, Biracial, Bisexual), arrived for therapy wearing her workout clothing and commented that she had not dressed very well and that she felt embarrassed about how she smelled. I reassured her that she can dress however she likes in therapy and we then went on to discuss feelings about class, clothing, and her body image issues. These two examples show the ways that markers of class and professionalism read/written onto the body—and the indirect and semi-direct ways that patients discuss this—constitute important subjects to not ignore in the therapy room.

Gendered bodies

The gendering of bodies—particularly with regard to conforming or not conforming to gender roles and gendered social scripts—also situates the body as having central importance in psychotherapy. Patients read onto the therapist ideas about sexual orientation, political beliefs, "good" motherhood or "good" wifely status, openness to their gender-nonconforming behaviors, drug use, and safety. For example, I see a number of trans and gender-nonconforming patients, including a sizable number of female-to-male patients and non-binary patients. My body figures centrally in how they imagine whether they can safely talk about these issues, and whether they perceive me as open to understanding their struggles. Many of these patients have Googled me and then read my scholarly work on body hair and gender nonconformity. They tell me that this makes them feel more comfortable talking about their bodies. Some patients ask about or comment upon my body hair choices; one patient, Janet (early-30s, Bi-racial, Queer and Trans) commented on my eyebrows and said that I "let them go like Frida Kahlo" and that this made her feel more comfortable with me. Another patient, Sana (mid-30s, White, Heterosexual and Non-Binary) commented when I wore crop pants one day that she "appreciated" seeing that I had some leg hair because it meant that I understood her. Both of these readings of my body allowed trans and non-binary patients to establish solidarity with me even while not reading me as trans and non-binary. Further, given that so many trans patients begin hormone therapy during our time together, being able to talk openly about their bodily changes and struggles with the body (e.g., increase in libido, acne, and so on) allows me to better support them through difficult aspects of transitioning (Atnas, Milton, & Archer, 2015; Klein, Krane, & Paule-Koba, 2018).

Markers of traditional femininity also have salience for many of my women patients, particularly as they think about their own "successes" and "failures" in the world of gender and bodies. My lack of wearing make-up, for example, is seen by some patients as relatable and down-to-earth and by others as strangely unprofessional. A patient named Sally (early-30s, White, Heterosexual) frequently expressed that she wanted to "look good" in the business world and that she needed to devote considerable time to getting ready in the morning to look how she wanted. She once said she envied my courage to not wear a lot of make-up, which we then followed up by talking about her history of being criticized for her looks by her parents (particularly her mother) and how she wishes she could be invisible instead of constructed as a sexualized woman while at her job.

This attention to my body also has occurred with patients who have had health issues that have impacted their "femininity." I had a patient, Crystal (early-40s, White, Heterosexual) who had undergone treatment for breast cancer, ultimately resulting in a mastectomy, who commented that she envied people with real breasts. Though this was never directed toward me overtly, she implied that she thought about this bodily comparison with many women. Another patient, Ruby (mid-50s, African-American, Heterosexual), who used a colostomy bag after treatment for cancer, said that I should realize how nice it is to not "carry around my own shit" all the time. These examples attest to how patients interact with the therapist's body to express and (in most cases) work to understand their own bodies.

Body weight and size have also become a common text in therapy, albeit one that operates just below the surface. Patients have at times expressed relief and solidarity about my body size, believing that I can better understand the fat-shaming behaviors of their families because of our "sameness." One patient, Rebecca (mid-20s, White, Bisexual), told me that she had never felt comfortable discussing her body weight with other therapists because she felt they were "twigs" who did not relate to her. Our perceived similarity allowed her to discuss her fears about fatness and explore some of the deeply held beliefs that she would never have a "good life." Another patient, Rose (late-teens, African-American, Heterosexual) talked at length about clothes shopping and how she felt that nothing fit her, asking me if I had those experiences too. We talked not only about the practical aspects of fatness, but also about how to resist internalized body shaming. Connecting as fat women allowed for a much more deep and impactful discussion than if we had different body sizes and this similarity also allowed for fat-affirmative work rather than fat-shaming work (McHugh & Chrisler, 2019). In my practice, I actively work against fat-shaming narratives with my clients, recognizing that many of them have serious imprints of trauma based on being shamed and mistreated by medical doctors because of their size (Davis-Coelho, Waltz, & Davis-Coelho, 2000; Kasardo & McHugh, 2015; Kinavey & Cool, 2018).

Discomfort about fatness has also appeared in the room, though this has typically been far more subtextual than overt. Some patients have apologized for complaining about "feeling fat," by saying, "I know I shouldn't say this, but … " or "This is hard to say around you." When we establish room for them to feel and express their authentic beliefs about bodies, or when we make room for them to imagine that I do not hate my own body, this can be productive for both of us. One of my fatter patients, Jim (mid-40s, Latino, Heterosexual), talked frequently about how difficult it is to lose weight but told me, "If you can do it, I can too." His projection onto me that I diet (or want to diet) was notable, as it also suggested that patients situate the therapist's body according to what they need at that moment. (Similar things have happened with sexual orientation, in that patients have imagined me as heterosexual, bisexual, or lesbian depending on the issues they are working out at that time.)

Thus, whether through direct or indirect comparisons, or conversation about the therapist's body and its meaning, the therapist's body clearly evokes for many patients feelings about their struggles and beliefs about how therapists can (or cannot) help them. Opportunities for projection and identifying with, or distancing from, therapists also often connect to how bodies are constructed during psychotherapy (Burka, 1996; Carroll, 2018; Rance, Clarke, & Moller, 2014; Stein, 2011). Ignoring the body in therapy—especially the more subtextual operations of the body—is deeply problematic for these reasons and likely leads therapists to missing huge amounts of information about patients' beliefs, attitudes, and ideologies.

Conclusion

These discussions of the how the corporeal, fleshy body enters the therapy room have important overlaps both with feminist pedagogy (that is, how feminist professors and teachers imagine their bodies and their students' bodies in the classroom) and qualitative feminist research (that is, how feminist researchers' bodies and the people they're interviewing imagine the importance of bodies). Feminist professors have begun to reflect more on how the body figures centrally in pedagogical practice, whether as a marker of status, race, class, or ability (R. C. Anderson, 2006; Lewis, 2011; Patton & Catching, 2009; Shapiro, 2005), as a way to resituate the experiential lived body as crucial for teaching effectively (Probyn, 2004), and as a tool for embodied praxis (Hunter, 2011).

With regard to feminist research, Sara McClelland's (2017) concept of *vulnerable listening* speaks to how researchers have moved to understand the role of the body in doing qualitative research. Reflecting on the materiality of her own breasts in rooms where she interviewed women dying of breast cancer, McClelland wrote, "Vulnerability encourages greater focus on the affective and embodied aspects of listening, as well as potential ethical considerations to support those listening to participants" (p. 338). Other researchers, too, have woven their bodies more into their analyses of interview data, whether through studying masculinity (Pascoe, 2011), examining pregnancy and motherhood (Ortbals & Rincker, 2009) analyzing "kink" or alternative sexualities (Bain & Nash, 2006; Plante, 2014), talking with participants about childbirth (Chadwick, 2012), or having visibly disabled bodies as researchers (Brown & Boardman, 2011). Embodied analysis—both for the researcher and participants—has emerged as having central relevance to impactful feminist research.

Certainly, in my role as a feminist professor, qualitative researcher, and practicing clinical psychologist, I have thought quite a lot about my body and the bodies of my students, research participants, and patients. In each of these spaces, the body is charged up with cultural ideas about normality and abnormality, conformity and nonconformity, visibility and hiddenness. In each of these spaces, it means something different to be marked as a woman, nonwhite, fat, working-class, and sexual minority than it does to be marked as a man, white, thin, upper or middle-class, and heterosexual. I reiterate here the value of *paying attention to the corporeal body* in all of these spaces, of imagining it as valuable and insightful, of seeing the body as worth looking at and talking about, of finding and making meaning in the seemingly mundane aspects of interpersonal relationships.

Note

1 Like Chapters 7 and 8, all names used in this chapter are pseudonyms, and all patients mentioned in this article gave formal consent through an Institutional Review Board-approved study for their stories to be used for research purposes.

References

Anderson, F. S. (2013). *Bodies in treatment: The unspoken dimension*. New York: Routledge.

Anderson, R. C. (2006). Teaching (with) disability: Pedagogies of lived experience. *The Review of Education, Pedagogy, and Cultural Studies, 28*(3–4), 367–379.

Atnas, C., Milton, M., & Archer, S. (2015). The transitioning process: The transitioning experiences of trans men. *Psychology of Sexualities Review, 6*(1), 5–17.

Bain, A., & Nash, C. (2006). Undressing the researcher: Feminism, embodiment and sexuality at a queer bathhouse event. *Area, 38*(1), 99–106.

Bhati, K. (2014). Effect of client-therapist gender match on the therapeutic relationship: An exploratory analysis. *Psychological Reports, 115*(2), 565–583.

Bordo, S. (2004). *Unbearable weight: Feminism, Western culture, and the body*. Berkeley, CA: University of California Press.

Braun, V., Tricklebank, G., & Clarke, V. (2013). "It shouldn't stick out from your bikini at the beach": Meaning, gender, and the hairy/hairless body. *Psychology of Women Quarterly, 37*(4), 478–493.

Brown, L., & Boardman, F. K. (2011). Accessing the field: Disability and the research process. *Social Science & Medicine, 72*(1), 23–30.

Burka, J. B. (1996). The therapist's body in reality and fantasy: A perspective from an overweight therapist. In B. Gerson (Ed.), *The therapist as a person: Life crises, life choices, life experiences, and their effects on treatment* (pp. 266–276). Hillsdale, NJ: Analytic Press.

Burnes, T. R., Singh, A. A., & Witherspoon, R. G. (2017). Graduate counseling psychology training in sex and sexuality: An exploratory analysis. *The Counseling Psychologist, 45*(4), 504–527.

Cabral, R. R., & Smith, T. B. (2011). Racial/ethnic matching of clients and therapists in mental health services: A meta-analytic review of preferences, perceptions, and outcomes. *Journal of Counseling Psychology, 58*(4), 537–554.

Caldwell, C. (1996). *Getting our bodies back: Recovery, healing, and transformation through body-centered psychotherapy*. Boulder, CO: Shambhala Publications.

Carroll, R. (2018). Four relational modes of attending to the body in psychotherapy. In K. White (Ed.), *Talking bodies* (pp. 11–39). New York: Routledge.

Chadwick, R. J. (2012). Fleshy enough? Notes toward embodied analysis in critical qualitative research. *Gay & Lesbian Issues & Psychology Review, 8*(2), 82–97.

Chrisler, J. C. (2011). Leaks, lumps, and lines: Stigma and women's bodies. *Psychology of Women Quarterly, 35*(2), 202–214.

Davis-Coelho, K., Waltz, J., & Davis-Coelho, B. (2000). Awareness and prevention of bias against fat clients in psychotherapy. *Professional Psychology: Research and Practice, 31*(6), 682–684.

Douglas, M. (2003). *Purity and danger: An analysis of concepts of pollution and taboo*. New York: Routledge.

Fahs, B. (2017). The dreaded body: Disgust and the production of "appropriate" femininity. *Journal of Gender Studies, 26*(2), 184–196.

Grosz, E. A. (1994). *Volatile bodies: Toward a corporeal feminism*. Bloomington, IN: Indiana University Press.

Hall, J. A., Harrigan, J. A., & Rosenthal, R. (1995). Nonverbal behavior in clinician— Patient interaction. *Applied and Preventive Psychology, 4*(1), 21–37.

Hunter, L. (2011). Re-embodying (preservice middle years) teachers? An attempt to reposition the body and its presence in teaching and learning. *Teaching and Teacher Education, 27*(1), 187–200.

Irigaray, L. (1997). *The logic of the gift: Toward an ethic of generosity* (Trans. A. D. Schrift). New York: Routledge.

Kasardo, A. E., & McHugh, M. C. (2015). From fat shaming to size acceptance: Challenging the medical management of fat women. In M. C. McHugh, & J. C. Chrisler (Eds.), *The wrong prescription for women: How medicine and media create a "need" for treatments, drugs, and surgery* (pp. 179–201). Santa Barbara, CA: ABC-CLIO.

Kinavey, H., & Cool, C. (2018). The broken lens: How anti-fat bias in psychotherapy is harming our clients and what to do about it. *Women & Therapy, 42*(1–2), 116–130.

Klein, A., Krane, V., & Paule-Koba, A. L. (2018). Bodily changes and performance effects in a transitioning transgender college athlete. *Qualitative Research in Sport, Exercise and Health, 10*(5), 555–569.

Korol, R. (1995). The impact of therapist pregnancy on the treatment process. *Clinical Social Work Journal, 23*(2), 159–171.

Kristeva, J. (1982). *Powers of horror: An essay on abjection.* New York: Columbia University Press.

Kuusisto, K., & Artkoski, T. (2013). The female therapist and the client's gender. *Clinical Nursing Studies, 1*(3), 39–56.

Lambert, M. J. (2016). Does client-therapist gender matching influence therapy course or outcome in psychotherapy? *Evidence Based Medicine and Practice, 2,* 2.

Levinson, F., & Parritt, S. (2006). Against stereotypes: Experiences of disabled psychologists. In D. Goodley, & R. Lawthom (Eds.), *Disability and psychology: Critical introductions and reflections* (pp. 111–122). New York: Macmillan.

Lewis, M. M. (2011). Body of knowledge: Black queer feminist pedagogy, praxis, and embodied text. *Journal of Lesbian Studies, 15*(1), 49–57.

Martin, E. (2001). *The woman in the body: A cultural analysis of reproduction.* Boston, MA: Beacon Press.

McClelland, S. I. (2017). Vulnerable listening: Possibilities and challenges of doing qualitative research. *Qualitative Psychology, 4*(3), 338–352.

McCluskey, M. C. (2016). The pregnant therapist: A qualitative examination of the client experience. *Clinical Social Work Journal, 45*(4), 301–310.

McHugh, M. C., & Chrisler, J. C. (2019). Making space for every body: Ending sizeism in psychotherapy and training. *Women & Therapy, 42*(1–2), 7–21.

Miller, J. A. (2000). The fear of the body in psychotherapy. *Psychodynamic Counselling, 6*(4), 437–450.

Miller-Young, M. (2014). *A taste for brown sugar: Black women in pornography.* Durham, NC: Duke University Press.

Orbach, S. (2004). What can we learn from the therapist's body? *Attachment & Human Development, 6*(2), 141–150.

Ortbals, C., & Rincker, M. (2009). Embodied researchers: Gendered bodies, research activity, and pregnancy in the field. *PS: Political Science & Politics, 42*(2), 315–319.

Pascoe, C. J. (2011). *Dude, you're a fag: Masculinity and sexuality in high school.* Berkeley, CA: University of California Press.

Patton, L., & Catching, C. (2009). "Teaching while black": Narratives of African American student affairs faculty. *International Journal of Qualitative Studies in Education, 22*(6), 713–728.

Plante, R. F. (2014). Sexual spanking, the self, and the construction of deviance. In P. J. Kleinplatz, & C. Moser (Eds.), *Sadomasochism* (pp. 69–90). New York: Routledge.

Price, J., & Shildrick, M. (2017). Openings on the body: A critical introduction. In J. Price, & M. Shildrick (Eds.), *Feminist theory and the body* (pp. 1–14). New York: Routledge.

Probyn, E. (2004). Teaching bodies: Affects in the classroom. *Body & Society, 10*(4), 21–43.

Rance, N. M., Clarke, V., & Moller, N. P. (2014). "If I see somebody … I'll immediately scope them out": Anorexia Nervosa clients' perceptions of their therapists' body. *Eating Disorders, 22*(2), 111–120.

Scott, J. A., & Mostyn, T. (2003). Women's experiences of breastfeeding in a bottle-feeding culture. *Journal of Human Lactation, 19*(3), 270–277.

Shapiro, S. (2005). *Pedagogy and the politics of the body: A critical praxis.* New York: Routledge.

Shildrick, M. (2015). *Leaky bodies and boundaries: Feminism, postmodernism and (bio) ethics.* New York: Routledge.

Shin, S. M., Chow, C., Camacho-Gonsalves, T., Levy, R. J., Allen, I. E., Leff, H. S., & Hansen, J. I. C. (2005). A meta-analytic review of racial-ethnic matching for African American and Caucasian American clients and clinicians. *Journal of Counseling Psychology, 52* (1), 45–56.

Simon, J. (1990). A patient-therapist's reaction to her therapist's serious illness. *American Journal of Psychotherapy, 44*(4), 590–597.

Stein, A. (2011). The tattooed therapist: Exposure, disclosure, transference. *Psychoanalysis, Culture & Society, 16*(2), 113–131.

Sterling, R., Gottheil, E., Weinstein, S., & Serota, R. (2001). The effect of therapist/ patient race- and sex-matching in individual treatment. *Addiction, 96*(7), 1015–1022.

Totton, N. (2014). Foreign bodies: Recovering the history of body psychotherapy. In T. Staunton (Ed.), *Body psychotherapy* (pp. 19–38). New York: Routledge.

White, K. (2014). *Talking bodies: How do we integrate working with the body in psychotherapy from an attachment and relational perspective?* London: Karnac.

Wintersteen, M. B., Mensinger, J. L., Diamond, G. S., & Kenkel, M. B. (2005). Do gender and racial differences between patient and therapist affect therapeutic alliance and treatment retention in adolescents? *Professional Psychology: Research and Practice, 36*(4), 400–408.

PART 4
All riled up

—

10

WARNING

Capitalism is destroying our sex lives

The relationship between sexuality and labor is abundant in the contemporary landscape of everyday sexuality. While much attention has been given to sex workers and the exchange of money for sex in the official labor force, in this chapter I direct attention instead toward the mundane aspects of sexual labor and the labor that connects to the logics and priorities of capitalism. Sex as a job, or as requiring emotional or physical labor, shows up in the contexts of everyday sex lives (see Chapters 1 and 2), pointing to important connections between mundane sexuality and the political frameworks of capitalism. In this chapter, I ask: What does it mean to have sex in a capitalist economy? How do the practices and priorities of capitalism, particularly as seen in the US, seep into the most intimate aspects of people's personal lives? How do people become subjected to, and subject others to, the logic of capitalism through sexual practices, choices, desires, fantasies, and actions? How do sexual problems that people have relate back to the economic and social structures within which they live?

Marxist and materialist feminists have long argued that women's oppression occurs primarily through systems of capitalism and private property and that women's liberation can only occur through a radical reconfiguration of the current capitalist economy (Hennessy & Ingraham, 2014; MacKinnon, 1982; Weeks, 2011). According to Marxist feminists like Margaret Benston and Peggy Morton, women are relegated to the (unpaid) reproductive labor sphere while men engage in (paid) productive labor, which allows for women's ongoing exploitation and relationships of dependence (Vogel, 2013). Benston and Morton claim that true equality between people cannot occur without an evening out of the economic relationships between them. By this logic, an equal partnership is impossible when one partner works a paid job, and one does not, or where income inequality is vast. Stay-at-home parents, jobless spouses, part-time workers, and teenagers can all attest to the somewhat bizarre character of maintaining family and love relationships under conditions of fundamental economic inequality. For Marxist feminists, these conditions disallow genuine exchange between partners because of the existence of economic dependence and hierarchical inequality. Even the various means by which people have tried to rectify this—paid labor for childcare, wages for housework, rebelling against housework, pushing for better income equality (Arruzza, 2013; Bryson, 2004; Federici, 1975; Hartmann, 1981)—have largely failed to address the seriousness of economic inequality and how it impacts social and sexual relationships.

Understanding capitalism as fundamentally altering the way that people relate to each other is essential if we want to truly see the insidious and destructive capacities of a capitalist economy. Modern American life routinely sees families burdened by mind-numbing jobs, shift work, longer and longer hours at work, crazed connections to smartphones, punishing commutes, and low pay. These facets of life all directly impact social and sexual life as well, including seemingly non-economic aspects of life like friendship, knowledge-production, leisure, gender relations, and sexuality. Under capitalism, social connections and intimate relationships are no longer treated as having *intrinsic* value but instead function as commodities, bought and sold to the highest bidder.

In this chapter, I take Marxist feminist arguments about capitalism's destructive impact on women a step further and invite consideration of the ways that capitalism fundamentally alters the way that people have sex. Further, living in a capitalist system prevents people from fully addressing their sexual problems and complaints, and limits expression of sexual freedom and enjoyment. Capitalism also profoundly affects the structures within and around which people have sex, including leisure time, vacation time, breaks from work, and rest/relaxation. I outline ten ways that capitalism is destroying people's sex lives, drawing on my experiences as a psychotherapist specializing in sexuality and as a teacher and researcher of women's sexuality. These are words of warning and also a call to action. After all, as Michel Foucault argued in *The history of sexuality, vol. 1*, "Power is only tolerable on condition that it masks a substantial part of itself. Its success is proportional to its ability to hide its own mechanisms" (Foucault, 1978, p. 86).

Aversion to leisure

One of the major assaults on people's sex lives today is the growing suspicion, particularly in the US, toward leisure time. American workers have the least amount of paid vacation time of workers in the Western world, with an average amount of 1–2 weeks of paid time off each year (and even that is entirely at the employer's discretion) (Mohn, 2013; US Department of Labor, 2017). Many American jobs offer no paid time off, and an increasing number of jobs have adopted a "contract" model where workers receive no benefits and no paid leave at all; instead, they only receive unpaid leave to the extent that it is required by federal law. The rise of the "gig economy," for example, means that greater numbers of workers have no safety net in the form of paid time off, paid sick leave, or disability insurance (De Stefano, 2015; Friedman, 2014). And, notably, even when American workers do have paid vacation time, they are among the *least* likely to actually use their vacation time, with half of the American workforce forfeiting their vacation time (Dickler, 2017; Sullivan, 2015). One study found that many people have become so accustomed to working and engaging in structured activities that they imagine leisure time as itself a source of stress (Haller, Hadler, & Kaup, 2013).

This normalization of working year-round (and sometimes around the clock) without rest or breaks—and the insistence that people "prove" their dedication to their jobs by overworking and not taking paid leaves even when they have earned them—introduces a cultural framework where leisure is met with suspicion, contempt, and hostility. In a capitalist economy, leisure time means lack of productivity; under capitalism, only the super wealthy deserve such "laziness." And, with regard to gender, women bear the brunt of this logic, as they are more likely than men to believe that they should work nonstop (all day long) in order to ensure that the family runs smoothly (Shaw, 2001).

Suspicion toward pleasure

In stark contrast with some of its pleasure-loving Western European counterparts (e.g., Italy, Spain, Greece, France, Australia) and other countries around the world that routinely build in naps and rest time during the day (the Philippines, Mexico, Costa Rica, Ecuador, Nigeria) the US has a strong suspicion toward pleasure, idleness, and rest. Americans are some of the least well-rested people in the developed world, clocking in an average of 6.8 hours per night (leaving 40% of Americans chronically sleep deprived) (Jones, 2013). A full 30% sleep less than six hours each day, with much higher numbers for workers in manufacturing and those who work night shifts, especially in transportation and health care (CDC, 2012).

Sleep deprivation has enormous consequences in multiple aspects of our lives. Sleep deprived people get into more accidents, fall asleep on the road, fight more with their partners and families, perform less well academically, and report more cognitive problems and health impairments (Almklov, Drummond, Orff, & Alhassoon, 2015; Gil-Jardiné et al., 2017; Jones, 2013; Patrick et al., 2017; Powell & Copping, 2010). Ours is not a culture of long naps, leisurely meals, and sensually passing the hours. Rather, American workers rarely nap, often eat meals at their desks or on the go while driving or otherwise multi-tasking, and construct leisure time as "non-productive."

This internalization of the notion that rest is a problem and pleasure is suspect has led, for US workers, to a variety of sexual symptoms that reveal the deep deprioritization of pleasure and the devaluing of slow-moving sex based on mutuality: less time for sex, more "quickies" or fast sex that is typically less pleasurable for women, more virtual sex and less in-person sex, more interest in BDSM than other countries, more interest in "doggy style" sex versus other positions, and more value placed on work and consumption rather than leisure and relaxation (Delmonico & Carnes, 1999; Döring et al., 2017; Eveleth, 2014; Gager & Yabiku, 2010; Mackay, 2001; Paiella, 2015). Even moments that should feel relaxing are increasingly intruded upon by work; Americans spend a substantial amount of time using their phone while on the toilet (75%), in the shower (12%), at church (19%), and *during* sex (9–20%) (Castillo, 2012; Sherman, 2013), which also increases their anxiety and decreases their life satisfaction (Lepp, Barkley, & Karpinski, 2014).

Orgasm as producing a product

As one of the more concrete ways that capitalism is destroying our sex lives, the emphasis on orgasm as a product—and the quest toward ever-more efficient means to arrive at orgasm—suggests that even the pleasurable aspects of sex have become surprisingly laborious and tedious. Sex has begun to mimic a corporate mentality that emphasizes the efficient control of workers' behaviors in order to optimize productivity and minimize the time it takes to complete different tasks.

The epidemic rates of women faking orgasm—producing the "product" expected from sex—speak to this crisis. In recent studies, at least 50% of women reported having faked an orgasm, with a significant percentage of those saying that they fake often (Fahs, 2011, 2014; Wiederman, 1997). When asked about why they fake orgasm, women described a plethora of reasons: fearing that their (male) partners would be hurt if they did not orgasm, fatigue/wanting the encounter to end, and worry about feeling "normal" (Fahs, 2011) alongside fear and insecurity about sex, or wanting to increase their own arousal (Cooper, Fenigstein, & Fauber, 2014).

Additionally, the "product" of orgasm has become an expectation of partnered sex and masturbation. Janet Hyde and John DeLamater (1997) have criticized this framework by arguing:

> Our discussions of sex tend to focus on orgasm rather than pleasure in general. Orgasm is the observable "product," and we are concerned with how many orgasms we have, much as the plant manager is concerned with how many cans of soup are produced on the assembly line each day.
>
> *(p. 261)*

This push toward *producing something* from sex has engendered an environment where women's emotional labor during sex—including their impulses to fake orgasm—are expected in order to support their partners' egos (Fahs & Swank, 2016; Frith, 2013, 2015).

Couples in therapy have described orgasm as necessary for sex to even "count" as sex; "What's the point otherwise?" is a claim often heard in the therapy office. Sex without orgasm, or sex that does not purposefully drive toward orgasm, is less and less validated as *good sex*. In one of my recent studies, several women described feeling pressured to orgasm in order to validate the "work" and "labor" that their partners put into them, as if sex without this validation of "work" and "labor" would be meaningless (Fahs, 2014). Orgasm has become an expected product and outcome of sex rather than sex serving as a form of (leisurely) pleasure and release. Also note that women do not experience orgasm through penetrative intercourse nearly as often as men, with between 8–25% of women reporting orgasm during penetrative intercourse (Dingfelder, 2011; Jannini et al., 2012) compared to 95% of men (Richters, de Visser, Rissel, & Smith, 2006). Consequently, the pressure to orgasm has resulted in a crisis of faking orgasm and outcome-oriented sexual exchanges.

"Good" sex means talking about sex rather than having sex

Gayle Rubin (1984) argued that we have created a number of hierarchies of sex, with an emphasis on married procreative sex and a devaluating of unmarried, non-procreative sex. This implies that "good" sex has increasingly stringent boundaries around it: in private, with a partner, married, for the purposes of having a child, not "kinky," or "weird," not using sex toys, not involving paid sexual labor, and so on. Such boundaries also quarantine sex as more and more personal, intimate, off-limits, vanilla, and separated from other aspects of our lives. Audre Lorde's (1984) call to value the erotic and the ability of eroticism to infuse other aspects of our lives such as work, parenting, friendship, and creativity seems hard to imagine in a capitalist economy. Lorde argues:

> The erotic functions for me in several ways, and the first is providing the power which comes from sharing deeply any pursuit with another person … Another important way in which the erotic connection functions is the open and fearless underlining of my capacity for joy.
>
> *(p. 341)*

Instead, the framework of efficiency, consumerism, and suspicion toward pleasure leads sex to become increasingly deprioritized. As Michel Foucault (1978) has written,

> We have at least invented a different kind of pleasure: pleasure in the truth of pleasure, the pleasure of knowing that truth, of discovering and exposing it, the fascination of seeing it and telling it, of captivating and capturing others by it, of confiding it in secret, of luring it out in the open—the specific pleasure of the true discourse on pleasure.
>
> *(p. 71)*

In other words, we enjoy the *talking about* and *thinking about* sex more than actually having sex, as the discourse proliferates, but sex itself does not. Capitalism predicts this, with an emphasis on work instead of rest (one can perhaps converse about sex at work, but one cannot typically *have sex* while working all day).

As a case in point: half of American adults had sex only a few times per month, with many having sex more infrequently than that (Laumann, Gagnon, Michael, & Michaels, 1994). At the high end, Americans have sex 6–8 times per month (Huber et al., 2014) and we can only imagine that these numbers will continue to sharply decline with the era of smartphones and hyper-connectivity to work and other life demands. (I have rarely met a couple in couple's therapy, for example, who does not fight about excessive cell phone use and its negative impact on their sex life. Some people consider life a distraction from their cell phone and not the other way around, see Roberts & David, 2016.) In short, people value discourse about sex more than sex itself, which then allows sex to become a *product* sold, talked about, and imagined in the public marketplace (Messner & Montez de Oca, 2005). People make less and less room for sex in their lives, have less and less time to devote to it, and have less and less acknowledgment of its value to their lives in general.

Insistence on "dirtiness" of sex

To describe the many ways that Americans fuse sex and "dirtiness" together is a daunting task, in large part because American sexual culture has insisted on this as the operating framework for its sexual politics. Numerous institutions and institutional practices insist upon and reinforce the "filthy" aspects of sexuality as a baseline truth about sexuality. Sex as "dirty" appears in how the Motion Picture Association of America (MPAA) ratings board rates different films, with its policies communicating that women on screen receiving oral sex is "obscene" and men receiving oral sex is standard-operating-procedure. Similarly, while films can display women's bodies fully nude, the depiction of men's genitals often earn films an NC-17 rating (Dick et al., 2006; Leone, 2002).

Institutional practices routinely treat sex as tarnishing, problematic, and shame-inducing. Churches discuss sex in connection to "sin" and "temptation" (more accurately, that *men* are led into temptation by salacious women). The church expends immense energy to contain and control sexuality and to disparage queer sexualities, particularly for teenagers (Burdette & Hill, 2009; Mak & Tsang, 2008). Some churches sponsor chastity or purity balls, where girls and their fathers attend a wedding-like event, and the girl receives a ring from her father in exchange for a pledge of chastity until marriage (Fahs, 2010; Gardner, 2011). Schools, when they teach sex education at all, insist on teaching sex as risky, disease-ridden, and frightening, prone to violence, the spread of contagions, and devoid of pleasure (Fine, 1988; Irvine, 2004). The military has all but ignored its problems of sexual violence and, in a broader sense, frames soldiers' routine and ordinary sexual lives as problematic (Turchik & Wilson, 2010).

Dirtiness also informs how people formulate sexual fantasies, both during partnered sex and during masturbation. Women learn to fantasize about and eroticize their own lack of agency and power (e.g., being *done to* rather than *doing* things to others) (Bivona & Critelli, 2009; Fahs, 2011). Porn is rife with depictions of women that show them as objects of humiliation, degradation, and violence (Dines, Jensen, & Russo, 2013). Talking dirty—an expression that itself shows the link between sexuality and "dirtiness"—has also become an increasingly popular way to express sexual desire (Adelman, 1992; Kehily, 2001). And, of course, even *studying* these phenomena as sex researchers carries a stigma for doing "dirty" work (Fahs, Plante, & McClelland, 2018; Irvine, 2014).

All of these examples collectively suggest that the ability to *imagine* sexuality outside of dirtiness and taboo has been severely limited. Using Audre Lorde's framework of the erotic vs. the pornographic—that is, the life-sustaining, joy-producing qualities of sex compared with the power-based, inequality-based, sex-as-dirty framework—it seems that people have moved away from the erotic and toward the pornographic. And, of course, this lack of imagination serves the interests of capitalism. If sex is dirty, people can only experience it as marked with disgust, shame, and taboo, and so sexuality gets cut off from other aspects of their lives. People tolerate pleasureless work lives and joyless office spaces, and they expect sex to (at best) allow them brief relief from the misery of daily life. We are a culture of desperate phone sex and quick masturbation rather than one of powerful and slow sexual creativity. The more that people rely on mediated versions of their sexuality—through pornographic fantasies, or through powerful institutions that reinforce sex as dirty and "bad"—the more that sex becomes a force of regression and oppression rather than one of fulfillment, resistance, imagination, or possibility.

Dominance/submission dynamics

Sex under capitalism also insists on power imbalances to infuse erotic thought and experience. People have become so accustomed to power structures, hierarchies, and inequalities in their work lives that they now eagerly recreate those dynamics in their sexual lives as well. The permeation of dominance/submission dynamics—or the insistence that one person is in charge, and the other is not—perpetuates the idea that people cannot share power equally. Sex as a surrendering of power, or a taking of power, has become normative. The more extreme iterations of this—dominatrix work, "top" and "bottom" identities, BDSM culture, rough sex, power-imbalanced role playing, the creation of "metrosexual" identities for heterosexual men, or the infliction of sexual pain between people—also work to recreate dynamics of fundamental inequality (one person *has power*, others *do not*). Feminist sexuality scholar Robert Jensen (2007, 2017) has argued that what we "get off" to as a culture tells us much about who we are, and that distinctions between "good" and "bad" men in a capitalist patriarchal economy are unproductive and problematic. He writes:

> We have to let go of a comforting illusion—that there is some bright line between men who rape and men who don't rape, between the bad guys and the good guys. That doesn't mean all guys are bad, or that we can't distinguish between levels of bad behavior. It means that if we want to end men's violence against women we have to acknowledge the effects of patriarchal socialization, and such critical self-reflection is rarely a pleasant task, individually or collectively.
>
> *(Jensen, 2017)*

Building on Jensen's arguments, I would also argue that what we "get off to" as a culture feeds off of and reinforces who we are in other aspects of our lives. In this way, it makes sense that Americans so routinely insist on sexual inequalities in the bedroom, on having a sexual "boss" or using language of control, domination, aggression, control, power, and "topping." As a sex researcher and critical feminist scholar, I care far less about whether dominance and submission "gets people off" than I do about the conditions within which dominance and submission start to feel familiar or desirable. These expressions of dominance and submission reflect back to people what they experience in their everyday lives: a loss of equality, an insistence on submitting to increasingly poor (and underpaid) working conditions, an overvaluation of authority and the power elite, and familiar feelings of humiliation as a condition of their everyday lives. Capitalism creates working conditions that fundamentally strip the humanity away from people: they perform emotional labor, they do work without feeling invested in it, they feel tired and stressed out, they dislike coworkers and bosses (and rarely feel solidarity with coworkers *against* their bosses), they endure long commutes and difficult working conditions, and they have little creativity, autonomy, or control over their work lives. Capitalism normalizes dominance and submission, control of labor and time, and fundamental inequalities among and between people/workers. In doing so, capitalism works against mutuality, shared decision-making, connectivity, and pleasure between partners.

Negativity toward emotions and desires

Under capitalist conditions, a good worker has tight control over his or her emotions and does not show "big" feelings on the job. Efficiency and product-oriented thinking are prioritized, while emotions, affect, intuition, and desires are not. All of this leads to a certain type of alienation in which people engage in meaningless actions and feel estranged from any sense of feelings within themselves. This equation also transfers into people's sex lives, as emotionless sex has gained traction in recent years. People avoid their emotions during sex or seek out sex without emotional connections. They look for (or tolerate) "friends with benefits" relationships where sex is "just sex," or want open relationships where they will not have romantic feelings for other partners (Fahs & Munger, 2015; Owen & Fincham, 2011; Zimmerman, 2012).

Similarly, sex as "sport" or the belief that emotions ruin or lessen sexual empowerment have also shown up in how people think and talk about sexuality. The recent push toward non-committed relationships and relationships without emotional connections has created a number of problems for people's sexual and emotional lives, particularly as people idealize emotionless sex and devalue emotional vulnerability. Research on "friends with benefits" relationships, for example, shows that people overvalue traditionally "masculine" ways of having sex/relationships (no emotions, no strings attached) and devalue "feminine" (or more emotional) ways of having sex (Bisson & Levine, 2009; Fahs & Munger, 2015). At best, friends with benefits relationships require a constant renegotiation about feelings and the meaning of the relationship (Levine & Mongeau, 2010). For women, they often felt more distress, guilt, and shame about casual sex than did men (Townsend & Wasserman, 2011). Further, casual sex rarely pushes back against "pervasive mononormativity" and instead all-too-often reinforces traditional gender and sexual scripts (Farvid & Braun, 2013).

Similarly, sexuality scholars and educators have paid little attention to understanding the social justice implications of people's sexual desires, especially the ways that desires can both reinforce and rebel against cultural stories about gender and power. While people could see sex as a creative force, they often instead treat it as a destructive one. Rather than viewing sexual desires as imaginative and inventive, they are instead seen as dangerous, "dirty," and problematic. For example, sex education programs do not typically mention sexual fantasy as part of early sexual life (Irvine, 2004), just as most partners do not regularly discuss sexual fantasies with each other (Fahs, 2011). In therapy, my clients are not typically curious about where their fantasies come from, or what they might mean, instead choosing to analyze the behavioral or negotiating aspects of their sexual lives (e.g., how often they have sex with their partners and whether to initiate or agree to sex) rather than the cerebral or imaginative/creative qualities of their sex lives. This is yet another way that capitalism has influenced thinking about sexuality, reducing sex to mechanical bodies producing a product (orgasm) rather than envisioning sexuality as a part of creativity and humanness.

Fusion of sex and consumerism

Capitalism also teaches people that (over)consumption is a necessary part of their everyday lives, and that they should direct all aspects of their lives toward the accumulation of more things. This infects people's sex lives in numerous ways. First, people allow pornography—a genre that largely lacks sexual creativity, especially for mainstream pornography—to train and reinforce certain kinds of sexual fantasies and desires at the expense of all others. Common themes in pornography include women as "servicing" men, violence against women, forced or coerced sex, stark power imbalances, role playing with women dressed as young girls, violations of taboos, and racist/sexist imagery (Dines, Jensen, & Russo, 2013). And, notably, men who watch internet pornography reported more sex with multiple partners, higher likelihood of paying for sex, and higher frequency of extramarital affairs (Wright & Randall, 2012).

Second, people have increasingly turned to sex toys to help them fulfill or enhance their sex lives. This means that women increasingly masturbate using sex toys instead of their fingers, and partnered sex more often includes devices and gadgets meant to enhance sexual pleasure. All of these must be purchased (and many are quite expensive), which again fuses sexuality with the pushing of products. And, while feminist sex toy shops have grown in number and visibility (Comella, 2017), most sex toy shops do not openly embrace feminist politics. Sex toys may also change people's sense of their sexual possibilities. In one of my recent studies on women's masturbation, several women mentioned to me that they did not know how to masturbate without a sex toy, and that the idea of masturbating without a toy felt unthinkable (Fahs & Swank, 2013).

Third, our leisure time—potentially time to rest, have sex, unwind, or socialize—has become increasingly shaped and molded by consumerism, in that people associate relaxation with consumption (e.g., shopping, traveling, beauty treatments). If relaxation becomes equated with buying things or consuming, our leisure time is then susceptible to corporate intrusions, the pressures of advertising, social comparisons with others, and the hazards of over-spending. By contrast, people direct little time and attention toward the pleasures of rest, social interaction outside of consuming, face-to-face interactions, spending time in nature, or simply wasting time.

Sex work without sex workers

An increasing number of critical feminist psychologists have started to look at "sex work" not just as paid sexual labor but as the unpaid sexual labor that occurs in the mundane sexual relationships women have with men (Cacchioni, 2007; Duncombe & Marsden, 1996). What would it mean to acknowledge that nearly all sexually-active women are engaging in "sex work"? If we broaden the traditional conceptualization of "sex workers" (that is, prostitutes, or people who explicitly take money for sex) to include those who associate sex with work (that is, those who labor to create sexual experiences for their partner, or those who consider sex a form of work or a job), the notion of who engages in sexual labor expands considerably. Traces of sex work, sexual labor, and emotional labor appear everywhere in women's descriptions of their sexual lives, from explicit sexual exchanges (e.g., women giving husbands oral sex in exchange for them doing the dishes) to implicit notions of validating sexual labor (e.g., loudly moaning during sex to show that a partner's sexual efforts had positive outcomes).

The link between sex and work appears in the cultural lexicon surrounding sex, thus providing a window into how language reflects the priorities and logic of capitalism. *Blow job* or *hand job* (mostly women *doing this* to men) implies that women giving men oral sex or performing manual sex is a form of *work* or *labor*. Traces of sex work and sexual labor show up in even the most mundane descriptions of sexuality, particularly the ways that women describe different kinds of sexual performances (e.g., moaning, showing enjoyment, mitigating damage to a partner's ego) or different ways of displaying "authentic" sexual feelings (Fahs, 2011; Frith, 2013). Conceptualizing these forms of labor as "sex work" shines a light on the everyday patterns of such labor rather than relegating it to a small subsection of sexual laborers (e.g., for-pay sex workers). Under capitalism, imagining sex as work rather than play has permeated people's sexual lives (even actors in pornography rarely laugh, goof around, or seem to be having any fun, despite the fact that porn began as a genre of humor, see Penley, 2006).

Foreclosure of sexual possibilities

Perhaps the single most dangerous way that capitalism destroys our sex lives is by foreclosing certain kinds of sexual possibilities. Similar to the ways that capitalism makes it difficult to imagine other kinds of economic and social structures (e.g., what would it mean to *not* work to increase of wealth for shareholders? How could people revalue money without the stock market?), sex under capitalism also lacks imagination. It becomes static, predictable, driven underground, quarantined to interior spaces of the bedroom, and cordoned off from other aspects of our lives. People stop asking what else sex could be, what else it could look like. They stop asking questions. They stop *imagining* differently.

The foreclosure of sexual possibilities means that sex no longer works as a creative force but as a regressive one. People cannot demand more of their sexual culture—movies, pornography, books, sex education curricula, schooling, partnerships, and more—because they, too, cannot imagine differently. I argue that we must insist on making room for new possibilities that construct a sexuality full of rebellious impulses, creativity, inspiration, fervor, energy, and power—ones that take seriously the tangled web of power relations and unequal discursive practices—while also imagining a sexuality that stands in opposition to capitalism. This does not suggest that people will ever cultivate a sexuality entirely free—of cultural constraints, problematic and oppressive practices and structures, and inequalities—but it does mean that *we are freer than we feel*. Could we imagine a sexuality that takes its time, loves leisure and fun and play, has no product or goal in mind, sees something else possible in partners and ourselves? Is there room for a sexuality that imagines that it is freer than it feels, that continually conjures something different? There is an urgency to this: to not allow capitalism to hollow out these sexual possibilities, to insist on something more.

References

Adelman, M. B. (1992). Sustaining passion: Eroticism and safe-sex talk. *Archives of Sexual Behavior, 21*(5), 481–494.

Almklov, E. L., Drummond, S. A., Orff, H., & Alhassoon, O. M. (2015). The effects of sleep deprivation on brain functioning in older adults. *Behavioral Sleep Medicine, 13*(4), 324–345.

Arruzza, C. (2013). *Dangerous liaisons: The marriages and divorces of Marxism and feminism.* London: Merlin Press.

Bisson, M. A., & Levine, T. R. (2009). Negotiating a friends with benefits relationship. *Archives of Sexual Behavior, 38*, 66–73.

Bivona, J., & Critelli, J. (2009). The nature of women's rape fantasies: An analysis of prevalence, frequency, and contents. *Journal of Sex Research, 46*(1), 33–45.

Bryson, V. (2004). Marxism and feminism: Can the "unhappy marriage" be saved? *Journal of Political Ideologies, 9*(1), 13–30.

Burdette, A. M., & Hill, T. D. (2009). Religious involvement and transitions into adolescent sexual activities. *Sociology of Religion, 70*(1), 28–48.

Cacchioni, T. (2007). Heterosexuality and "the labour of love": A contribution to recent debates on female sexual dysfunction. *Sexualities, 10*(3), 299–320.

Castillo, M. (2012). Survey: 75 percent of Americans admit to using phone while in bathroom. *CBS News.* www.cbsnews.com/news/survey-75-percent-of-americans-admit-to-using-phone-while-in-bathroom/.

Centers for Disease Control and Prevention (CDC). (2012). Short sleep duration among workers—United States, 2010. *MMWR, 61*(16), 281–285.

Comella, L. (2017). *Vibrator nation: How feminist sex-toy stores changed the business of pleasure.* Durham, NC: Duke University Press.

Cooper, E. B., Fenigstein, A., & Fauber, R. L. (2014). The faking orgasm scale for women: Psychometric properties. *Archives of Sexual Behavior, 43*(3), 423–435.

De Stefano, V. (2015). The rise of the just-in-time workforce: On-demand work, crowd-work, and labor protection in the gig-economy. *Comparative Labor Law & Policy Journal, 37*, 461–471.

Delmonico, D. L., & Carnes, P. J. (1999). Virtual sex addiction: When cybersex becomes the drug of choice. *CyberPsychology & Behavior, 2*(5), 457–463.

Dick, K., Dick, K., Schmidt, E., Patterson, M., Waters, J., Smith, K., … Bello, M. (2006). *This Film is not yet rated.* IFC Films.

Dickler, J. (2017). US workers forfeit half their vacation time. *CNBC.* www.cnbc.com /2017/06/19/u-s-workers-forfeit-half-their-vacation-time.html.

Dines, G., Jensen, B., & Russo, A. (2013). *Pornography: The production and consumption of inequality.* New York: Routledge.

Dingfelder, S. F. (2011). Understanding orgasm. *APA Monitor.* www.apa.org/monitor/ 2011/04/orgasm.aspx.

Döring, N., Daneback, K., Shaughnessy, K., Grov, C., Byers, E., Döring, N., & Byers, E. S. (2017). Online sexual activity experiences among college students: A four-country comparison. *Archives of Sexual Behavior, 46*(6), 1641–1652.

Duncombe, J., & Marsden, D. (1996). Whose orgasm is this anyway? "Sex work" in long-term heterosexual couple relationships. In J. Weeks, & J. Holland (Eds.), *Sexual cultures* (pp. 220–238). London: Palgrave Macmillan.

Eveleth, R. (2014). Americans are more into BDSM than the rest of the world. *Smithsonian Magazine.* www.smithsonianmag.com/smart-news/americans-are-more-bdsm-rest-world-180949703/.

Fahs, B. (2010). Daddy's little girls: On the perils of chastity clubs, purity balls, and ritualized abstinence. *Frontiers: A Journal of Women Studies, 31*(3), 116–142.

Fahs, B. (2011). *Performing sex: The making and unmaking of women's erotic lives.* Albany, NY: State University of New York Press.

Fahs, B. (2014). Coming to power: Women's fake orgasms and best orgasm experiences illuminate the failures of (hetero)sex and the pleasures of connection. *Culture, Health & Sexuality, 16*(8), 974–988.

Fahs, B., & Munger, A. (2015). Friends with benefits? Gendered performances in women's casual sexual relationships. *Personal Relationships, 22,* 188–203.

Fahs, B., Plante, R. F., & McClelland, S. I. (2018). Working at the crossroads of pleasure and danger: Feminist perspectives on doing critical sexuality studies. *Sexualities, 21*(4), 503–519.

Fahs, B., & Swank, E. (2013). Adventures with the "plastic man": Sex toys, compulsory heterosexuality, and the politics of women's sexual pleasure. *Sexuality & Culture, 17*(4), 666–685.

Fahs, B., & Swank, E. (2016). The other third shift? Women's emotion work in their sexual relationships. *Feminist Formations, 28*(3), 46–69.

Farvid, P., & Braun, V. (2013). Casual sex as "not a natural act" and other regimes of truth about heterosexuality. *Feminism & Psychology, 23*(3), 359–378.

Federici, S. (1975). *Wages against housework.* Bristol: Falling Wall Press.

Fine, M. (1988). Sexuality, schooling, and adolescent females: The missing discourse of desire. *Harvard Educational Review, 58*(1), 29–54.

Foucault, M. (1978). *The history of sexuality* (Vol. 1, Trans. Robert Hurley). New York: Pantheon.

Friedman, G. (2014). Workers without employers: Shadow corporations and the rise of the gig economy. *Review of Keynesian Economics, 2*(2), 171–188.

Frith, H. (2013). Labouring on orgasms: Embodiment, efficiency, entitlement and obligations in heterosex. *Culture, Health & Sexuality, 15*(4), 494–510.

Frith, H. (2015). Visualising the "real" and the "fake": Emotion work and the representation of orgasm in pornography and everyday sexual interactions. *Journal of Gender Studies, 24*(4), 386–398.

Gager, C. T., & Yabiku, S. T. (2010). Who has the time? The relationship between household labor time and sexual frequency. *Journal of Family Issues, 31*(2), 135–163.

Gardner, C. J. (2011). *Making chastity sexy: The rhetoric of evangelical abstinence campaigns.* Berkeley, CA: University of California Press.

Gil-Jardiné, C., Née, M., Lagarde, E., Schooler, J., Contrand, B., Orriols, L., & Galera, C. (2017). The distracted mind on the wheel: Overall propensity to mind wandering is associated with road crash responsibility. *Plos ONE, 12*(8), 1–10.

Haller, M., Hadler, M., & Kaup, G. (2013). Leisure time in modern societies: A new source of boredom and stress? *Social Indicators Research, 111*(2), 403–434.

Hartmann, H. (1981). The unhappy marriage of Marxism and feminism: Towards a more progressive union. In C. McCann, & S. Kim (Eds.), *Feminist theory reader* (pp. 187–199). New York: Routledge.

Hennessy, R., & Ingraham, C. (2014). *Materialist feminism: A reader in class, difference, and women's lives.* New York: Routledge.

Huber, L., Lyerly, J., Young, A., Dmochowski, J., Vick, T., & Scholes, D. (2014). Comparison of prospective and retrospective measurements of frequency of sexual intercourse. *Maternal & Child Health Journal, 18*(6), 1293–1299.

Hyde, J. S., & DeLamater, J. D. (1997). *Understanding human sexuality.* New York: McGraw-Hill.

Irvine, J. M. (2004). *Talk about sex: The battles over sex education in the United States*. Berkeley, CA: University of California Press.

Irvine, J. M. (2014). Is sexuality research "dirty work"? Institutionalized stigma in the production of sexual knowledge. *Sexualities*, *17*(5–6), 632–656.

Jannini, E. A., Rubio-Casillas, A., Whipple, B., Buisson, O., Komisaruk, B. R., & Brody, S. (2012). Female orgasm(s): One, two, several. *Journal of Sexual Medicine*, *9*(4), 956–965.

Jensen, R. (2007). *Getting off: Pornography and the end of masculinity*. Cambridge, MA: South End Press.

Jensen, R. (2017). On good guys and bad buys. *Common Dreams*. www.commondreams.org/views/2017/11/06/good-guys-and-bad-guys.

Jones, J. M. (2013). In U.S., 40% get less than recommended amount of sleep. *Gallup*. http://news.gallup.com/poll/166553/less-recommended-amount-sleep.aspx.

Kehily, M. (2001). Bodies in school: Young men, embodiment, and heterosexual masculinities. *Men and Masculinities*, *4*(2), 173–185.

Laumann, E. O., Gagnon, J. H., Michael, R. T., & Michaels, S. (1994). *Sex in America: A definitive survey*. Boston, MA: Little, Brown and Co.

Leone, R. (2002). Contemplating ratings: An examination of what the MPAA considers "too far for R" and why. *Journal of Communication*, *52*(4), 938–954.

Lepp, A., Barkley, J. E., & Karpinski, A. C. (2014). The relationship between cell phone use, academic performance, anxiety, and satisfaction with life in college students. *Computers in Human Behavior*, *31*, 343–350.

Levine, T. R., & Mongeau, P. A. (2010). Friends with benefits: A precarious negotiation. In W. O. Stephens (Ed.), *College sex: Philosophy for everyone: Philosophers with benefits* (pp. 91–109). New York: Wiley-Blackwell.

Lorde, A. (1984). The uses of the erotic: The erotic as power. In H. Abelove, M. A. Barale, & D. M. Halperin (Eds.), *The lesbian and gay studies reader* (pp. 339–343). New York: Routledge.

Mackay, J. (2001). How does the United States compare with the rest of the world in human sexual behavior? *Western Journal of Medicine*, *174*(6), 429–433.

MacKinnon, C. A. (1982). Feminism, Marxism, method, and the state: An agenda for theory. *Signs*, *7*(3), 515–544.

Mak, H. K., & Tsang, J. A. (2008). Separating the "sinner" from the "sin": Religious orientation and prejudiced behavior toward sexual orientation and promiscuous sex. *Journal for the Scientific Study of Religion*, *47*(3), 379–392.

Messner, M. A., & Montez de Oca, J. (2005). The male consumer as loser: Beer and liquor ads in mega sports media events. *Signs*, *30*(3), 1879–1909.

Mohn, T. (2013). U.S. is the only advanced economy that does not require employers to provide paid vacation time, report says. *Forbes*. www.forbes.com/sites/tanyamohn/2013/08/13/paid-time-off-forget-about-it-a-report-looks-at-how-the-u-s-compares-to-other-countries/#2f0cc3426f65.

Owen, J., & Fincham, F. D. (2011). Effects of gender and psychosocial factors on "friends with benefits" relationships among young adults. *Archives of Sexual Behavior*, *40*(2), 311–320.

Paiella, G. (2015). The big differences between how Americans and Europeans have sex. *Maxim*. www.maxim.com/maxim-man/europeans-and-americans-sexual-habit-survey-2015-9.

Patrick, Y., Lee, A., Raha, O., Pillai, K., Gupta, S., Sethi, S., & Moss, J. (2017). Effects of sleep deprivation on cognitive and physical performance in university students. *Sleep & Biological Rhythms*, *15*(3), 217–225.

Penley, C. (2006). Crackers and whackers: The white trashing of porn. In P. Lehman (Ed.), *Pornography: Film and culture* (pp. 99–117). New Brunswick: Rutgers University Press.

Powell, R., & Copping, A. (2010). Sleep deprivation and its consequences in construction workers. *Journal of Construction Engineering & Management, 136*(10), 1086–1092.

Richters, J., de Visser, R., Rissel, C., & Smith, A. (2006). Sexual practices at last heterosexual encounter and occurrence of orgasm in a national survey. *Journal of Sex Research, 43*(3), 217–226.

Roberts, J. A., & David, M. E. (2016). My life has become a major distraction from my cell phone: Partner phubbing and relationship satisfaction among romantic partners. *Computers in Human Behavior, 54*, 134–141.

Rubin, G. (1984). Thinking sex: Notes for a radical theory of the politics of sexuality. In C. S. Vance (Ed.), *Pleasure and danger: Exploring female sexuality* (pp. 267–294). London: Pandora.

Shaw, S. M. (2001). Conceptualizing resistance: Women's leisure as political practice. *Journal of Leisure Research, 33*(2), 186–201.

Sherman, E. (2013). Cell phone use during sex? Believe it. *CBS News*. www.cbsnews.com/news/cell-phone-use-during-sex-believe-it/.

Sullivan, P. (2015, August 22). What it takes to get a workaholic to chill out. *New York Times*, pp. B1–B3.

Townsend, J. M., & Wasserman, T. H. (2011). Sexual hookups among college students: Sex differences in emotional reactions. *Archives of Sexual Behavior, 40*(6), 1173–1181.

Turchik, J. A., & Wilson, S. M. (2010). Sexual assault in the US military: A review of the literature and recommendations for the future. *Aggression and Violent Behavior, 15*(4), 267–277.

United States Department of Labor. (2017). Vacation leave. *Department of Labor*. www.dol.gov/general/topic/workhours/vacation_leave.

Vogel, L. (2013). *Marxism and the oppression of women: Toward a unitary theory*. Chicago, IL: Haymarket Books.

Weeks, J. (2011). Un-/Re-productive maternal labor: Marxist feminism and chapter fifteen of Marx's capital. *Rethinking Marxism, 23*(1), 31–40.

Wiederman, M. W. (1997). Pretending orgasm during sexual intercourse: Correlates in a sample of young adult women. *Journal of Sex & Marital Therapy, 23*(2), 131–139.

Wright, P. J., & Randall, A. K. (2012). Internet pornography exposure and risky sexual behavior among adult males in the United States. *Computers in Human Behavior, 28*(4), 1410–1416.

Zimmerman, K. J. (2012). Clients in sexually open relationships: Considerations for therapists. *Journal of Feminist Family Therapy, 24*(3), 272–289.

11

"FREEDOM TO" AND "FREEDOM FROM"

A new vision for sex-positive politics

Walking through the exhibit hall at the Society for the Scientific Study of Sexuality conference, the displays featured a vast array of new possibilities for sexual expression: dildos shaped like tongues, edgy books and journals on bisexuality and polyamory, videos for helping heterosexual women gain comfort with penetrating their (receptive) boyfriends and husbands, and even a pamphlet for an "autoerotic asphyxiation support club." Clearly, the sex-positive movement—inclusive of those who argue against all restrictions on sexuality aside from issues of safety and consent—has made significant advances in how scholars, feminists, practitioners, and the public think about, feel about, and "do" sexuality. For example, women's access to feminist sex toy shops, pornography, blogs, and representations of queer sexuality have increased dramatically in the past several decades (Loe, 1999; Queen, 1997a, 1997b). Despite the relentless attacks from conservatives in the US, people today generally have more expansive options for how they express "normal" sexuality, and they can do so more openly and with more formal and social support. Sex-positive feminists have, in many ways, turned upside-down the notion of the once highly-dichotomous public/private, virgin/whore, and deviant/normal. The sex-positive movement has helped to decriminalize sex work (Jenness, 1993), expand representations in pornography (McElroy, 1995), teach people how to embrace sexuality as normal and healthy (Queen, 1997a, 1997b), explore "sexual enhancement" devices (Reece, Herbenick, & Sherwood-Puzello, 2004), advocate comprehensive sex education (Irvine, 2002; Peterson, 2010; Spencer, Maxwell, & Aggleton, 2008), and challenge overly simplistic notions of "good" and "bad" sex (Rubin, 1993). From Annie Sprinkle showing her cervix as a "Public Cervix Announcement" (Shrage, 2002), to Carol Queen (1997a) arguing against "whore stigma," to Gayle Rubin

(1993) fighting tirelessly against a fixed (and faulty) construction of sex offending, sex positivity has laid the groundwork to depathologize sexuality, particularly for women, sexual minorities, people of color, and sex workers.

Still, the whole scene—clearly intent on a "progress narrative" of sexuality—gives me a strong sense of unease, as many contradictions still overwhelm women's sexual lives. Along with these newfound modes of pleasure-seeking and knowledge-making, women struggle within a plethora of urgent contemporary challenges: alarming rates of sexual violence (Luce, 2010), body shame (Salk & Engeln-Maddox, 2012), eating disorders (Calogero & Pina, 2011), pressure to orgasm (Fahs, 2011a; Farvid & Braun, 2006), distance from their bodily experiences (Martin, 2001), disempowerment with childbirth (Lyerly, 2006; Martin, 2001), masochistic sexual fantasies (Bivona & Critelli, 2009), and a host of other sexual and political crises. Women increasingly associate sexual freedom with consumerism, fashion, and commodities (Hakim, 2010). Women internalize normative pressures to hate their pubic hair and body hair (Bercaw-Pratt, 2012; Fahs, 2011b; Riddell, Varto, & Hodgson, 2010) and hide their menstrual cycles from others (Bobel, 2006; Mandziuk, 2010). Across demographic categories, women suffer immensely from feeling disempowered to speak, explore, and embrace the kinds of sexual lives they most want.

In this chapter, I examine this vast contradictory moment—that is, living between celebrations of progress and alarmingly regressive notions of women's sexual "empowerment"—to explore the problems of (uncritical) sex positivity in this post-sexual-revolution age. Drawing from anarchist theories from the past two centuries—particularly the notion that true liberation and freedom must include *both* the freedom *to* do what we want to do *and* the freedom *from* oppressive structures and demands—I argue that the sex-positive movement must advance its politics to include a more serious consideration of the "freedom from" repressive structures (or "negative liberty"). More specifically, by outlining several ways that the "freedom from" and the "freedom to" are currently in conversation in discourses of women's sexuality, I argue that the integration of these two halves could lead to a subtler and more complete understanding of contemporary sexual politics, particularly around tensions that arose during the infamous "sex wars" of the 1980s, thus helping to build a more cohesive and powerful feminist movement as a whole.

Anarchism and sexuality

> There is a long history of association between anarchism and sexual freedom, but sexual freedom means different things to different people at different times, and has complex connections to ideas about nature, bodies, gender, power, and social organization.
>
> *(Greenway, 1997)*

While anarchy and political theory may not seem like an intuitive bedfellow for feminists who study sex, the political and social bases of anarchy have much to teach feminists interested in bodies and sexualities as sites of social (in)justice.

Anarchists have long espoused important divisions between those interested in individualist versus social anarchism. On the one hand, individualist anarchism, what Isaiah Berlin (1969) termed "negative liberty," argued for freedom from the state and corporate apparatuses. On the other hand, social anarchism advocated for both negative liberty (freedom from the state) and positive liberty (freedom to do what we want to do). True economic freedom, anarchists argue, must include the simultaneous freedom from rules that lead to worker exploitation and the freedom to take actions to ensure worker control of organizations. Both sides, however, embrace negative liberty as a central tenet of freedom. In fact, the concept of negative liberty appeared quite early, as Thomas Hobbes (1651) alluded to it in *Leviathan*, while Hegel is credited as the originator of the concept (Carter, 2012). As early as the nineteenth century, Marxists constructed the freedom *to* and the freedom *from* as two complementary halves that advance the project of social justice, liberty, and freedom for all; some Marxists considered negative and positive liberty indistinguishable and therefore difficult to outline as separate entities (Carter, 2012; Fromm, 1941/1966). In other words, one cannot have true freedom without both the freedom *to* do what we want and the freedom *from* having to do what others tell us to do. This dialectic between negative and positive liberty formed a central tension in political theories of freedom, sovereignty, and morality over the last century (Carter, Kramer, & Steiner, 2007; Flikschuh, 2007).

Both within and outside of anarchist communities, tensions arose between those interested in negative liberty and positive liberty. For example, while Emma Goldman (1917) fought for the freedom *from* state-sponsored marriage, many prominent social theorists argued for the freedom to pursue our full potential (Fromm, 1966), the freedom to self-govern (e.g., Rousseau), and the ability to have "free will" (e.g., Hegel) (Carter, 2012). Feminist anarchists like Goldman, Voltairine de Cleyre, and Lucy Parsons fought to integrate individualist and social anarchism by uniting ideas, the social imaginary, and the gendered self (Ferguson, 2010, 2011; Passet, 2003), particularly as the notion of the "individual" became increasingly less relevant to Goldman and her contemporaries (Day, 2007). Anarcha-feminists were among the first who refused to conceptualize love, relationships, and domesticity as separate from state politics, calling for an end to "sex slavery" (de Cleyre, 1914), jealousy (Goldman, 1998), oppression through motherhood, marriage, and love (Goldman, 1917; Marso, 2003), and control of love and relationships (Haaland, 1993; Molyneux, 2001). In the 1960s, riffing on the work of anarchists, radical feminists—many of whom came from Marxist backgrounds that prioritized the elimination of class inequalities and the importance of structural equalities—fought for the "freedom to" as much as the "freedom from," simultaneously advancing ideas about women *gaining* access to certain previously impenetrable spheres (e.g., all-male faculty clubs, all-male jobs) and *blocking* access to others (e.g., all-women consciousness-raising groups, all-women classrooms, all-women music festivals). (While freedom to and freedom from rarely serve as precise opposites, the ability to willfully *separate* has been considered more a "freedom from" than a "freedom to".) Though radical feminists rarely referred directly to anarchism as their inspiration, these same ideological concepts (negative and positive liberty) informed the center of their political claims about the pathological implications of patriarchy. Radical feminist circles explored the varying modes of power imbalances between men and women (and, later, between women) and attended to distinctions between "power over" (domination and oppression), "power to" (freedom to do and act), and "power with" (collective power to do and act) (Allen, 2008). Far from the over-simplified notion of a singular, rebellious anarchy, they argued for a multi-faceted approach to understanding the workings of power, the state, and social relationships (Fahs, 2018).

Still, despite the clear retrospective links we can draw between radical feminism and anarchism in the late 1960s and early 1970s, particularly surrounding notions of how women interact with state interventions about abortion, the tenets of anarchism have not typically linked up with the theories and practices of women's *sexuality* (practices, identities, attitudes). While anarcha-feminists did focus on institutions that affected *women* (e.g., marriage, love, motherhood), anarchism as a political movement has typically failed to construct the individual, corporeal body as a relevant site of interest (Ward, 2004), often preferring to focus on "freedom from" external social forces found in regimes, dictatorships, or authority (broadly defined). How people have sex, or what power dynamics they bring to sex, has remained largely absent from this rhetoric, even while communities formed around sexual identity (e.g., LGBT movements) garner attention. Even when these connections have existed (e.g., *The Joy of Sex* author, Alex Comfort, published numerous anarchist pamphlets, see Rayner, 2000), the relationship between anarchism and sexuality has rarely received much attention. And, despite the feminist plea that "the personal is political," the overwhelming interest in 1960s counterculture and the sexual revolution, and the (highly commercialized) notion of "girl power" and "sexual empowerment," sex and the body have typically fallen outside the modalities of anarchist political activism and have not formed a central component of most anarchist movements (Greenway, 1997; Heckert & Cleminson, 2011).

As one rare exception, Jamie Heckert (2010, 2011) has interrogated links between sex, love, the body, and anarchism as fundamentally intertwined, particularly as anarchism helps shed light on phenomena like monogamy and polyamory, friendship, and the power of the erotic (Heckert, 2010; Heckert & Cleminson, 2011). To counter the "phallicized whiteness" of capitalism, Heckert and Cleminson (2011) argue that processes and relationships themselves have value, that the conversations, connections, love relationships, and collegial bonds that *produce* knowledge do matter, perhaps more than the *outcomes* or *products* of those interactions. More precisely:

> Love and solidarity can be articulated in the sphere of sexuality and beyond within societies that may seem ever-more disconnected, atomized, and authoritarian … rather than supporting charity, anarchism favors solidarity where all practices of freedom are recognized as interconnected.
>
> *(Heckert & Cleminson, 2011, p. 4)*

Even though anarchist theories of rebellion from the state form an intuitive companion to claims for sexual "freedom," sexuality and anarchy have not typically joined forces (with Greenway, 1997; Heckert & Cleminson, 2011; Passet, 2003 as notable exceptions). Nevertheless, the two share an important set of common goals, particularly around the "freedom from" oppressive structures, mandates, statutes, and interventions. As Gustav Landauer wrote, "The state is not something which can be destroyed by a revolution, but is a condition, a certain relationship between human beings, a mode of human behavior; we destroy it by contracting other relationships, by behaving differently" (Heckert, 2010). Sexuality, then, allows us to "relate differently" and "behave differently," to reimagine our relationships to sex, love, friendship, and kinship (Heckert, 2011), to forego the boredom and monotony capitalism engenders (CrimethInc, 2012). If we understand sexuality as a tool of creativity, as a force that reconsiders power, equality, and freedom, it becomes a perfect companion for anarchist sensibilities. Sexuality as *process* rather than *outcome* (as desire rather than merely orgasm, as exchange rather than merely physical release) links up with the political sentiments of anarchy by suggesting that interaction between people—ideally devoid of power imbalances—matters far more than goal-oriented drives toward an *end*. Thus, drawing upon these claims, I argue that merging the "freedom from" and the "freedom to" with sexuality may result in a powerful overhaul of fragmented segments of social and political life: the personal and political, the corporeal and the cognitive, the "sex-positive" and the "radical feminist."

Sex positives and the "freedom to"

Though sex-positive feminists as currently constituted would likely not categorize themselves exclusively as fighting for the "freedom to," the vast majority of their work has centered on the expansion of sexual rights, freedoms, and modes of expression (Queen, 1997a, 1997b). The movement emerged in response to highly repressive discourses of sexuality, particularly those that they perceived as embracing a state-centered, conservative ideology of "good sex"—as heterosexual, married, monogamous, procreative, non-commercial, in pairs, in a relationship, same generation, in private, no pornography, bodies only, and vanilla—and "bad sex"—as homosexual, unmarried, promiscuous, non-procreative, commercial, alone or in groups, casual, cross-generational, in public, pornography, with manufactured objects, and sadomasochistic (Rubin, 1993). Though the sex wars of the 1980s—where feminists battled about pornography in particular—suggest that sex positivity arose in response to the supposedly pro-censorship notions from radical feminists (though that, too, is highly controversial), in fact sex positivity more clearly rebelled against conservatism, evangelical culture, homophobia, and religious dogma (Duggan & Hunter, 1995). In this way, the sex wars have arguably falsely framed sex positives as the "enemy" of radical feminists, causing much destruction and havoc to the feminist movement as a whole (Ferguson, 1984).

Sex positives fought fiercely for the "freedom to" have diverse, multiple, expansive, and agentic sexual expression; that is, to dislodge histories of repression, sex positives argued that women (and men) should freely embrace new modes of experiencing and expressing their sexuality. Often taking a sort of libertarian perspective on sexual freedom, some wings of the sex-positive movement value lack of government intervention into sex as their top priority (Weeks, 1990) while other aspects of the sex-positive movement more clearly value education and expansion of sexual knowledge (Irvine, 2002). Sex positives share a concern with external limitations placed on sexual expression and with the moralizing judgments placed upon diverse sexualities. For example, Carol Queen defined sex positivity as a community of people who "don't denigrate, medicalize, or demonize any form of sexual expression except that which is not consensual" (Queen, 1997a, p. 128).

One of the key battlegrounds for sex positives—sex education—has also been (arguably) its most successful terrain. Sex positives fought against abstinence-only sex education in favor of comprehensive sex education that would support not only *more* knowledge about STIs and birth control, but also more expansive ideas about queer sexuality, pleasure, "alternative" families, and options for abortion (Irvine, 2002). Further, as an offshoot of the push toward *more* sex education, feminist-owned sex toy shops began to open (and thrive) throughout the country (e.g., Good Vibrations in San Francisco, Smitten Kitten in Minneapolis, Early to Bed in Chicago, Aphrodite's Toy Box in Atlanta, and several others). These stores state that they promoted safe, fun, non-sexist ways to enjoy sex toys, pornography, and erotica, and have worked hard to navigate the tricky terrain of selling commercial products while nurturing an inclusive, community-based, potentially activist space (Attwood, 2005; Loe, 1999). The conflicts between supposedly promoting sex education while also embracing commercial gains presents tricky territory for feminist critics.

As another key victory for sex-positive feminists, they have fought for heightened awareness about, and advocacy for, queer sexualities. This has included the expansion of trans rights (Currah, Juang, & Minter, 2006), more legal and social rights for lesbians and gay men (Bevacqua, 2004; Sycamore, 2004), and acceptance for bisexuality within the queer movement (Garber, 1995). Sex positives have rejected anti-gay-marriage statutes even while exploring marriage as fundamentally flawed (Sycamore, 2004), encouraged better social services for queer youth (McCabe & Rubinson, 2008; Orecchia, 2008), and worked to understand sexuality as fluid, flexible, and not beholden to dogmatic and religious doctrines (Diamond, 2009). In doing so, they have embraced a diversity of bodies, expressions, and identities and have critically examined the all-too-narrow construction of the "sexual body" as white, heterosexual, young, female, and passive. Instead, sex positives have moved to recognize the sexualities of those on the "fringe": fat bodies (Johnston & Taylor, 2008), older bodies (Chrisler & Ghiz, 1993), people of color (Landrine & Russo, 2010; Moore, 2012), gender queer (Branlandingam, 2011), and "alternative" bodies (Hughes, 2009). These "freedom to" victories have certainly helped the feminist movement link up with other move-ments for social and political justice, particularly as sex positives reject claims of "deviance" for any particular group (Showden, 2012).

Radical feminists and the "freedom from"

At the same time that sex positives argued to decriminalize, expand, and embrace sexuality—often constructing pornography as positive, educational, and anti-repressive—radical feminists countered these claims by looking at the "free-dom from" (MacKinnon, 1989). While radical feminists have often been seen as the *opposite* of, or contrary to, the beliefs of sex positivity, I argue that radical feminists have merely wanted *more* recognition of "negative liberty," or the "freedom from" oppressive structures that most women confront on a daily basis. (Not all sex positives have totally neglected the "freedom from," but rather, have *deprioritized* the *freedom from* in comparison to other goals and prior-ities, see Fahs, 2018.) Advocating caution about the unconditional access to women that is built into the sex-positive framework, radical feminists essentially said that, without women's "freedom from" patriarchal oppression, women lacked freedom at all. Real sexual freedom, radical feminists claimed, must include the "freedom from" the social mandates to have sex (particularly the enforcement of sex with men) and "freedom from" treatment as sexual objects.

Looking collectively at the work of Teresa De Lauretis (1988), Marilyn Frye (1997), Adrienne Rich (1980), Audre Lorde (2007), Andrea Dworkin (1997), and Catharine MacKinnon (1989), they all share the belief that men's access to women is a *taken-for-granted* assumption often exercised on women's bodies and sexualities. Indeed, all powerful groups demand unlimited access to less powerful groups, while less powerful groups rarely have access to more powerful groups. As Marilyn Frye (1997) said, "Total power is unconditional access; total powerlessness is being unconditionally accessible. The creation and manipulation of power is constituted of the manipulation and control of access" (p. 411). For example, the poor rarely have access to the rich (particularly if demanded by the poor), while the rich almost always have access to the poor (e.g., buying drugs or sex in poor neighborhoods and returning to their "safe" communities). Affluent whites often live in gated com-munities, in part to deny access to people of color, while middle-class whites live in segregated suburban cul-de-sacs. Men notoriously operate in spheres of power that exclude women (e.g., country clubs, golf circles, "good ol' boys" hiring practices, and so on). At its core, radical feminism argues against the patriarchal assumption that men have the *right* to access women (and the patriarchal notion that women must internalize this mandate).

Lesbian separatism, particularly *political* lesbian separatism not based specifically or primarily on the sexual desire for women (Atkinson, 1974; Densmore, 1973), represents a rebellion against this mandated access. By revealing the assumptions of access embedded within sexuality—namely that men can always access the bodies of women for their sexual "needs"—lesbian separatists make a clear case for the "freedom from." All-women spaces that excluded men did not merely allow women to physically separate from men, but also to rebel against the constant surveillance of the male gaze and men's *assumptions of access* (Fahs, 2011a). These separatists understood that the "free love" of the 1970s, far from a celebratory moment of progress for women, merely allowed men's sexual access to *more* women and largely ignored women's experiences with "brutalization, rape, submission [and] someone having power over them" (Dunbar, 1969, p. 56). They also (rightly) noted that women's assertion of their "freedom from" interacting with men provokes dangerous resistances, anger, and hostilities.

Moving forward to the 1980s, scholars like Dworkin (1997) and MacKinnon (1989) made similar claims about sexual access when they argued for the "freedom from" messages and images embedded in pornography that portrayed women as "hot wet fuck tubes" (Dworkin, 1991). Further, they called out the power-imbalanced practices of sexual intercourse and theorized about the dangers of women tolerating their own oppression (e.g., not reporting rape). By calling out sexuality as a site of dangerous power imbalances between men and women, their version of "freedom from" became particularly threatening within and outside of feminist circles. Recall that both MacKinnon and Dworkin received death threats and had to retain security personnel for even *suggesting* that women can and should assert their "freedom from" pornography and power-imbalanced sex (MacKinnon & Dworkin, 1998). Taken together, these examples reveal that the "freedom from" provokes greater threat from men and the culture at large, with increasingly hostile backlashes against those who assert their right to negative liberty. To suggest that women *deny access to men* undercuts core cultural assumptions about gender politics and patriarchal power.

Cycles of liberation

Looking at these histories together, a clear pattern emerges: rarely does the feminist movement (or the queer movement, or sexuality studies) adequately address the dialectic between the "freedom from" and the "freedom to." I am particularly concerned about the degree to which sex positivity neglects the "freedom from", particularly when the rhetoric of sex positivity often inadvertently allows for the unconditional access to women that many of their projects, goals, and narratives rely upon. That said, I also worry about the ways that negative liberty (ironically) could create new norms that require women to label their (heterosexual, pornographic, masochistic, etc.) desires as necessarily patriarchal (e.g., Showden, 2012 has suggested that sex positivity must become a "politics of *maybe*" rather than a "politics of *yes*"). The relative crisis of women's "sexual freedom"—along with the hazards of *solving* this "problem"—becomes increasingly clear when examining contemporary dilemmas and quandaries women face in their sexual lives. In the following seven examples, I outline the ways that the "freedom from" has fallen more and more out of focus, even as the "freedom to" achieves small victories. These seven themes are organized by first emphasizing the more (supposedly) positive and personal aspects of sexuality (orgasm, sexual satisfaction), followed by an examination of how cultural norms infect women's sexual lives (treatments of sexual dysfunction, rape and sexual coercion, body hair), and ending with an examination of how women function in the cultural imaginary (same-sex eroticism, sexual fantasy). Each of these elements reveals the tenuous nature of sexual empowerment and showcases the absolute necessity of uniting positive and negative liberty. I reiterate the anarchist principle outlined above: one cannot have true freedom without *both* the "freedom to" and the "freedom from".

Orgasm

In my previous work (Fahs, 2011a), I looked at what I consider to be the most dangerous aspect of defining sexual freedom: it is subject to continued appropriations and distortions, and it requires continual reinvention. Sexual freedom has no fixed definition and is not static. Rather, because freedoms are easily co-opted, all definitions of freedom (sexual or otherwise) are transient and transitory, require constant re-evaluation and reassessment, and present an ongoing set of new challenges to each cohort and generation. In the articulation of freedom, co-optation is not only possible, but *probable*, particularly when addressing issues of women's sexuality. As a key example, consider a brief history of women's orgasms. During the sexual revolution, women fought hard for the right to have the clitoris recognized as a site of legitimate pleasure. Until the late 1960s, it was assumed (largely due to the influence of psychoanalysis) that vaginal orgasm represented "maturity" and clitoral orgasm represented "immaturity" (studies by medical doctors—quite recently—still argue this! See Brody & Weiss, 2011; Costa & Brody, 2011); still more, women were expected to prioritize phallic male pleasure over anything clitoral, often resulting in harsh pressures for women to vaginally orgasm. As Ti-Grace Atkinson (1974) said, "Why *should* women learn to vaginal orgasm? Because that's what men want. How about a facial tic? What's the difference?" (p. 7). During the sexual revolution, the convergence of the queer movement, the women's movement, and the sexual revolution led to a concerted interest in dethroning the vaginal orgasm in favor of the clitoral orgasm (Gerhard, 2000). If women valued and recognized the power of the clitoris, some argued, they could embrace sex with other women, orgasm more easily and efficiently, and enjoy the same sexual pleasures men had always enjoyed (Koedt, 1973).

This celebration of progress on the orgasm front—notably something radical feminists expressed some concerns about even then—had a short-lived period of revolutionary potential. At the tail end of the sexual revolution, radical feminists like Dana Densmore (1973) and Roxanne Dunbar (1969) began to worry that all of this focus on women's clitoral orgasms could lead to an "orgasm frenzy" where women would feel *mandated* to orgasm and men would use clitoral orgasms as yet another tool to oppress women. Dunbar believed that sexual liberation became equated with "the 'freedom' to 'make it' with anyone anytime" (p. 49), while Sheila Jeffreys (1990) claimed retrospectively that "sexual liberation" from the 1960s and 1970s merely substituted one form of oppression for another. Indeed, over the next 20 years, clitoral orgasms evolved from a much-fought-for occurrence to a social mandate between (heterosexual) sex partners. Fast-forward to 2012 and we find some startling data: over half of women have faked orgasms, often regularly (Wiederman, 1997), and women describe faking orgasms for reasons that still ensure male dominance and power: they want to support the egos of their (male) partners; they want to end the encounter (primarily intercourse), often because they feel exhausted; and they imagine that orgasms make them "normal" (Fahs, 2011a; Roberts, Kippax, Waldby, & Crawford, 1995). This suggests that, though orgasm once served a symbolic role as a tool of liberation (a new "freedom to" personal desire), orgasm eventually reverted to being another tool of patriarchy as orgasm became a marker of male prowess. Given the high rates of faking orgasm (Fahs, 2011a; Roberts et al., 1995) now seen among women, many women may now need the "freedom from" orgasm as a *mandate*; further, the orgasm mandate exists not primarily to please women themselves, but to please their (male) partners.

Sexual satisfaction

As an offshoot of the "orgasm problem," recent research on sexual satisfaction has pointed to some disturbing trends. While popular culture (particularly movies, music, and magazines) generally advocates women's "freedom to" have sexual pleasure and satisfaction, little attention is paid to how women themselves *construct* satisfaction or how women's sexual satisfaction still showcases men's overwhelming sexual power. What does a "satisfied woman" say about her sexual experiences? Studies consistently suggest correlations between sexual satisfaction and intimacy, close relationships (Pinney, Gerrard, & Denney, 1987; Sprecher, Barbee, & Schwartz, 1995), emotional closeness (Trompeter, Bettencourt, & Barrett-Connor, 2012), reciprocal feelings of love, and versatile sexual techniques (Haavio-Mannila & Kontula, 1997). These findings underlie the relational dimensions of women's sexual satisfaction (and undermine pop culture's "bodice ripping" stereotypes). In this regard, women may have the "freedom to" sexual pleasure as long as it remains in the stereotyped confines of marriage and romantic love. This may represent a sign of progress, or it may signify the trappings of traditional femininity. Similarly, studies also show that sexually satisfied women typically have better body image (Meltzer & McNulty, 2010), lower rates of eating disorders, lower self-objectification tendencies (Calogero & Thompson, 2009; Frederickson & Roberts, 1997), thereby suggesting other modest victories for the association between sexual expression and personal empowerment even while raising questions about women's interpretation of "satisfaction."

When looking more closely at data about women's sexual satisfaction, particularly measures of "deservingness" and "entitlement," women fall far short of full equality with men with regard to seeking pleasure, though differing definitions and assessments of satisfaction make these gender findings increasingly complicated (McClelland, 2010, 2011). For example, the same relational dimensions that may help women equate sexual satisfaction with emotional closeness also demand that they prioritize their partner's (especially men's) pleasure over their own. When asked why they want to orgasm, women say that their partners' pleasure matters more than their own and that their partners' pleasure is a conditional factor that determines their own pleasure (Nicolson & Burr, 2003), calling into question *whose* pleasure women value when assessing their own satisfaction. Compared to men, women also more often equate sex with submissiveness, and when they do so, this leads to lower rates of sexual arousal, autonomy, and enjoyment (Sanchez, Kiefer, & Ybarra, 2006). Further, compared to men, women also describe orgasm as a far less important component of their sexual satisfaction (Kimes, 2002).

Additionally, sexual satisfaction is certainly not static or equally distributed *between* all women, as different demographic groups report vastly different sexual satisfaction. Strong correlations between sexual satisfaction, sexual activity, and social identities have been found, as lower status women (e.g., women of color, less educated women, working-class women) reported having more *frequent* but less satisfying sex, particularly compared to white, upper-class (typically higher status) women (Fahs & Swank, 2011). That is, women without as much social and political power still have sex, but they have to endure less satisfying sex on a much more regular basis than women with more power. This suggests, most specifically, that lower status women more often lack the "freedom from" unwanted sex or unsatisfying sex even while they have the apparent "freedom to" have frequent sexual activity. Compared to higher status women, lower status women do not have the same social permissions to deny others access to their bodies, and they do not feel as entitled to refuse sex when not satisfied.

Treatment for sexual dysfunction

Medicalization has also served as a tool for ensuring women's lack of "freedom from" sex, as women who abstain from sex, refuse sex, or construct themselves as asexual or celibate have been labeled as fundamentally dysfunctional by the medical community. For example, to turn a social problem into something supposedly derived from women's inadequacies, a recent study characterized a staggering 43.1% of women as "sexually dysfunctional," even though far fewer women reported subjective distress about such sexual "problems" (Shifren, Monz, Russo, Segreti, & Johannes, 2008). When the medical community decides that women have dysfunction if they do not conform to some medically defined prescription of the "normal," they do not account for women's own narratives about their sexual experiences. Rarely do studies account for partner abilities, contextual factors in women's lives, or women's personal narratives about their "dysfunction." As it stands now, women can receive a psychiatric diagnosis of sexual dysfunction if they refuse penetration, fail to orgasm, have "inadequate" lubrication or swelling response, refuse to have sex with partners, and feel aversion toward sexuality in general. (These diagnoses are labeled hypoactive sexual desire disorder, sexual aversion disorder, female sexual arousal disorder.) Such diagnoses normalize heterosexuality and penetrative intercourse as the pinnacle of "healthy sex" while setting clear and monolithic standards for sexual normality.

As a more precise example of the dangerous power of medicalization, consider the (especially egregious) recent treatments developed by the medical community to cure vaginal pain disorders like vaginismus. One recent treatment advises doctors to inject Botox into three sites of the vagina in order to allow women to "tolerate" penetrative intercourse (Ghazizadeh & Nikzad, 2004). Another common treatment advises doctors to insert vaginal dilators into women's vaginas in order to stretch out their vaginal opening to allow for penile penetration (Crowley, Goldmeier, & Hiller, 2009; Grazziotin, 2008; Raina et al., 2007). These treatments ensure that women's vaginas can effectively ingest a penis, thereby constructing "normal" vaginas and "normal" sex as penile-vaginal intercourse. Normal sex becomes that which meets men's sexual needs even if it induces pain in women. Even if women can orgasm through manual or oral stimulation, even if women report sexual violence and abuse histories, and even with reliable statistics that consistently point to penile-vaginal intercourse as an unreliable facilitator of women's orgasms (Hite, 1976), these treatments are considered standard and routine for sexual pain disorders. Women do not have the "freedom from" penile-vaginal intercourse, even if it causes them physical or psychological discomfort and pain. If sociocultural scripts mandate that a "normal" woman has "normal" sex, the medical community will ensure that she complies.

Rape and sexual coercion

In an age so often characterized as "empowering" for women—and with so much rhetoric devoted to women's supposed choices about their bodies and sexualities—the occurrence of rape and sexual coercion of women serve as a sobering reminder of patriarchy's widespread influence. In addition to the staggering rates of reported sexual violence both within the US (Elwood et al., 2011) and globally (Koss, Heise, & Russo, 1994), women also deal (sometimes on a daily basis) with their lack of "freedom from" sexual harassment, street harassment, pornography, objectification, and coercion. Women typically minimize coercive encounters they have had, often to avoid the stigma and label of "rape victim" (Bondurant, 2001; Kahn, Jackson, Kully, Badger, & Halvorsen, 2003). They also protect boyfriends, husbands, family members, and dating partners as "not rapists" by denying or minimizing the coercion that these men enact (Fahs, 2011a), often while endorsing "rape myth" beliefs that women deserve rape or brought it on themselves (Haywood & Swank, 2008). While women may have the "freedom to" experiment with their sexuality in new ways, such experimentation often goes hand-in-hand with coercion, abuses of power, pressure, and lopsided power dynamics.

Women's lack of "freedom from" coercion and harassment also extends into their relationship with space itself. Women construct "outside" as unsafe and "inside" as safe, refuse to walk alone at night (Valentine, 1989), and imagine their (benevolent) boyfriends, husbands, brothers, male acquaintances, and male friends as "protectors," even when these men most often perpetrate sexual violence (Fahs, 2011a). Women's relative lack of freedom to occupy public space, travel alone, protect themselves from violence, or ensure non-coercive sexual exchanges represents a major component of women's sexual consciousness, even if they have not experienced violent rape or clear-cut coercion. The literature on "sexual extortion"—where women engage in sexual acts to avoid domestic violence—also speaks to this continuum between rape and not rape (DeMaris, 1997). Their lack of "freedom from" violence is, for many women, an everyday occurrence that harms their well-being and blocks access to institutions that men use as sources of their power (e.g., better-paying jobs, education, public space).

Body hair as "personal choice"

As a reminder of the invisibility of power, women also imagine that they have far more personal freedom when "choosing" how to groom and present their bodies to the outside world and to friends, partners, and families. As a prime example, women, particularly younger women, generally endorse the idea that removing body hair (particularly underarm, leg, and pubic hair) is a "personal choice" that they simply "choose" to do. That said, when women refuse to remove their body hair, they often face intense negative consequences: homophobia, harassment, objectification, partner disapproval, family disapproval, coworker disapproval, threats of job loss, anger and stares from strangers, and internal feelings of discomfort and disgust (Fahs, 2011b). Women who do not remove body hair are labeled by others as "dirty" or "gross" (Toerien & Wilkinson, 2004), and are seen as less sexually attractive, intelligent, happy, and positive compared to hairless women (Basow & Braman, 1998). Women who do not shave their body hair were also judged as less friendly, moral, or relaxed, and as *more* aggressive, unsociable, and dominant compared to women who removed their body hair (Basow & Willis, 2001). While older age, feminist identity, and lesbian identity predicted less negative attitudes toward body hair (Toerien, Wilkinson, & Choi, 2005), few women receive full protection from the cultural negativity surrounding women's body hair.

These findings reveal that women overwhelmingly lack the "freedom from" regulating their bodies through shaving. With increasingly vicious rhetoric directed toward their "natural" body hair as inherently dirty, disgusting, and unclean, women spend great energy and time fighting against these stereotypes in an effort to have acceptable bodies, particularly for already stigmatized groups like women of color and working-class women (Fahs, 2011b; Fahs & Delgado, 2011). With trends indicating that increasing numbers of women in the US remove pubic hair, the hairlessness norms seem only to expand, particularly in the last decade (Herbenick, Schick, Reece, Sanders, & Fortenberry, 2010). Women may have the "freedom to" groom their pubic hair into triangles, landing strips, or vajazzled ornaments (thanks to the growth of corporate techniques of hair maintenance, see Bryce, 2012), but they cannot go *au naturelle* or not shave their bodies without serious social punishments (Toerien et al., 2005).

Same-sex eroticism

For several decades, the queer movement has fought to expand legal and social rights for same-sex couples, increase the representation of same-sex eroticism, and garner cultural acceptance of LGBT identities as normative and non-"deviant" (Clendinen & Nagourney, 2001; Swank & Fahs, 2011). In particular, women have more *freedoms to* express their sexual interests in other women and to explore same-sex eroticism more openly, with blatant hostile homophobia diminishing some in the last decades (Loftus, 2001). That said, these supposed "freedoms" have also been appropriated by the patriarchal lens and converted into actions that women undertake to gain acceptance and approval in certain settings: bars, fraternity parties, clubs, bars, and so on (Yost & McCarthy, 2012). Women "making out" and "hooking up" with other women in these settings constitutes an increasingly normative practice, as long as men *watch* women doing this behavior and as long as the women fit stereotypical standards of "sexiness" for male viewers. Increasing numbers of women report *pressure* to kiss and have sex with other women in front of men, either by "hooking up" at bars, engaging in threesomes (male partner initiated, only involving multiple women and one man), or allowing men to watch women kiss in public (Fahs, 2009; Yost & McCarthy, 2012).

Such pressures exist regardless of women's sexual identity, as queer women report pressures to "hook up" in front of men just as heterosexual women say their boyfriends and male friends ask them to "pretend" to enjoy same-sex eroticism for their viewing benefit (Fahs, 2009). Women increasingly describe these pressures toward "bisexuality" as compulsory (Fahs, 2009), as 33% of college women had engaged in this behavior, while 69% of college students had observed this behavior (Yost & McCarthy, 2012). Thus, large segments of women lack the relative "freedom from" mandated same-sex eroticism that is performed *in front of* men and for the sake of men's pleasure. The rebellious, transformative qualities of same-sex eroticism have also been distorted to serve the interests of men (and patriarchy) by ensuring that men are physically and psychologically present during these encounters. No wonder, then, that such "performative bisexuality" (Fahs, 2009) has *not*, for the women engaging in these acts, consistently translated into shifts in political consciousness like increased identification with bisexuality, more support for gay marriage laws, and more LGBT activism (Fahs, 2009, 2011a).

Sexual fantasy

As a final example—and likely the one most directly contrasting with sex positivity—women lack the "freedom from" a sexuality that corresponds with mainstream (pornographic?) fantasies. They also lack the freedom from internalized heterosexist beliefs that distorts their imagination about what constitutes "exciting" sex. Even when women enjoy pornography without internalizing pornographic fantasies as *real*, they still grapple with increasingly narrow definitions of "the sexual." When examining women's sexual fantasies, an incredible amount of internalized passivity, lack of agency, and desire for domination appears (Bivona & Critelli, 2009; Fahs, 2011a). In particular, women report fantasies of men dominating them as their most common sexual fantasies, even when their best lived sexual experiences do not include such content. When women described their most pleasurable sexual encounters, these descriptions did not include dominance and power narratives, yet when women described their sexual fantasies, themes of power, coercion, dominance, and passivity appeared (Fahs, 2011a). In addition to fantasy, women described pressures from their partners to engage in (increasingly rough) anal sex (Štulhofer & Ajduković, 2011), threesomes (Fahs, 2009), forceful encounters (Koss et al., 1994), role playing, and dominance (Bivona & Critelli, 2009), indicating that many women negotiate these themes not only in their minds, but also in their partnered practices.

While women have certainly made advances in their *freedoms to* expand sexual expression and ideas about sexuality, they now face their relative lack of "freedom from" such dynamics both in their imaginations and in their body practices. Pornographic fantasies have entered mainstream consciousness in many ways: body and hair grooming (Fahs, 2011b), new procedures like anal bleaching, increasing desires for "designer vaginas" and labiaplasty surgeries (Braun & Tiefer, 2010), and pressures for women to conform to men's desires for threesomes, painful anal sex (Štulhofer & Ajduković, 2011), and rougher sex in general. Sexual fantasy cannot be dismissed as mere frivolity, as rape fantasies have become increasingly common (Bivona & Critelli, 2009), and men's treatment of women often closely reflects the messages and themes they absorb from pornography (Jensen, 2007).

New visions for sex positivity

The tensions between "freedom to" and "freedom from" in women's sexuality constitute a central dialectic in the study of, and experience of, women's sexuality (Vance, 1984). In order to move toward the ever-elusive "sexual liberation," women need to be able to deny access to their bodies, say no to sex as they choose, and engage in sexual expression free of oppressive homophobic, sexist, and racist intrusions. Women should have, when they choose, the "freedom from" unwanted, mediated versions of their sexuality (e.g., Facebook, internet intrusions, "sexting"), heterosexist constructions of "normal sex," and sexist assumptions about what satisfies and pleases them. If women cannot have "freedom from" these things without social penalty, they therefore lack a key ingredient to their own empowerment.

Those who avoid sex, choose asexuality, embrace celibacy (either temporary or permanent), or otherwise feel disinclined toward sex (perhaps due to personal choice, histories of sexual violence, health issues, hormonal fluctuations, irritation or emotional distance with a partner, and so on) should be considered healthy and *normal* individuals who are making healthy and normal choices. Recent studies have begun to look at "sexual assertiveness," sexual autonomy, and the importance of women's right to refuse sex (Morokoff et al., 1997; Sanchez, Crocker, & Boike, 2005). The assumption that women must have consistency in their sexual expression, desire, and behavior does not fit with the way sexuality ebbs and flows and responds to circumstances in their lives. Sexual freedom means both the "freedom to" enjoy sexuality, and "freedom from" having to "enjoy" it, just as reproductive freedom means the "freedom to" have children when desired *and* the "freedom from" unwanted pregnancies.

As a new vision for sex positivity, I argue that we need three broadly defined goals, each of which contributes to a larger vision that prioritizes a complex, multi-faceted sexual freedom that fuses the political goals of both sex positives and radical feminists; first, *more* critical consciousness about any vision of sexual liberation. Definitive and universal claims about freedom and choice for all women must be met with caution or even downright suspicion. For example, while sex toys can represent a positive aspect of women's lives—they allow for more efficient masturbation for some, exploration for others, and fun and quirkiness for still others—these toys still exist within a capitalistic framework. While sex toys can be empowering, pleasurable, fun, and exciting, they also equate liberated sexuality with *purchasing power*, buying things, and (perhaps) distancing women from their bodies (not to mention that the labor politics around making such toys, where women's labor in developing countries is often exploited in the name of mediated versions of pleasure). These debates also overlap with notions of "sexual citizenship" and the ways capitalism shapes not only sexual rights but also desire itself (see Evans, 2002). Also, when women masturbate with sex toys, they learn *not* to touch their vaginas in the same way. When couples "spice things up" with accessories, they often avoid the harder conversations about their goals, desires, and relationship needs. Further, sex toy packaging and marketing fall into the all-too-common associations between acquiring objects and achieving personal happiness (not to mention that sex toy companies often use poor quality plastics and exploit their workers, another decidedly "unsexy" side to the industry). In short, the relentless insistence upon a critical consciousness regarding sexual liberation (and claims of what is "sexually liberating") is a *requirement* if we want to illuminate the complexities of women's sexual freedom.

Second, *more* attention should be paid to how sexual access functions in the lives of lower status people (particularly women). Those with lower socially-inscribed statuses—women, people of color, queer people, working-class and poor people, less educated people (etc.)—are often expected, in numerous areas in their lives, to provide *access* to higher status people. Their bodies are expected to provide certain kinds of labor that serve the interests of high-status people (e.g., physical, sexual, emotional labor) (Barton, 2006). Thus, it is especially important that lower status people not equate sexual liberation with sexual access. These groups should not equate sexual empowerment with providing sexual access to others; rather, their sexual empowerment might derive from the "freedom from" such access to their bodies and (eroticized) labor.

Third, *more* attention must be devoted to the insidious aspects of disempowerment. There is no single definition of "liberated sex." Rather, sexual empowerment is a constantly moving target that requires continual critique, revision, self-reflexiveness, and (re)assessment of our own practices, cultural norms, ideologies, and visions for the self. Even my own vision of better incorporating the "freedom from" into ideas of sexual empowerment carries with it many dangerous trappings that must be cautiously navigated (e.g., not creating new norms and hierarchies of "good" and "bad" sex; forgetting about the "politics of maybe"). Because our culture so often pathologizes "non-normative" sexual behavior, many individuals spend much time and energy defending their sexual choices, behaviors, and lifestyles against conservative, religious, politically regressive individuals and institutions. While this work is much needed and often politically effective, particularly in our current political climate, these defenses *cannot* preclude a *critical assessment* of how our sexual choices still often reflect and per-petuate sexist, classist, racist, and homophobic ideals. We must release our attachment to certain forms of negative liberty that defend us against critical "intruders." In other words, when we insist upon radically examining, critiquing, and unpacking our own sexual lives—even at the cost of unsettling and dislodging the barricades that defend us against intrusions and judgments from the far right—we move ever closer to a fully-realized notion of sexual liberation, sexual empowerment, and sexual equality for all.

References

Allen, A. (2008) Feminist perspectives on power. *Stanford encyclopedia of philosophy*. http://plato.stanford.edu/entries/feminist-power/.

Atkinson, T. (1974). *Amazon odyssey: The first collection of writings by the political pioneer of the women's movement*. New York: Links Books.

Attwood, F. (2005). Fashion and passion: Marketing sex to women. *Sexualities, 8*(4), 392–406.

Barton, B. C. (2006). *Stripped: Inside the lives of exotic dancers*. New York: New York University Press.

Basow, S. A., & Braman, A. C. (1998). Women and body hair: Social perceptions and attitudes. *Psychology of Women Quarterly, 22*(4), 637–645.

Basow, S. A., & Willis, J. (2001). Perceptions of body hair on white women: Effects of labeling. *Psychological Reports, 89*(3), 571–576.

Bercaw-Pratt, J. L. (2012). The incidence, attitudes, and practices of the removal of pubic hair as a body modification. *Journal of Pediatric & Adolescent Gynecology, 25*(1), 12–14.

Berlin, I. (1969). *Four essays on liberty*. New York: Oxford University Press.

Bevacqua, M. (2004). Feminist theory and the question of lesbian and gay marriage. *Feminism & Psychology, 14*(1), 36–40.

Bivona, J., & Critelli, J. (2009). The nature of women's rape fantasies: An analysis of prevalence, frequency, and contents. *Journal of Sex Research, 46*(1), 35–45.

Bobel, C. (2006). "Our revolution has style": Contemporary menstrual product activists "doing feminism" in the third wave. *Sex Roles, 54*(5), 331–345.

Bondurant, B. (2001). University women's acknowledgment of rape: Individual, situational, and social factors. *Violence Against Women, 7*(3), 294–314.

Branlandingam, B. (2011). Hot piece of hipster: Summer genderqueer hair. *The Queer Fat Femme Guide to Life*. http://queerfatfemme.com/2011/05/29/hot-piece-of-hipster-summer-genderqueer-hair/.

Braun, V., & Tiefer, L. (2010). The "designer vagina" and the pathologisation of female genital diversity: Interventions for change. *Radical Psychology, 8*(1). www.radicalpsychology.org/vol8-1/brauntiefer.html.

Brody, S., & Weiss, P. (2011). Simultaneous penile-vaginal intercourse orgasm is associated with satisfaction (sexual, life, partnership, and mental health). *The Journal of Sexual Medicine, 8*(3), 734–741.

Bryce. (2012). I got vajazzled (and had a camera crew). *The Luxury Spot*. www.theluxuryspot.com/features/i-got-vajazzled-and-had-a-camera-crew/.

Calogero, R. M., & Pina, A. (2011). Body guilt: Preliminary evidence for a further subjective experience of self-objectification. *Psychology of Women Quarterly, 35*(3), 428–440.

Calogero, R. M., & Thompson, J. K. (2009). Potential implications of the objectification of women's bodies for women's sexual satisfaction. *Body Image, 6*(2), 145–148.

Carter, I. (2012). Positive and negative liberty. *Stanford Encyclopedia of Philosophy*. http://plato.stanford.edu/archives/spr2012/entries/liberty-positive-negative/

Carter, I., Kramer, M., & Steiner, H. (2007). *Freedom: A philosophical anthology* (Vol. 22). Oxford: Wiley-Blackwell.

Chrisler, J. C., & Ghiz, L. (1993). Body images of older women. *Women & Therapy, 14*(1–2), 67–75.

Clendinen, D., & Nagourney, A. (2001). *Out for good: The struggle to build a gay rights movement in America*. New York: Simon & Schuster.

Costa, M. R., & Brody, S. (2011). Sexual satisfaction, relationship satisfaction, and health are associated with greater frequency of penile-vaginal intercourse. *Archives of Sexual Behavior, 41*(1), 9–10.

CrimethInc Ex-Workers Collective. (2012). Your politics are boring as fuck. *CrimethInc*. www.crimethinc.com/texts/selected/asfuck.php.

Crowley, T., Goldmeier, D., & Hiller, J. (2009). Diagnosing and managing vaginismus. *BMJ, 339*, 2284.

Currah, P., Juang, R. M., & Minter, S. (2006). *Transgender rights*. Minneapolis, MN: University of Minnesota Press.

Day, J. E. (2007). The "individual" in Goldman's anarchist theory. In P. A. Weiss, & L. Kensinger (Eds.), *Feminist interpretations of Emma Goldman* (pp. 109–136). University Park, PA: Pennsylvania State University Press.

de Cleyre, V. (1914). Sex slavery. In *Selected Works of Voltairine de Cleyre* (pp. 342–358). New York: Mother Earth Publishing Association.

De Lauretis, T. (1988). Sexual indifference and lesbian representation. *Theatre Journal, 40*(2), 155–177.

DeMaris, A. (1997). Elevated sexual activity in violent marriages: Hypersexuality or sexual extortion? *Journal of Sex Research, 34,* 361–373.

Densmore, D. (1973). Independence from the sexual revolution. In A. Koedt, E. Levine, & A. Rapone (Eds.), *Radical Feminism* (pp. 107–118). New York: Quadrangle Books.

Diamond, L. M. (2009). *Sexual fluidity: Understanding women's love and desire.* Cambridge, MA: Harvard University Press.

Duggan, L., & Hunter, N. D. (1995). *Sex wars: Sexual dissent and political culture.* New York: Routledge.

Dunbar, R. (1969). Sexual liberation: More of the same thing. *No More Fun and Games, 3,* 49–56.

Dworkin, A. (1991). *Woman hating.* New York: Plume.

Dworkin, A. (1997). *Intercourse.* New York: Simon & Schuster.

Elwood, L. S., Smith, D. W., Resnick, H. S., Gudmundsdottir, B., Amstadter, A., Hanson, R. F., … Kilpatrick, D. G. (2011). Predictors of rape: Findings from the National Survey of Adolescents. *Journal of Traumatic Stress, 24*(2), 166–173.

Evans, D. T. (2002). *Sexual citizenship: The material construction of sexualities.* New York: Routledge.

Fahs, B. (2009). Compulsory bisexuality? The challenges of modern sexual fluidity. *Journal of Bisexuality, 9*(3), 431–449.

Fahs, B. (2011a). *Performing sex: The making and unmaking of women's erotic lives.* Albany, NY: State University of New York Press.

Fahs, B. (2011b). Dreaded "otherness": Heteronormative patrolling in women's body hair rebellions. *Gender & Society, 25*(4), 451–472.

Fahs, B. (2018). *Firebrand feminism: The radical lives of Ti-Grace Atkinson, Kathie Sarachild, Roxanne Dunbar-Ortiz, and Dana Densmore.* Seattle, WA: University of Washington Press.

Fahs, B., & Delgado, D. A. (2011). The specter of excess: Race, class, and gender in women's body hair narratives. In C. Bobel, & S. Kwan (Eds.), *Embodied resistance: Breaking the rules, challenging the norms* (pp. 13–25). Nashville, TN: Vanderbilt University Press.

Fahs, B., & Swank, E. (2011). Social identities as predictors of women's sexual satisfaction and sexual activity. *Archives of Sexual Behavior, 40*(5), 903–914.

Farvid, P., & Braun, V. (2006). "Most of us guys are raring to go anytime, anyplace, anywhere": Male and female sexuality in *Cleo* and *Cosmo. Sex Roles, 55*(5), 295–310.

Ferguson, A. (1984). Sex war: The debate between radical and libertarian feminists. *Signs, 10*(1), 106–112.

Ferguson, K. (2010). Anarchist counterpublics. *New Political Science, 32*(2), 193–214.

Ferguson, K. (2011). *Emma Goldman: Political thinking in the streets.* New York: Rowman & Littlefield.

Flickschuh, K. (2007). *Freedom: Contemporary liberal perspectives.* Cambridge: Polity Press.

Frederickson, B. L., & Roberts, T.-A. (1997). Objectification theory: An explanation for women's lived experience and mental health risks. *Psychology of Women Quarterly, 21,* 173–206.

Fromm, E. (1966). *Fear of freedom.* London: Routledge & Kegan Paul.

Frye, M. (1997). Some reflections on separatism and power. In D. T. Meyers (Ed.), *Feminist social thought: A reader* (pp. 406–414). New York: Routledge.

Garber, M. B. (1995). *Vice versa: Bisexuality and the eroticism of everyday life.* New York: Simon & Schuster.

Gerhard, J. (2000). Revisiting "the myth of the vaginal orgasm": The female orgasm in American sexual thought and second wave feminism. *Feminist Studies, 26*(2), 449–476.

Ghazizadeh, S., & Nikzad, M. (2004). Botulinum Toxin in the treatment of Refractory Vaginismus. *Obstetrics & Gynecology, 104*(5), 922–925.

Goldman, E. (1917). Marriage and love. In E. Goldman (Ed.), *Anarchism and other essays* (2nd ed., pp. 227–239). New York: Dover Publications.

Goldman, E. (1998). Jealousy: Causes and a possible cure. In A. K. Shulman (Ed.), *Red Emma speaks: An Emma Goldman reader* (pp. 214–221). Amherst, NY: Humanity Books.

Grazziotin, A. (2008). Dyspareunia and vaginismus: Review of the literature and treatment. *Current Sexual Health Reports, 5*(1), 43–50.

Greenway, J. (1997). Twenty-first century sex. In J. Purkis, & J. Bowen (Eds.), *Twenty-first century anarchism: Unorthodox ideas for a new millennium* (pp. 170–180). London: Continuum Books.

Haaland, B. (1993). *Emma Goldman: Sexuality the impurity of the state*. Montreal: Black Rose Books.

Haavio-Mannila, E., & Kontula, O. (1997). Correlates of increased sexual satisfaction. *Archives of Sexual Behavior, 26*(4), 399–419.

Hakim, C. (2010). Erotic capital. *European Sociological Review, 26*(5), 499–518.

Haywood, H., & Swank, E. (2008). Rape myths among Appalachian college students. *Violence and Victims, 23*, 373–389.

Heckert, J. (2010). Love without borders? Intimacy, identity, and the state of compulsory monogamy. In M. Barker, & D. Langdridge (Eds.), *Understanding non-monogamies* (pp. 255–265). New York: Routledge.

Heckert, J. (2011). Fantasies of an anarchist sex educator. In J. Heckert, & R. Cleminson (Eds.), *Anarchism & sexuality: Ethics, relationships, and power* (pp. 154–180). London/New York: Routledge.

Heckert, J., & Cleminson, R. (2011). Ethics, relationships, and power: An introduction. In J. Heckert, & R. Cleminson (Eds.), *Anarchism & sexuality: Ethics, relationships, and power* (pp. 1–22). London/New York: Routledge.

Herbenick, D., Schick, V., Reece, M., Sanders, S., & Fortenberry, J. D. (2010). Pubic hair removal among women in the United States: Prevalence, methods, and characteristics. *The Journal of Sexual Medicine, 7*(10), 3322–3330.

Hite, S. (1976). *The Hite report: A nationwide study of female sexuality*. New York: Macmillan.

Hobbes, T. (1651). Leviathan. In I. Carter, M. Kramer, & H. Steiner (Eds.), *Freedom: A philosophical anthology* (pp. 6–8). New York: Wiley-Blackwell.

Hughes, B. (2009). Wounded/monstrous/abject: A critique of the disabled body in the sociological imaginary. *Disability & Society, 24*(4), 399–410.

Irvine, J. M. (2002). *Talk about sex: The battles over sex education in the United States*. Berkeley, CA: University of California Press.

Jeffreys, S. (1990). *Anticlimax: A feminist perspective on the sexual revolution*. New York: New York University Press.

Jenness, V. (1993). *Making it work: The prostitute's rights movement in perspective*. New York: Aldine de Gruyter.

Jensen, R. (2007). *Getting off: Pornography and the end of masculinity*. Cambridge: South End Press.

Johnston, J., & Taylor, J. (2008). Feminist consumerism and fat activists: A comparative study of grassroots activism and the Dove real beauty campaign. *Signs, 33*(4), 941–966.

Kahn, A. S., Jackson, J., Kully, C., Badger, K., & Halvorsen, J. (2003). Calling it rape: Differences in experiences of women who do or do not label their sexual assault as rape. *Psychology of Women Quarterly, 27*(3), 233–242.

Koedt, A. (1973). The myth of the vaginal orgasm. In A. Koedt, E. Levine, & A. Rapone (Eds.), *Radical feminism* (pp. 199–207). New York: Quadrangle Books.

Koss, M. P., Heise, L., & Russo, N. F. (1994). The global health burden of rape. *Psychology of Women Quarterly, 18*(4), 509–537.

Landrine, H., & Russo, N. F. (2010). *Handbook of diversity in feminist psychology.* New York: Springer.

Loe, M. (1999). Dildos in our toolbox: The production of sexuality at a pro-sex feminist sex toy store. *Berkeley Journal of Sociology, 43,* 97–136.

Loftus, J. (2001). America's liberalization in attitudes toward homosexuals. *American Sociological Review, 66,* 762–782.

Lorde, A. (2007). *Sister outsider: Essays and speeches.* Berkeley, CA: Crossing Press.

Luce, H. (2010). Sexual assault of women. *American Family Physician, 81*(4), 489–495.

Lyerly, A. D. (2006). Shame, gender, birth. *Hypatia, 21,* 101–118.

MacKinnon, C. A. (1989). *Toward a feminist theory of state.* Cambridge, MA: Harvard University Press.

MacKinnon, C. A., & Dworkin, A. (1998). *In harm's way: The pornography civil rights hearings.* Cambridge, MA: Harvard University Press.

Mandziuk, R. M. (2010). "Ending women's greatest hygienic mistake": Modernity and the mortification of menstruation in Kotex advertising, 1921–1926. *Women's Studies Quarterly, 38*(2), 42–62.

Marso, L. J. (2003). A feminist search for love: Emma Goldman on the politics of marriage, love, sexuality, and the feminine. *Feminist Theory, 4*(3), 305–320.

Martin, E. (2001). *The woman in the body: A cultural analysis of reproduction.* Boston, MA: Beacon Press.

McCabe, P. C., & Rubinson, F. (2008). Committing to social justice: The behavioral intention of school psychology and education trainees to advocate for lesbian, gay, bisexual, and transgendered youth. *School Psychology Review, 37*(4), 469–486.

McClelland, S. I. (2010). Intimate justice: A critical analysis of sexual satisfaction. *Social and Personality Psychology Compass, 4*(9), 663–680.

McClelland, S. I. (2011). Who is the "self" in self-reports of sexual satisfaction? Research and policy implications. *Sexuality Research and Social Policy, 8*(4), 304–320.

McElroy, W. (1995). *XXX: A woman's right to pornography.* New York: St. Martin's Press.

Meltzer, A. L., & McNulty, J. K. (2010). Body image and marital satisfaction: Evidence for the mediating role of sexual frequency and sexual satisfaction. *Journal of Family Psychology, 24*(2), 156–164.

Molyneux, M. (2001). *Women's movements in international perspective: Latin America and beyond.* London: Palgrave MacMillan.

Moore, M. R. (2012). Intersectionality and the study of black, sexual minority women. *Gender & Society, 26*(1), 33–39.

Morokoff, P. J., Quina, K., Harlow, L. L., Whitmire, L., Grimley, D. M., Gibson, P. R., & Burkholder, G. J. (1997). Sexual Assertiveness Scale (SAS) for women: Development and validation. *Journal of Personality and Social Psychology, 73*(4), 790–804.

Nicolson, P., & Burr, J. (2003). What is "normal" about women's (hetero)sexual desire and orgasm? A report of an in-depth interview study. *Social Science & Medicine, 57*(9), 1735–1745.

Orecchia, A. C. (2008). Working with lesbian, gay, bisexual, transgender, and questioning youth: Role and function of the community counselor. *Graduate Journal of Counseling Psychology, 1*(1), 66–77.

Passet, J. E. (2003). *Sex radicals and the quest for women's equality*. Urbana, IL: University of Illinois Press.

Peterson, Z. D. (2010). What is sexual empowerment? A multidimensional and process-oriented approach to adolescent girls' sexual empowerment. *Sex Roles, 62*(5–6), 307–313.

Pinney, E. M., Gerrard, M., & Denney, N. W. (1987). The Pinney Sexual Satisfaction inventory. *Journal of Sex Research, 23*(2), 233–251.

Queen, C. (1997a). Sex radical politics, sex-positive feminist thought, and whore stigma. In J. Nagle (Ed.), *Whores and other feminists* (pp. 125–135). New York: Routledge.

Queen, C. (1997b). *Real, live, nude girl: Chronicles of sex-positive culture*. San Francisco, CA: Cleis Press.

Raina, R., Pahlajani, G., Khan, S., Gupta, S., Agarwal, A., & Zippe, C. D. (2007). Female sexual dysfunction: Classification, pathophysiology, and management. *Fertility & Sterility, 88*(5), 1273–1284.

Rayner, C. (2000). Obituary: Alex Comfort. *The Guardian.* www.guardian.co.uk/news/2000/mar/28/guardianobituaries.

Reece, M., Herbenick, D. M., & Sherwood-Puzello, C. (2004). Sexual health promotion and adult retail stores. *Journal of Sex Research, 41*(2), 173–180.

Rich, A. (1980). Compulsory heterosexuality and lesbian existence. *Signs, 5*(4), 631–660.

Riddell, L., Varto, H., & Hodgson, Z. G. (2010). Smooth talking: The phenomenon of pubic hair removal in women. *Canadian Journal of Human Sexuality, 19*(3), 121–130.

Roberts, C., Kippax, S., Waldby, C., & Crawford, J. (1995). Faking it: The story of "Ohh!". *Women's Studies International Forum, 18*(5–6), 523–532.

Rubin, G. (1993). Thinking sex: Notes for a radical theory of the politics of sexuality. In M. A. Barale, H. Abelove, & D. M. Halperin (Eds.), *The lesbian and gay studies reader* (pp. 3–44). New York: Routledge.

Salk, R. H., & Engeln-Maddox, R. (2012). Fat talk among college women is both contagious and harmful. *Sex Roles, 66*(9–10), 636–645.

Sanchez, D., Crocker, J., & Boike, K. R. (2005). Doing gender in the bedroom: Investing in gender norms and the sexual experience. *Personality and Social Psychology Bulletin, 31* (10), 1445–1455.

Sanchez, D., Kiefer, A. K., & Ybarra, O. (2006). Sexual submissiveness in women: Costs for sexual autonomy and arousal. *Personality and Social Psychology Bulletin, 32*(4), 512–524.

Shifren, J. L., Monz, B. U., Russo, P. A., Segreti, A., & Johannes, C. B. (2008). Sexual problems and distress in United States women: Prevalence and correlates. *Obstetrics and Gynecology, 112*(5), 970–978.

Showden, C. (2012). Theorising maybe: A feminist/queer theory convergence. *Feminist Theory, 13*(1), 3–25.

Shrage, L. (2002). From reproductive rights to reproductive Barbie: Post-porn modernism and abortion. *Feminist Studies, 28*(1), 61–93.

Spencer, G., Maxwell, C., & Aggleton, P. (2008). What does "empowerment" mean in school-based sex and relationships education? *Sex Education, 8*(3), 345–356.

Sprecher, S., Barbee, A., & Schwartz, P. (1995). "Was it good for you, too?" Gender differences in first sexual intercourse experiences. *Journal of Sex Research, 32*(1), 3–15.

Štulhofer, A., & Ajdukovi⬚, D. (2011). Should we take anodyspareunia seriously? A descriptive analysis of pain during receptive anal intercourse in young heterosexual women. *Journal of Sex & Marital Therapy, 37*(5), 346–358.

Swank, E., & Fahs, B. (2011). Pathways to political activism among Americans who have same-sex sexual contact. *Sexuality Research and Social Policy, 8*(2), 126–138.

Sycamore, M. B. (2004). *That's revolting: Queer strategies for resisting assimilation*. Berkeley, CA: Soft Skull Press.

Toerien, M., & Wilkinson, S. (2004). Exploring the depilation norm: A qualitative questionnaire study of women's body hair removal. *Qualitative Research in Psychology, 1*(1), 69–92.

Toerien, M., Wilkinson, S., & Choi, P. Y. (2005). Body hair removal: The "mundane" production of normative femininity. *Sex Roles, 52*(5–6), 399–406.

Trompeter, S. E., Bettencourt, R., & Barrett-Connor, E. (2012). Sexual activity and satisfaction in healthy community-dwelling older women. *The American Journal of Medicine, 125*(1), 37–43.

Valentine, G. (1989). The geography of women's fear. *Area, 21*(4), 385–390.

Vance, C. (1984). *Pleasure and danger: Exploring female sexuality*. New York: Routledge & Kegan Paul.

Ward, C. (2004). *Anarchism: A very short introduction*. Oxford: Oxford University Press.

Weeks, J. (1990). *Sexuality and its discontents: Meanings, myths, and modern sexualities*. New York: Routledge.

Wiederman, M. W. (1997). Pretending orgasm during sexual intercourse: Correlates in a sample of young adult women. *Journal of Sex & Marital Therapy, 23*(2), 131–139.

Yost, M. R., & McCarthy, L. (2012). Girls gone wild? Heterosexual women's same-sex encounters at college parties. *Psychology of Women Quarterly, 36*(1), 7–24.

12

COUNTER-EROTICS

Sex as a form of resistance

One of the great pleasures of studying sexuality is the recognition of its nearly limitless potential as a force of oppression and resistance. Both for individuals and in social life, sexuality sits in a permanent state of tension—between, on the one hand, the worst impulses of our culture and, on the other hand, some of the most crafty and impactful forms of resistance imaginable. My work argues that these tensions remain durable and never fully resolve; rather, feminist scholar-activists work within and between them, trying to redirect sexuality toward its more hopeful possibilities while minimizing the potential damage it can do both to individuals and to the culture at large.

We are living through times that have revealed in vivid detail some of the destructive possibilities of sex, from the overt outing of sexual abuse and sexual harassment (e.g., Harvey Weinstein and the #MeToo movement) to the blatantly patriarchal and misogynistic framing of sexual assault survivors as liars, manipulators, and figures of vengeance (e.g., Supreme Court hearings of 2018). Girls learn to imagine themselves as the *object* of others' desire and not as the *subject* of their own desires (Tolman, 2009). Pornography continues to highlight racism, misogyny, and homophobia as a core part of people's erotic diets ("2017 year in review", 2018). At the same time, sex can serve as a tool for exposing hidden truths, challenging assumptions in discourse, and making public the struggles for recognizing women's sexuality as powerful. When seen as a force of collective struggle, sexuality can rightly intervene to push, expose, and modify outdated beliefs and practices about gender, identity, and power.

In this final chapter, I look at sex from a justice-based perspective, imagining how sex can become a form of resistance and can advance the cause of social justice for those too-often disempowered by it. More specifically, I envision what I term "counter-erotics," that is, an orientation to sexuality that emphasizes its ability to counter oppressive practices and regimes, to oppose the disempowerment of women, people of color, poor people, and queer-identified people most specifically. Counter-erotics is, in essence, a mentality or a framework that wants to emphasize sexuality as a collective, political entity. To explore this, I work from four key frames, first looking at critical sexuality studies and "intimate justice," followed by an examination of how sex might function as a form of hidden or covert resistance. I then consider the complexities of sexual power and how conceptualizing sexual agency in different ways can both reinforce and undermine people's sexual choices. I conclude with a closer look at sex as a form of collective resistance, moving it away from individual (or couple) experiences and into a more explicitly political and sociological realm. The value of a counter-erotics mentality—one that prioritizes the positioning of sex as a social and political tool—is highlighted, along with a word of warning about our contradictory sexual futures.

Sex and social justice

While tensions between sex as a biological/"natural" aspect of life versus sex as a social construction have long plagued the world of sex research—pitting traditionalists and biologists against feminists, sociologists, and social theorists—the framing of sex as a conduit for justice is relatively new. Researchers often think of sex as merely an individual phenomenon; on rarer occasions, researchers consider sexuality as an experience of the couple (Butzer & Campbell, 2008; Mark, 2012). Less often, however, do researchers truly reframe sex and sexuality to allow for a broader vision of social identities in relation to projects of social justice. And yet, as an emerging body of research in critical sexuality studies and feminist psychology suggests, thinking seriously about how things like gender, race, and sexual identity might influence our understanding of sexual expectations and sexual possibilities is a crucial step toward reframing sexuality as a *political* entity (Butler & MacGrogan, 2014; Fahs & McClelland, 2016; McClelland, 2010, 2014; Sanchez, Fetterolf, & Rudman, 2012). This shift toward imagining sex as political also maps onto work in other disciplines, as social movement scholars have for years linked sexuality with political struggles writ large, including LGBT rights (Bernstein, 1997), anti-sexual violence activism (Ferree & Martin, 1995), AIDS activism (Epstein, 1996), and reproductive rights struggles (Staggenborg, 1991).

Sara McClelland coined the term *intimate justice* in her work on sexual satisfaction. In this work, she argued that what people *expect* from sex, and how people imagine their sexual satisfaction, exists in relation to social identities that either enable or strip away these beliefs. In other words, some people expect to satisfy a partner rather than themselves, while others imagine they are entitled to orgasm and feeling satisfied (McClelland, 2010). McClelland (2010) writes of *intimate justice*:

> Intimate justice is a theoretical concept that encompasses the physical and psychological dimensions of a person's intimate and sexual life. At one level, this

theory describes how proximal and distal experiences of inequity impact individuals' sexual and relational well-being. Intimate justice also concerns the development of entitlement to justice in the intimate domain—including both freedom from harm and coercion, as well as experiences of pleasure and satisfaction. In other words, intimate injustice focuses our attention on how social and political inequities impact intimate experiences, affecting how individuals imagine, behave, and evaluate their intimate lives. Without explicitly pairing intimacy and justice, intimate matters are often examined at the individual level, using theories and methods that strip the social from view.

(p. 672)

Building on this, the emergence of critical sexuality studies—a subfield of sexuality studies that argues for an overtly critical lens toward the study of sexuality—has called for far more critical attention paid toward the language of sexuality and the development of different concepts (e.g., sexually active, agency, sexual subjectivity), the subtle and not-so-subtle ways that heterosex (and heterosexism) are prioritized, and attention to the material qualities of abject bodies (Fahs & McClelland, 2016). For example, Fahs and McClelland (2016) argue:

we envision a thriving field of critical sexuality studies that is politically minded, deeply informed by its feminist roots, and shameless about its connections to social movements, political rebellion, and the practices and priorities of social justice. Critical sexuality studies, at its core, aims to always attend to the ways that sex and power collide and, ultimately, who is asked to pay for this collision.

(p. 408)

In short, a critical sexuality studies perspective allows researchers to envision new questions about *how* we study things, *what* we study, *why* we study these things, and *what possibilities and limitations* are present in different areas of study. How we know things, and *why we want to know things* sit at the forefront of critical sexuality studies work. This builds in not only a renewed call to closely examine research methodologies (that is, the sorts of questions asked to different populations, and the design of research questions, and intentions of the research altogether), but also to look at the larger frames for how sex, sexuality, and sexual identities might undermine or further the aims of social justice. Critical sexuality studies profoundly informs the project of counter-erotics, particularly if we want to reframe some of the key questions circulating in sex research today.

To give a few examples, consider the case of sexual harassment and rape advocacy work. Advancing the visibility of these problems relies upon survivors to press charges and tell their stories publicly. The onus for believing survivors lies in the reliability and believability of their testimony rather than in an inherent understanding that sexual harassment and rape form a *central, not marginal*, part of women's sexual lives (see Chapter 5). A counter-erotics perspective that draws on critical sexuality studies would instead argue that, in order to make progress for women on the issues of sexual harassment and rape, we first have to critically understand the ways in which sexual harassment and rape lie at the heart of women's sexual lives. These are not marginalized experiences of a few; they are core experiences that border on near-universal status. And, further than that, the refusal to take women seriously about rape and sexual harassment connects to a variety of other ways that conservatives want to erode women's rights, particularly as the framework for both abortion rights and rape advocacy are premised on *believing* women (Lithwick, 2018).

A counter-erotics perspective might instead ask: What do men learn about sexuality, masculinity, and power/dominance, and *how* do they learn this? What hazards are present in the cultural framings of women's sexuality as passive and men's sexuality as active and dominant? What cultural institutions promote and maintain ideologies that encourage women's sexualized passivity and men's dominance? How can people undermine, challenge, and resist these institutions beyond relying upon victims to come forward? What problems exist in the framing of sexual assault survivors as "victims" or "survivors"? How does differentiating sexual harassment and rape experiences as "better" or "worse" trivialize and invisibilize the entirety of the problem, that is, the *normalizing power imbalances* and *eroticizing powerlessness for women*? In other words, a counter-erotics perspective assumes that we typically ask the wrong questions and that we too often allow conservative ideologies to shape the very kinds of questions we ask.

Consider another case, this time one that feels more intimate and personal to most people: the case of the orgasm gap. What we know about the orgasm gap between women and men is astonishing by any standard. Over half to two-thirds of women have faked or pretended orgasm (Darling & Davidson, 1986; Muehlenhard & Shippee, 2010; Opperman, Braun, Clarke, & Rogers, 2014; Sloan, 2017; Wiederman, 1997). Women report orgasming far less often than men, with one study showing that 69% of women had an orgasm in their last sexual encounter compared with 95% of men (Richters, de Visser, Rissel, & Smith, 2006). Most studies consistently show a 20–30% gap between men and women's rates of orgasming (Garcia, Lloyd, Wallen, & Fisher, 2014). Further, 5–10% of women never orgasm (Brewer, Abell, & Lyons, 2016), mostly because they did not get enough clitoral stimulation and/or that they did not get the right kind of stimulation (too hard, too soft, not direct enough, too direct) (Sloan, 2017).

A typical perspective in traditional sexuality studies would ask: How can we get women to orgasm more regularly, efficiently, and easily? Instead, a counter-erotics perspective might argue that this question is based on a variety of hidden assumptions that need some unpacking: 1) orgasms are good; 2) all women want to orgasm; 3) orgasm unquestionably has a special place in sex; 4) more orgasms are better than fewer orgasms; 5) women should orgasm *as much as* men (but not that men should orgasm less often!); and 6) efficiency of orgasming (for women, especially) is an important skill.

We could start to chip away at these assumptions by asking instead things like: What are orgasms and why do they matter? Are they just a reflex? Why should orgasm have a prized place in sex instead of other things (like affection, for example)? Should men orgasm less? Should people organize their sex lives instead around less efficient orgasm for men? Is orgasming efficiently merely a capitalistic impulse to produce more product-like outcomes? Should orgasm be de-emphasized in its importance, or should it balance with other sexual practices? What leads people to feel the most satisfied sexually, and why does orgasm matter only to some people? The list could go on, but the general premise here is that the assumptions made about the orgasm gap often betray a deep investment in the preservation of the status quo, one where penetrative intercourse (which largely disadvantages women during heterosex) is prioritized over other kinds of sexual activities that far more often lead to orgasm. Further, assumptions about the importance of orgasm—or its role and function—are rarely questioned in existing research. What if instead we prioritized *inefficient, productless* sex? (See Chapters 1 and 10.) What if orgasm happened only en route to other kinds of sexual exploration?

These sorts of questions also tie in with larger projects that question the fundamental bases of how we think about and imagine sexuality. For example, counter-erotics ties in with critical asexualities work that argues against compulsory sexuality (or mandated sexuality) (Przybylo, 2016) and counters the beliefs that all people can and should want to have sex. It also draws from many queer readings of sex that argue against the norms of heterosex and the prioritization of heterosexuality above other expressions of sexuality (Warner, 1993). In this model, critical heterosexualities asks whether the prioritization of orgasm and the insistence on penetrative sex have also become mandates rather than mutually-enjoyable aspects of sexuality (Fischer, 2013; Jackson, 2006). The links between sex and social justice here—in particular, the re-reading of how we understand sexuality studies—constitutes a major goal of counter-erotics thinking.

Sex and everyday resistance

A fully-realized counter-erotics philosophy and practice would also entail an embrace of mundane, everyday forms of resistance in tandem with more organized forms of collective resistance. Mundane forms of resistance rely more on individuals engaging in small acts of resistance rather than more collective, public, and movement-based resistance. Michel Foucault (1990) argued:

> Hence there is no single locus of great Refusal, no soul of revolt, source of all rebellions, or pure law of the revolutionary. Instead there is a plurality of resistances, each of them a special case: resistances that are possible, necessary, improbable; others that are spontaneous, savage, solitary, concerted, rampant, or violent; still others that are quick to compromise, interested, or sacrificial;

by definition, they can only exist in the strategic field of power relations ... And it is doubtless the strategic codification of these points of resistance that makes a revolution possible.

(p. 96).

In essence, Foucault believed that resistance mimics the transmission of power,
and because power operates in diffuse, multiple, hidden, "everyday" ways—for
example, the transmission of political and corporate ideologies through our cell
phones on an everyday, all day long basis—resistance to those forms of power
will also be diffuse, small, and persistent.

The concept of resistance has garnered much attention from scholars interested in studying social justice and social processes (Scott, 1990). Two key questions that emerge in this literature ask: Must resistance be intentional? And, does
resistance need to be recognized by others to count as a valid form of resistance?
Jocelyn Hollander and Rachel Einwohner (2004) have argued that resistance can
exist in multiple styles and modalities, including material resistance, violent
resistance, direct and indirect resistance, symbolic resistance, silent resistance, and
across a variety of scales (from tiny to large-scale). This suggests that resistance
can hide from more powerful authorities in unexpected places or be enacted by
unexpected individuals or groups. Further, Michael Hanchard (2006) has argued
for the concept of *congulation*, which he calls "a practice devised and employed
to forge circumstantial, incidental alliances between members of subordinate
groups, without an overarching theory of resistance to daily acts of domination"
(p. 16). This conceptualization reminds us that resistance need not be *coordinated*
or even theoretically cohesive in order to be both valid and powerful.

Sociologists have discussed the notion of "hidden resistance" (or covert resistance)—defined as "acts that are intentional yet go unnoticed (and, therefore,
unpunished) by their targets, although they are recognized as resistance by other,
culturally aware observers" (Hollander & Einwohner, 2004, p. 541)—for some
time. Researchers of hidden or covert resistance have argued that individuals can
engage in hidden resistance at home, work, and in the public sphere, and that
they do this because they lack access to more traditional avenues for power in
the public sphere (Hollander, 2002; Hollander & Einwohner, 2004). (In many
cases, people engage in hidden resistance because they do not have enough
power to contest oppression in face-to-face interactions.) First developed in
1985 by anthropologist James C. Scott, hidden resistance was conceptualized as
a practice that had multiple dimensions: 1) it was historically entangled with
power; 2) it changed according to the exercise of power in the public sphere;
and 3) it was highly intersectional (with different notions of oppression evident
at different points) (Vinthagen & Johansson, 2013).

James C. Scott argued that, under circumstances in which public resistance is
blocked or impossible, people without much power must create public transcripts that appear deferential to powerful people, but then, in a more hidden
sense, engage in resistance that preserves their power and respect unbeknownst

to those in power. In short, hidden resistance allows people to quietly get back their back power, under-the-radar and without obvious signs that they are doing so. Common actions such as foot-dragging, not paying attention, escape, sarcasm and humor, gossip, passivity, refusal, laziness, disloyalty, wordplay, slander, procrastination, theft, and avoidance all constitute elements of hidden resistance when enacted by groups without a significant amount of socially-inscribed power (Scott, 1990).

With regard to sexuality, many forms of hidden and covert resistance operate as a way to fight back against oppressive structures that disadvantage women. Some examples of hidden resistance in sexuality that can move from private to public resistance include: reframing the language around rape (Weiss, 2009), reconceptualizing stigma around sexuality, abortion, and sexually-transmitted infections (Chrobot-Mason, Button, & DiClementi, 2001; Cockrill & Nack, 2013; Fullec, Chang, & Knox, 2016; Nack, 2000), managing the complexities of exotic dancing (Mavin & Grandy, 2013), and working to improve adolescent girls' sense of sexual agency (Frieh & Smith, 2018; Tolman, Anderson, & Belmonte, 2015). Hidden resistance can also occur on a larger scale, particularly if many different versions of hidden resistance collide to become more collective. Since the 1970s, for example, anti-rape mobilizations have created a slew of legal changes for sexual assault alongside the creation of a widespread system of domestic violence shelters (Htun & Weldon, 2012). Jo Reger (2014) has argued for the existence of "micro-cohorts" in response to the emergence of SlutWalk (see below), while Alexandra Hawkey, Jane Ussher, and Janette Perz (2018) have argued that migrant and refugee women have engaged in hidden resistance as a community of women when negotiating premarital sexuality and expectations of sexual "purity."

On a much smaller and personal scale, hidden and covert resistance can also appear in the language of sexuality and within sexual negotiations. The ways that women say no to sex, either directly or indirectly, constitutes a form of hidden resistance (Kitzinger & Frith, 1999), just as women's expressions of sexual ambivalence (Fahs & Swank, under review; Muehlenhard & Peterson, 2005) can help them to negotiate a culture that demands a constant "yes to sex" from them. Further, women may engage in "emotion work"—that is, the managing of their own feelings or of their sexual partners' feelings—in order to maintain the relationship. While emotion work has mostly been framed as a taxing and difficult aspect of women's sexual lives—particularly as they do things like fake orgasms, minimize sexual pain, and (over)value their partners' desires and fantasies—it may also open up an avenue for other kinds of hidden or covert forms of resistance (Fahs & Swank, 2016; Frith, 2015; Frith & Kitzinger, 1998). Emotion work may, for example, allow women to end sexual encounters (e.g., feigning a headache) or get other sexual needs met via emotion work (e.g., boosting a partners' ego in order to change the kind of sex they have, etc.). Ultimately, the recognition of covert resistance as a key element of how women might fight back against broader structures of power that disadvantage them is central to a counter-erotics mentality.

The complexities of sexual power

Counter-erotics also argues for the necessity of complicating rather than simplifying our understanding of sexual empowerment and sexual agency. Debates about what constitutes empowered sexuality have long plagued the feminist literature in sexuality studies. What does it mean to "have" sexual agency (or not)? How might one go about having *more* sexual agency? Should we conceptualize this along a continuum or as a dichotomy? How can we measure sexual power, empowerment, and agency? These questions do not offer easy or tidy answers.

Studies that have tried to address sexual agency have argued that all-too-often sexual agency gets trapped within neoliberal discourses of individual empowerment through consumption (Bay-Cheng, 2015; Gill & Scharff, 2013). Girls and women learn that, in order to feel like they have sexual agency, they should buy into the trappings of traditional femininity and "become" empowered via clothing, outward appearance, make-up, and the performances of femininity. As Rosalind Gill (2008) wrote:

> Acts as trivial as purchasing a pair of shoes or eating a particular brand of cereal bar are now recognized as gestures of female empowerment just as surely as participating in a demonstration or pushing for a stronger voice in politics.
>
> *(p. 37)*

In this model, girls and women have sexual agency when they feel more confident, assertive, and able to make healthy decisions as individuals (Klein, Becker, & Štulhofer, 2018; Seabrook, Ward, Cortina, Giaccardi, & Lippman, 2017). They "achieve" agency when engaging in certain kinds of sex—for example, friends with benefits relationships (Jovanovic & Williams, 2018), sexting (Garcia-Gomez, 2017), self-touch, orgasm, and directing and initiating sex (Fritz & Paul, 2017). Further, agentic sexuality is thought to arise from good, comprehensive sex education (Froyum, 2010; Hall, Sales, Komro, & Santelli, 2016), though the mechanisms of how girls *become* empowered through sex education are less clear.

This model of sexual agency—one in which certain behaviors and personality characteristics emerge as agentic—is worth unpacking and more closely examining. Often this model of thinking is overly individualistic and ignores the social and structural contexts in which girls and women make sexual choices or imagine themselves as sexual beings, particularly with regard to things like state control of bodies and intersectional understandings of how girls differ from each other in expectations for empowerment (Lerum & Dworkin, 2015). Rosalind Gill (2008), for example, has argued that when we conceptualize women's sexual agency as being about "voice" and assertiveness, we actually *reinforce* rather than resist discourses that require women to be beautiful/sexy and always available for sex. In other words, all of this emphasis on sexual agency as something women have when they are assertive, confident, knowledgeable, self-aware, and engaging in the "right" sexual behavior does not necessarily ask the more radical question of: Why *should* women have sexual agency in the first place, and might their sexual agency also serve as a tool of patriarchy? When we teach women and girls to assert their sexual needs and have a voice in their sexual exchanges, are we also molding them to have certain kinds of sexual choices (e.g., sexually active, heterosexual, interested in sexual variety, etc.)?

This reframing also points to another key project of counter-erotics: asking new/different questions, and, more importantly, asking about *who benefits* when we envision "powerful" sexuality. Counter-erotics instead asks: Is there a more sinister or problematic goal in mind within the framing of women and girls as sexually empowered? Is there room for sexual refusal or asexuality or celibacy or women *not* wanting sex? Do the very things we use to counter the powerful narratives of sexuality—for example, that all girls and women want sex, that girls and women should be equipped to have safe sex whenever they want, etc.—also reinforce some of the worst aspects of patriarchy and misogyny? And if sexual power cannot arise from overly simplistic notions of sexual agency—or the corresponding behaviors we typically associate with women's sexual agency—then how might we imagine something like sexual power?

Sex as a collective resistance

The shift from private to public—or, more accurately, the making of *fluid boundaries* between the two—also serves an important function in the study of sexuality. Because sex is so often considered deeply private and personal, quarantined to the bedroom, and split off from other aspects of our lives (for a good critique of this, see Lorde, 1993), the notion that sex can and should serve a public role in our social and political lives can seem foreign and confusing to some. What would it mean to not only talk openly about sex, but firmly enter it into the discourses of the public sphere? What does this public-ness do and why does it matter? Feminists, especially radical feminists, have long argued that sexuality, the body, and love all constitute core parts of women's *political* lives (Fahs, 2018).

If we take menstrual activism as a model for the successes of fusing the private and the public, it becomes easier to imagine the value of merging the private and public for matters of the body and sexuality. Menstrual activism—a movement that emerged in the 1970s as a combination of artistic, political, and social interventions designed to reduce menstrual stigma, shape public policy about menstrual health, push back against corporate intrusions into menstruation, and reframe language and inclusivity—drew from the women's health movement of the late 1960s. Menstrual activism has had tactics as diverse as reducing the tampon tax, increasing access to menstrual education, normalizing menstrual blood, fighting back against harmful materials in single-use tampons and pads, rabblerousing and troublemaking, recognizing the broader community of menstruators, and creating art and performance pieces that both celebrate menstruation and critically examine its abject status. This movement—in both its liberal and more radical capacities—has been remarkably successful in its short (and somewhat small) lifespan. Menstrual activists have passed legislation, raised awareness, furthered menstrual education throughout the world, staged controversial art shows, organized conferences, instigated academic subfields and corresponding journals (e.g., *Women's Reproductive Health*), challenged "pre-menstrual syndrome" and "premenstrual dysphoric disorder" as medical problems worthy of diagnostic labels, forged alliances between women in the Global North and Global South, and they have worked to make more mainstream so-called "alternative" menstrual products like cups and pads. More importantly, menstrual activists have fought back against stigma, normalizing periods not as "gross" or as "amazing" but as a realistic and unremarkable part of girls' and women's lives (Bobel, 2006, 2010, 2018; Fahs, 2016; Bobel & Fahs, 2018; Bobel & Fahs, in press).

A counter-erotics perspective also advocates for sexuality to enter the public sphere, particularly in the form of rambunctious multi-faceted activism. Like menstrual activist work, this shift toward a public politics of sexual resistance would entail more than the mere "moving sex into the public eye"; rather, it would require a re-envisioning of sex itself as a political and social force. It would push through stigma and shame and silence and move instead into collectivity and unapologetic defiance of traditional and conservative discourses of sex. It would, in short, weaponize sex as a force of social justice.

US women in some ways lag behind the rest of the world in imagining sexuality as a force of public and politicized resistance. Sex strikes (that is, women coordinating efforts to refuse sex in order to achieve a sociopolitical goal) have been used in multiple countries throughout the world to mobilize mass numbers of women around a variety of political causes, often to much success.

The use of sex strikes as a way of mobilizing groups of women in solidarity with each other has a long and compelling history. In the 1600s, Iroquois women refused to have sex in order to stop unregulated warfare; men at the time controlled when and against whom they declared a war. The sex strike successfully earned them veto power concerning future wars and allowed them to control when they went to war (Global Non-Violent Database, n.d.). More recently, in 2001 Turkish women started a sex strike in order to protest a lack of running water, a problem which required them to wait in lines for hours at a time and walk several miles home with the water (CNN, 2001). In 2003, Liberian leader Leymah Gbowee organized what is now seen as perhaps the world's most famous sex strike in protest of their civil war, which resulted in an end to the violence, the passage of the Comprehensive Peace Agreement (CPA) after the 1989–2003 civil war, and Gbowee receiving the Nobel Peace Prize for these efforts (Agbedahin, 2014; Morales, 2013; *Pray the Devil Back to Hell*, 2008). In 2006, wives and girlfriends of Columbian gang members in the city of Pereira started a sex strike (what they called "una huelga de piernas cruzadas" or a "strike of crossed legs") to demand civilian disarmament and an end to gang violence (Harris, 2006). This resulted in a reduction of the murder rate by 26.5% three years later, which, as Shaw writes, was a "huge accomplishment for a city that had a homicide rate twice the national average when the sex strike began" (Shaw, 2017). In 2011, Columbian women in Barbacoas started a sex strike again in order to protest the lack of investment in getting their isolated town paved; after three and a half months, they succeeded in getting what they wanted, arguing that it was unsafe to bring children into the world where they could not travel safely on the main road (*Telegraph*, 2011).

A number of other sex strikes have proven successful in recent years. In 2009, Kenyan women organized a sex strike together with local prostitutes to protest the country's political infighting; accordingly, within one week the government had stabilized (BBC, 2009). More recently, a 2011 sex strike in the Philippines led to peace in Mindanao Island Village, a place known for intense violence (Shaw, 2017). In 2012, women in Togo started a sex strike to call for a resignation of the country's president; "We have many means to oblige men to understand what women want in Togo," said Isabelle Ameganvi, the strike's leader (Stanglin, 2012). Also, in 2012, Canadian women organized a "Got a gun? You get none" campaign to encourage women to refuse sex with men who owned a gun (Kalinauskas, 2012). And in 2014, in the wake of the Russian annexation of Crimea, Ukrainian women waged a sex strike against Russian men to protest this political action; "Don't Give It to a Russian" encourages women to "fight the enemy by whatever means" (Khazan, 2014). That same year, Japanese women in Tokyo called for a sex strike to protest sexist gubernatorial candidate Yoichi Masuzoe's statements about women, including his claim that menstruation makes women unfit for government (Agence-France Presse, 2014).

Sex strikes have also appeared in plays and literature, including the ancient absurdist Greek play *Lysistrata* where women band together in a sex strike in order to end the Peloponnesian War. This has inspired the phrase "Lysistratic non-action," meaning the withholding of sex in order to achieve political gains (Raghuram, 2016). Spike Lee's 2015 film, *Chi-Raq*, draws from these themes to explore, in a comedic way, the impact of sex strikes on American gun violence. Film critic Dan Hyman (2015), wrote, "Lee's film employs the original play's verse-based rhyming dialogue, but it sees the women of Chicago's South Side withholding sex until the men in their lives end the ongoing violence." Critical reception of the film was mixed; while some described it as serious, biting, necessary, and impactful, others described it as going "wildly astray," insulting black women, and unfocused or messy ("*Chi-Raq* Reviews," 2015). In 2017, singer Janelle Monáe called for a sex strike as a priority of the women's rights movement. She said, "People have to start respecting the vagina. Until every man is fighting for our rights, we should consider stopping having sex" (Shaw, 2017). In 2019, Alyssa Milano called for a sex strike in response to ongoing assaults on US abortion rights, including the "heartbeat law" (Holcombe & Kaur, 2019).

Not everyone has shown full-throttled support for sex strikes, with some critics describing them as an unfortunate side effect of denying women other kinds of power besides *sexual* power, and other critics saying that women should not have to exchange sex for power (Bowen, 2017; Martinson, 2013). Clearly, sex strikes do have serious limitations, including an emphasis on heterosexuality, the implicit belief that women should "return" to sex, the notion that women operate as gatekeepers of sex and do not themselves always "want" sex, the lack of attention to queer sexualities and how queerness might fit into a sex strike, and the relative unpopularity of these strikes among US women. That said, sex strikes map onto a broader framework of labor rights. Sex strikes, like other kinds of domestic labor and paid labor strikes, seek to make visible women's invisible labor and to explicitly situate sex as a form of work. Supporters of sex strikes argue for "pussy power" as a means to achieve political gains and argue that a clearly achievable goal like paid maternity leave and/or abortion rights would make it more likely to succeed (Shaw, 2017). I argue that this has its merits. When combined with other kinds of political action, particularly other forms of public solidarity among women, sex strikes can achieve remarkable results, including legislative change, media coverage, threats of future solidarity between diverse groups of women, and overthrow of governments.

A counter-erotics perspective on sex strikes would argue that mobilizing sex as a tool for social justice in this way—by linking sex and inequality in the public eye and by seeing women as collectively powerful when exercising their right to the *freedom from* having to have sex—can be, in certain circumstances, both positive and productive. Women's solidarity with each other is often deeply undermined on the political stage. Coalitional politics, where people come together to support each other's causes even if they occupy different identities, is also undermined in favor of seeing women as "cat fighting" and in perpetual competition with each other. Going on strike—and supporting women going on strike, even if striking is imperfect—is a step toward pushing back against the fragmentation of women's solidarity. Counter-erotics thinking is oriented toward *messing with sex*, seeing it as a force of collectivity, using sex as a political tool.

And, of course, sex strikes are not the only way that sex can be mobilized in the public sphere as a collective form of resistance. As an example of a public gesture of thinking collectively about seemingly "private" aspects of sexuality, San Francisco's "Masturbate-a-Thon" fundraising events for the Center for Sex and Culture founded by sexologist Carol Queen epitomize the fusion of personal and political. Created in 1999 as a way to normalize self-pleasure and make the masturbate-a-thon as mainstream as a walk-a-thon, participants are encouraged to masturbate with the support of sponsors in order to raise money for charities. Events like this have also taken place in London (2006) to raise money for sexual and reproductive health agencies, in Portland, Oregon (2008), in Shenzhen, China (2012) to raise money for HIV and AIDS prevention, and in Montreal, Canada (2013) to raise money for youth sex education outreach (Deans, 2007; Thomas, 2012). The events have inspired people to be more open about masturbation and to think about masturbation as a fun, politicized, and collective experience (the record for masturbating is 9 hours and 58 minutes), even while clear hazards have emerged (e.g., voyeurs masturbating, too many men participating and too few women participating, etc.) (Beckett, 2010). These events point to a collective way to reduce shame around masturbation and encourage people to politicize sexuality in a public way—to varying degrees of success.

When addressing sexual violence, a wide swath of activist work has changed rape laws, created rape crisis centers, altered laws about sexual violence, and engaged in intensive public education campaigns (Matthews, 2005). The prominence of SlutWalk marches, which began in Toronto in 2011, highlighted women's resistance to cultural framings of women as "sluts" when raped or sexually assaulted. These marches began after a Toronto police officer suggested that "women should avoid dressing like sluts" (Bell, 2011) as a way to avoid sexual assault. SlutWalk marches have typically featured women speakers who have disclosed their identity as rape survivors. Also, women who march dress in a purposefully provocative manner as an act of defiance against victim-blaming ideologies that hold women responsible for their own sexual assaults. Hailed as one of the great feminist grassroots movements of the 2010s, SlutWalk marches symbolize the fusion between social justice and experiences of sexual violence even as some feminists expressed unease with the full-throttled embrace of the word "slut" or the public, visual embrace of a derogatory framework of women's sexuality (Herriot, 2015; Hill, 2016; Mendes, 2015; Miriam, 2012; O'Reilly, 2012).

More recently, of course, #MeToo activism, where women have come forward publicly on social media and in many other public spaces to disclose their sexual assault and sexual harassment experiences, has become a full-fledged movement. Though conceptualized much earlier (in 2006) by activist Tarana Burke, #MeToo came to fruition as a movement in October 2017 in the wake of the Harvey Weinstein sexual harassment scandal as a way to further publicize and *normalize* women's disclosures of sexual harassment. Actress Alyssa Milano used the hashtag #MeToo to encourage women to tweet about it to "give people a sense of the magnitude of the problem" (Khomami, 2017). There were 12 million posts using the hashtag within 24 hours (Santiago & Criss, 2017). This then spawned a variety of moments where a reckoning about sexual harassment was long overdue, including church, politics, the financial sector, media, government, music and entertainment, and the pornography industry. #MeToo also spread globally, sparking a number of governments around the world to reconsider how they have handled sexual harassment claims and how to better advance social justice for women.

These examples point to the possibilities of what happens when we remove sexuality from quarantine (in private, in the bedroom, in couples only, etc.) and instead think about it more collectively as a form of *justice-making*, public troublemaking, or something that shifts public policy. These examples also show that activists can move between different registers, from humorous and absurd

(Masturbate-a-Thon) to anti-corporate and anarchist (menstrual activism), to policy and outcome-oriented (sex strikes) to consciousness-raising and solidarity (#MeToo and SlutWalk). Given that women have been pushed to a breaking point in recent years with the rise of alt-right ideologies and misogyny through-out much of the world, a counter-erotics mentality about sex would *expect* fur-ther forms of organized—formal and informal—resistance to emerge around sexuality, the body, and things once deemed "personal" and "private."

A counter-erotics mentality

If counter-erotics is an orientation to sexuality that emphasizes its ability to counter oppressive practices and regimes and is firmly committed to working against the disempowerment of lower status groups, we should think more closely about what such an orientation might look like. We have seen examples of sexuality serving the cause of social justice, and we have noted how sex might inform a politics of hidden or covert resistance. We have also briefly con-sidered some of the hazards of imagining sexual power or empowerment too narrowly or glibly, along with the difficulties of imagining sexual freedoms that do not then themselves become another mandate for women's sexuality. We have also taken cues from worldwide efforts to collectively combat misogyny and sexual oppression via things like sex strikes, masturbate-a-thons, and Slut-Walks. Taken together, these inform what I see as a *mentality shift* we need for sexual politics in an age where sex is too often seen through the lens of oppres-sive, crazy-making, chaotic power structures that strip women's sexuality of its potential as a political and social force of justice.

Counter-erotics takes as its primary goal the need to push sex more toward collectivity and social justice. What this means in practice is a conglomerate of things. For example, we might prioritize upsetting the status quo, insisting upon sex moving out of the private (and therefore unspeakable, unshareable) realm of life. Counter-erotics asks us to sabotage our existing ways of thinking about sex and imagine new possibilities for it. This might be an orientation toward think-ing in anti-capitalist ways about sexuality or valuing the erotics of everyday life. Such thinking might embrace justice rather than merely pleasure—and as such might use justice as the primary metric of satisfying sex rather than more per-sonal things like orgasm or relaxation. Counter-erotics asks for an embrace of sex (or non-sex) on the margins, perhaps in the form of allowing more space for asexuality, diverse bodies, sexualities across the lifespan (in a far wider range than our current sexual imagination allows), a deep and unabiding critical orien-tation toward the racialization of sexuality, and sexual activisms that encourage overlap between movements, identities, and causes.

As a starting point, consider this ten-part counter-erotics wish list:

1. Comprehensive sex education would also teach issues of sex and social just-ice, including skills for how to fight back against misogyny and racism in

everyday sexual practices. This might include better training about sexual communication, *critical* analysis of pornography and its representations of race and gender, and self-reflection on how sexual fantasies can be influenced by cultural norms.

2. Far more acknowledgment and awareness will exist for those who refuse sex, do not want to have sex, start sex and then want to stop, identify as asexual, want to engage in temporary or permanent celibacy, or imagine sex as irrelevant, off-putting, or a non-issue.

3. A commitment to anti-capitalist ways of thinking about sex will be at the fore of our minds. This might mean more "goalless" sex, where orgasm as a *product* is not expected or prioritized. This might mean distancing from industries that "sell" us on how to have sex, and which products to use during or around sex. This might also mean a reframing of the concept of leisure time and work so that sex is not crammed in between other things in people's busy schedules. A cautious approach toward power imbalance and dominance/submission themes will also be necessary if we want to create distance from capitalistic mentalities of sexuality.

4. An orientation toward public considerations about sex will be valued. This means that sex and sexuality as a justice issue will be discussed in the public sphere, in mainstream media, in the workplace, within families, and within other institutions. A dogged insistence on not replicating oppressive practices (e.g., silencing, fetishizing, abusing others' sexuality, etc.) will be a priority.

5. Sex and activism will go hand-in-hand. This means that thinking and acting collectively—whether through absurd performances, organized policy activism, public displays of collective action, transformative pedagogies, and so on—will appear more often.

6. Complicating overly simplistic notions of "good sex" or "empowered sexuality" will happen consistently. Traditionally and stereotypically "masculine" ways of having sex (e.g., without emotions, as frequently as possible, etc.) will not be prized over relationality, emotions, justice, patience, vulnerable listening, and diversity of sexualities.

7. An intense investment in making room for sexualities on the margin will be prioritized, whether through making spaces for bodies typically marked as abject to imagine themselves as sexual, or through a widening of our existing lens about who is sexual and who is not. We will demand of our cultural representations (e.g., TV, movies, art, culture, etc.) that they, too, work to embrace sexualities and bodies on the margins.

8. A reframing of the successes and failures of social justice will be necessary. The recognition that even when all groups do not benefit equally, a "win" for one group is a win for all will become a dominant way of thinking about sexual and social justice. Linking arms with people who occupy different bodies and identities—and may have different needs and priorities— will feel intuitive and politically necessary. We will champion coalitional politics.

9. We will expect policy shifts and institutionalized changes to how sexuality is talked about, legislated, and imagined in public. In this regard, we will recognize the value of expecting liberal (within system) perspectives on sexuality and social justice to take a more radical (going to the roots) turn in the realm of law and public policy.
10. Imagining new possibilities for sex—what it can be, what it could look like, how it could better advance social justice for all—will be a huge priority of both academic studies in sexuality studies and political and social activism around sexuality. This work will better challenge the sorts of problems women encounter in their sexual lives, many of which I outlined in this book.

A word of warning

While I have mostly considered a positive vision of sexuality in this final chapter, I also want to end with a word of warning about the current state of sexual politics. We are now living through times of immense despair and darkness for many, dominated by dogged and appalling selfishness of conservatives combined with ever-intensifying misogyny and racism that is in ascendancy throughout the world. These political contexts inevitably impact how people see, feel, and experience sexuality, and they will continue to do so in ways not always immediately visible to us at this current moment in time. We are asked right now to live not only with a sense of fear about the future, but also with a heavy burden of uncertainty about whether things will change or improve, particularly for people already made vulnerable by sexism, racism, classism, and homophobia.

We also know that co-optation of discourses of sexual empowerment happens quickly, turning the rhetoric of power and resistance against us. That which we identify as empowering may in only a few short years (or even months) be taken up and turned against us. This has happened too many times to name. When the medical industries touted Viagra as a drug to "empower" men with erectile dysfunction, everlasting erections then became the norm (much to the dismay of many older women!). When menstrual activists advocated for alternative menstrual products like cups, sponges, and homemade reusable menstrual pads, the entire landscape of menstrual activism became dominated by product-focused, money-making schemes to disseminate menstrual products to all, ignoring nearly all of the other major concerns of menstrual activists. These are just a few examples in a vast landscape of co-optation of empowerment stories. We must stay one step ahead of this co-optation, but this will require an immense amount of work and struggle. Co-optation essentially means that we can never fully rest; we can never set this work down in a permanent sense.

We should also remember that it takes work to redeem sex from its more destructive and painful manifestations. To see sex as potentially empowering requires self-awareness and cautious optimism, particularly in an age where terrifying signs of sexual oppression appear in abundance. Mainstream pornography, for example, continues to get worse and worse, with themes of incest, rape, and fetishization of teenage girls topping the charts ("2017 year in review," 2018). There are profound assaults on even the most basic of sexual and reproductive rights in the US, including a chipping away at comprehensive sex education (Valenti, 2018), threats to Roe v. Wade and abortion rights (LeTourneau, 2018), the confirmation of both a Supreme Court justice and the election of a president accused by multiple women of sexual assault, and a declining faith in the prospects of sexual justice (Chira, 2018).

Ultimately, I have argued both in this chapter and throughout this book that sex is full of contradictions, and as such has the potential to become deeply disempowering or, in contrast, a nourishing avenue that connects us to each other. In this sense, the *potential* of sex is what a politics of counter-erotics illuminates—that is, what sex *could become, could be, might be* if it enters a framework of justice. Sex and politics go hand-in-hand and are delicately woven together and interconnected. Because our culture is saturated with madness and chaos about sexuality—burdened greatly by its treatment of sexuality as "dirty" and by its vicious disregard for women's sexual subjectivities—this makes it all the more necessary to have clarity and vision for social change *as a collective* rather than as individuals.

My ultimate claim is this: Perhaps sex is so wrapped up in cultural madness, so tied together with irredeemably crazy thinking and acting, that it can only become empowering through the collective reframing of it as a justice project. As such, working to use sexuality to counter oppressive regimes and advance the cause of social justice for all will be difficult, perhaps at times impossible. Nevertheless, seeing sex as a matter of justice allows us to work collaboratively, to be a little less lonely or short-sighted in the project of envisioning sexual empowerment, and to create something full of imaginative possibilities.

References

"2017 year in review." (2018). *PornHub*. www.pornhub.com/insights/2017-year-in-review

Agbedahin, K. (2014). Interrogating the Togolese historical sex strike. *International Journal on World Peace*, *31*(1), 7–26.

Agence-France Presse. (2014). Tokyo women call for "sex strike" over sexist gubernatorial candidate. *The Guardian*. www.theguardian.com/world/2014/feb/07/tokyo-women-sex-strike-yoichi-masuzoe.

Bay-Cheng, L. Y. (2015). The agency line: A neoliberal metric for appraising young women's sexuality. *Sex Roles*, *73*(7–8), 279–291.

Beckett, L. (2010). Behind the scenes at masturbate-a-thon 2010. *SF Weekly*. https://archives.sfweekly.com/thesnitch/2010/06/01/behind-the-scenes-at-masturbate-a-thon-2010-pics-nsfw.

Bell, S. (2011). Slutwalk London: "Yes means yes and no means no." *BBC News*. www.bbc.com/news/uk-13739876.

Bernstein, M. (1997). Celebration and suppression: The strategic uses of identity by the lesbian and gay movement. *American Journal of Sociology*, *103*(3), 531–565.

Bobel, C. (2006). "Our revolution has style": Contemporary menstrual product activists "doing feminism" in the third wave. *Sex Roles, 54*(5–6), 331–345.

Bobel, C. (2010). *New blood: Third-wave feminism and the politics of menstruation.* New Brunswick: Rutgers University Press.

Bobel, C. (2018). *The managed body: Developing girls and menstrual health in the global south.* London: Palgrave.

Bobel, C., & Fahs, B. (2018). The messy politics of menstrual activism. In J. Reger (Ed.), *Nevertheless they persisted: Feminisms and continued resistance in the U.S. women's movement* (pp. 161–179). New York: Routledge.

Bobel, C., & Fahs, B. (in press). From private to public: Shifting from the politics of bloodless respectability to radical menstrual embodiment. *Signs.*

Bowen, S. (2017). Why Janelle Monáe needs to rethink her strategy for combatting sexism. *Refinery, 29.* www.refinery29.com/2017/04/149338/janelle-monae-respect-vagina-sex-strike-gender-equality-Bowen-2017.

Brewer, G., Abell, L., & Lyons, M. (2016). Machiavellianism, pretending orgasm, and sexual intimacy. *Personality and Individual Differences, 96,* 155–158.

Butler, J., & MacGrogan, M. (2014). *Erotic welfare: Sexual theory and politics in the age of epidemic.* London: Routledge.

Butzer, B., & Campbell, L. (2008). Adult attachment, sexual satisfaction, and relationship satisfaction: A study of married couples. *Personal Relationships, 15*(1), 141–154.

Chira, S. (2018). Resigned or determined? After Kavanaugh, women are pulled in opposite directions. *New York Times.* www.nytimes.com/2018/10/16/us/politics/kavanaugh-women-supreme-court.html.

"*Chi-Raq* reviews." (2015). *Rotten Tomatoes.* www.rottentomatoes.com/m/chi_raq/reviews/.

Chrobot-Mason, D., Button, S. B., & DiClementi, J. D. (2001). Sexual identity management strategies: An exploration of antecedents and consequences. *Sex Roles, 45*(5–6), 321–336.

Cockrill, K., & Nack, A. (2013). "I'm not that type of person": Managing the stigma of having an abortion. *Deviant Behavior, 34*(12), 973–990.

"Colombian women end 'crossed legs' abstinence protest for new road." (2011). *Telegraph.* www.telegraph.co.uk/news/worldnews/southamerica/colombia/8830666/Colombian-women-end-crossed-legs-abstinence-protest-for-new-road.html.

Darling, C. A., & Davidson, J. K. (1986). Coitally active university students: Sexual behaviors, concerns, and challenges. *Adolescence, 21*(82), 403.

Deans, J. (2007). "Wank week" postponed. *The Guardian.* www.theguardian.com/media/2007/feb/02/broadcasting.channel4.

Epstein, S. (1996). *Impure science: AIDS, activism, and the politics of knowledge.* Berkeley, CA: University of California Press.

Fahs, B. (2016). *Out for blood: Essays on menstruation and resistance.* Albany, NY: State University of New York Press.

Fahs, B. (2018). *Firebrand Feminism: The Radical Lives of Ti-Grace Atkinson, Kathie Sarachild, Roxanne Dunbar-Ortiz, and Dana Densmore.* Seattle, WA: University of Washington Press.

Fahs, B., & McClelland, S. I. (2016). When sex and power collide: An argument for critical sexuality studies. *The Journal of Sex Research, 53*(4–5), 392–416.

Fahs, B., & Swank, E. (2016). The other third shift? Women's emotion work in their sexual relationships. *Feminist Formations, 28*(3), 46–69.

Fahs, B., & Swank, E. (under review). Refusals, reciprocity, and sexual labor: Women discuss negotiations around oral and anal sex with men.

Ferree, M. M., & Martin, P. Y. (Eds.). (1995). *Feminist organizations: Harvest of the new women's movement.* Philadelphia, PA: Temple University Press.

Fischer, N. L. (2013). Seeing "straight," contemporary critical heterosexuality studies and sociology: An introduction. *The Sociological Quarterly*, *54*(4), 501–510.

Foucault, M. (1990). *The history of sexuality: An introduction, volume I* (Trans. Robert Hurley). New York: Vintage.

Frieh, E. C., & Smith, S. H. (2018). Lines of flight in sex education: Adolescents' strategies of resistance to adult stereotypes of teen sexuality. *Sexualities*, *21*(1–2), 174–193.

Frith, H. (2015). Visualising the "real" and the "fake": Emotion work and the representation of orgasm in pornography and everyday sexual interactions. *Journal of Gender Studies*, *24*(4), 386–398.

Frith, H., & Kitzinger, C. (1998). Emotion work as a participant resource: A feminist analysis of young women's talk-in-interaction. *Sociology*, *32*(2), 299–320.

Fritz, N., & Paul, B. (2017). From orgasms to spanking: A content analysis of the agentic and objectifying sexual scripts in feminist, for women, and mainstream pornography. *Sex Roles*, *77*(9–10), 639–652.

Froyum, C. M. (2010). Making "good girls": Sexual agency in the sexuality education of low-income black girls. *Culture, Health & Sexuality*, *12*(1), 59–72.

Fullec, A. I., Chang, J., & Knox, D. (2016). Female sexual hedonism: Navigating stigma. *College Student Journal*, *50*(1), 29–34.

Garcia, J. R., Lloyd, E. A., Wallen, K., & Fisher, H. E. (2014). Variation in orgasm occurrence by sexual orientation in a sample of US singles. *The Journal of Sexual Medicine*, *11* (11), 2645–2652.

Garcia-Gomez, A. (2017). Teen girls and sexual agency: Exploring the intrapersonal and intergroup dimensions of sexting. *Media, Culture & Society*, *39*(3), 391–407.

Gill, R. (2008). Empowerment/sexism: Figuring female sexual agency in contemporary advertising. *Feminism & Psychology*, *18*(1), 35–60.

Gill, R., & Scharff, C. (Eds.). (2013). *New femininities: Postfeminism, neoliberalism and subjectivity*. London: Palgrave.

Global Non-Violent Database. (n.d.). Iroquois women gain power to veto wars, 1600s. https://nvdatabase.swarthmore.edu/content/iroquois-women-gain-power-veto-wars-1600s.

Hall, K. S., Sales, J. M., Komro, K. A., & Santelli, J. (2016). The state of sex education in the United States. *The Journal of Adolescent Health*, *58*(6), 595–597.

Hanchard, M. (2006). *Party/politics: Horizons in black political thought*. Oxford: Oxford University Press.

Harris, L. (2006). Colombian women launch "strike of crossed legs". *Salon*. www.salon.com/2006/09/13/colombia_strike/.

Hawkey, A. J., Ussher, J. M., & Perz, J. (2018). Regulation and resistance: Negotiation of premarital sexuality in the context of migrant and refugee women. *Journal of Sex Research*, *55*(9), 1116–1133.

Herriot, L. (2015). SlutWalk: Contextualizing the movement. *Women's Studies International Forum*, *53*, 22–30.

Hill, A. (2016). SlutWalk as perifeminist response to rape logic: The politics of reclaiming a name. *Communication & Critical/Cultural Studies*, *13*(1), 23–29.

Holcombe, M., & Kaur, H. (2019). Alyssa Milano called for a sex strike to protest strict abortion laws. Women were not having it. *CNN*. www.cnn.com/2019/05/12/entertainment/alyssa-milano-abortion-sex-strike/index.html.

Hollander, J. A. (2002). Resisting vulnerability: The social reconstruction of gender in interaction. *Social Problems*, *49*(4), 474–496.

Hollander, J. A., & Einwohner, R. L. (2004). Conceptualizing resistance. *Sociological Forum*, *19*(4), 533–554.

Htun, M., & Weldon, S. L. (2012). The civic origins of progressive policy change: Combating violence against women in global perspective, 1975–2005. *American Political Science Review*, *106*(3), 548–569.

Hyman, D. (2015). What the controversy over Spike Lee's *Chi-Raq* is really about. GQ. www.gq.com/story/chi-raq-controversy-spike-lee.

Jackson, S. (2006). Interchanges: Gender, sexuality and heterosexuality: The complexity (and limits) of heteronormativity. *Feminist Theory*, *7*(1), 105–121.

Jovanovic, J., & Williams, J. C. (2018). Gender, sexual agency, and friends with benefits relationships. *Sexuality & Culture*, *22*(2), 555–576.

Kalinauskas, N. (2012). "Guns get none": Toronto woman encourages gang members' girlfriends to withhold sex. *Yahoo News Canada*. https://ca.news.yahoo.com/blogs/dailybrew/guns-none-toronto-woman-encourages-gang-members-girlfriends-170856445.html.

"Kenyan women hit men with sex ban." (2009). *BBC News*. http://news.bbc.co.uk/2/hi/africa/8025457.stm.

Khazan, O. (2014). Ukrainian women have launched a sex strike against Russian men. *The Atlantic*. www.theatlantic.com/international/archive/2014/03/ukrainian-women-have-launched-a-sex-strike-against-russian-men/284614/.

Khomami, N. (2017). #MeToo: How a hashtag became a rallying cry against sexual harassment. *The Guardian*. www.theguardian.com/world/2017/oct/20/women-worldwide-use-hashtag-metoo-against-sexual-harassment.

Kitzinger, C., & Frith, H. (1999). Just say no? The use of conversation analysis in developing a feminist perspective on sexual refusal. *Discourse & Society*, *10*(3), 293–316.

Klein, V., Becker, I., & Štulhofer, A. (2018). Parenting, communication about sexuality, and the development of adolescent women's sexual agency: A longitudinal assessment. *Journal of Youth and Adolescence*, *47*(7), 1486–1498.

Lerum, K., & Dworkin, S. L. (2015). Sexual agency is not a problem of neoliberalism: Feminism, sexual justice, & the carceral turn. *Sex Roles*, *73*(7–8), 319–331.

LeTourneau, N. (2018). How to prepare for the day when Roe v. Wade is overturned. *Washington Monthly*. https://washingtonmonthly.com/2018/10/18/how-to-prepare-for-the-day-when-roe-vs-wade-is-overturned/.

Lithwick, D. (2018). The GOP doesn't trust women. *Slate*. https://slate.com/news-and-politics/2018/10/abortion-roe-overturned-christine-blasey-ford-believe-women.html.

Lorde, A. (1993). The uses of the erotic: The erotic as power. In H. Abelove, M. A. Barale, & D. Halperin (Eds.), *The lesbian and gay studies reader* (pp. 339–343). New York: Routledge.

Mark, K. P. (2012). The relative impact of individual sexual desire and couple desire discrepancy on satisfaction in heterosexual couples. *Sexual and Relationship Therapy*, *27*(2), 133–146.

Martinson, J. (2013). Do sex strikes really work, and isn't it time we moved on? *The Guardian*. www.theguardian.com/lifeandstyle/womens-blog/2013/oct/24/do-sex-strikes-really-work.

Matthews, N. A. (2005). *Confronting rape: The feminist anti-rape movement and the state*. New York: Routledge.

Mavin, S., & Grandy, G. (2013). Doing gender well and differently in dirty work: The case of exotic dancing. *Gender, Work, & Organization*, *20*(3), 232–251.

McClelland, S. I. (2010). Intimate justice: A critical analysis of sexual satisfaction. *Social and Personality Psychology Compass*, *4*(9), 663–680.

McClelland, S. I. (2014). "What do you mean when you say that you are sexually satisfied?" A mixed methods study. *Feminism & Psychology*, *24*(1), 74–96.

Mendes, K. (2015). *SlutWalk: Feminism, activism, and media*. London: Palgrave.

Miriam, K. (2012). Feminism, neoliberalism, and SlutWalk. *Feminist Studies*, *38*(1), 262–266.

Morales, H. (2013). Aristophanes' Lysistrata, the Liberian "sex strike," and the politics of reception. *Greece and Rome*, *60*(2), 281–295.

Muehlenhard, C. L., & Peterson, Z. D. (2005). Wanting and not wanting sex: The missing discourse of ambivalence. *Feminism & Psychology*, *15*(1), 15–20.

Muehlenhard, C. L., & Shippee, S. K. (2010). Men's and women's reports of pretending orgasm. *Journal of Sex Research*, *47*(6), 552–567.

Nack, A. (2000). Damaged goods: Women managing the stigma of STDs. *Deviant Behavior*, *21*(2), 95–121.

O'Reilly, A. (2012). Slut pride: A tribute to SlutWalk Toronto. *Feminist Studies*, *38*(1), 245–250.

Opperman, E., Braun, V., Clarke, V., & Rogers, C. (2014). "It feels so good it almost hurts": Young adults' experiences of orgasm and sexual pleasure. *The Journal of Sex Research*, *51*(5), 503–515.

"Pray the devil back to hell." (2008). www.forkfilms.net/pray-the-devil-back-to-hell/.

Przybylo, E. (2016). Introducing asexuality, unthinking sex. In N. Fischer, & S. Seidman (Eds.), *Introducing the new sexuality studies reader* (pp. 181–191). New York: Routledge.

Raghuram, N. (2016). No rights, no sex: The powerful history of women going on strike. *Broadly*. https://broadly.vice.com/en_us/article/gyxbw3/no-rights-no-sex-the-powerful-history-of-women-going-on-strike.

Reger, J. (2014). Micro-cohorts, feminist discourse, and the emergence of the Toronto SlutWalk. *Feminist Formations*, *26*(1), 49–69.

Richters, J., de Visser, R., Rissel, C., & Smith, A. (2006). Sexual practices at last heterosexual encounter and occurrence of orgasm in a national survey. *Journal of Sex Research*, *43*(3), 217–226.

Sanchez, D. T., Fetterolf, J. C., & Rudman, L. A. (2012). Eroticizing inequality in the United States: The consequences and determinants of traditional gender role adherence in intimate relationships. *Journal of Sex Research*, *49*(2–3), 168–183.

Santiago, C., & Criss, D. (2017). An activist, a little girl, and the heartbreaking origin of "Me too." *CNN*. www.cnn.com/2017/10/17/us/me-too-tarana-burke-origin-trnd/index.html/.

Scott, J. C. (1990). *Domination and the arts of resistance: Hidden transcripts*. New Haven, CT: Yale University Press.

Seabrook, R. C., Ward, L. M., Cortina, L. M., Giaccardi, S., & Lippman, J. R. (2017). Girl power or powerless girl? Television, sexual scripts, and sexual agency in sexually active young women. *Psychology of Women Quarterly*, *41*(2), 240–253.

"Sex ban lifted in Turkish village." (2001). *CNN World*. http://edition.cnn.com/2001/WORLD/europe/08/16/turkey.women/index.html.

Shaw, M. (2017). History shows that sex strikes are a surprisingly effective strategy for political change. *Quartz*. https://qz.com/958346/history-shows-that-sex-strikes-are-a-surprisingly-effective-strategy-for-political-change/.

Sloan, K. (2017). The orgasm gap: Why equality in the bedroom is as important as equality in the boardroom. *Herizons*. www.thefreelibrary.com/The+Orgasm+Gap%3A+Why+Equality+in+the+Bedroom+is+as+Important+as…-a0513759370.

Staggenborg, S. (1991). *The pro-choice movement: Organization and activism in the abortion conflict*. New York: Oxford University Press.

Stanglin, D. (2012). Togo women call sex strike to force president's resignation. *USA Today*. https://content.usatoday.com/communities/ondeadline/post/2012/08/togo-women-call-sex-strike-to-force-presidents-resignation/1#.VkEKi7erRaR.

Thomas, E. (2012). Masturbation contest in China held to celebrate safe sex on world AIDS day. *Huffington Post*. www.huffingtonpost.com/2012/12/03/chinese-wankathon_n_2232063.html.

Tolman, D. L. (2009). *Dilemmas of desire: Teenage girls talk about sexuality*. Cambridge, MA: Harvard University Press.

Tolman, D. L., Anderson, S. M., & Belmonte, K. (2015). Mobilizing metaphor: Considering complexities, contradictions, and contexts in adolescent girls' and young women's sexual agency. *Sex Roles, 73*(7–8), 298–310.

Valenti, J. (2018). Under Trump, the lies of abstinence-only sex education are back. *The Guardian*. www.theguardian.com/commentisfree/2018/mar/14/trump-lies-abstinence-only-sex-education.

Vinthagen, S., & Johansson, A. (2013). "Everyday resistance": Exploration of a concept and its theories. *Resistance Studies Magazine, 1*(1), 1–46.

Warner, M. (Ed.). (1993). *Fear of a queer planet: Queer politics and social theory*. Minneapolis, MN: University of Minnesota Press.

Weiss, K. G. (2009). "Boys will be boys" and other gendered accounts: An exploration of victims' excuses and justifications for unwanted sexual contact and coercion. *Violence Against Women, 15*(7), 810–834.

Wiederman, M. W. (1997). Pretending orgasm during sexual intercourse: Correlates in a sample of young adult women. *Journal of Sex & Marital Therapy, 23*(2), 131–139.

ACKNOWLEDGMENTS

Given the true pleasures and dangers of working and writing on sexuality as a critical feminist scholar, I owe an enormous debt to those scholars and thinkers who fill our small circle with such rewarding exchanges. In particular, I thank Sara McClelland, a longtime friend and collaborator, whose work stands alone as exceptional, thoughtful, and sharp. I thank Rebecca Plante, Ela Przybylo, Leonore Tiefer, Virginia Braun, Thea Cacchioni, Sandy Caron, Jessa Crispin, Deborah Tolman, Monica Casper, Janet Hyde, Hannah Frith, Jill Wood, Carla Golden, Patrick Grzanka, Maureen McHugh, David Frost, Jane Caputi, Rosalind Gill, Tomi-Ann Roberts, and Joan Chrisler for epitomizing the best of what we do and for being so generous with me for so many years. And to Jane Ussher, feminist sex researcher extraordinaire, this book exists only because of your belief in me—thank you!

I whole-heartedly thank my mentors, many of whom have read and cheered on my work on sexuality for years. To Elmer Griffin, who nurtured me along during my first 100-page missive on women's orgasms, without you none of this would exist. To Abby Stewart, who built my knowledge of methods and feminist psychology, you have been a beacon of light these many years. To Sarah Stage, whose deep grounding in feminist history has inspired so much of what I do, I adore you. Thank you also to the brilliant and kind Marlene Tromp, a singular force of nature who has always had my back, and thanks (again and again) to Chris Bobel, Larin McLaughlin, and Amy Scholder.

To my wonderful research group, the Feminist Research on Gender and Sexuality Group—"The FROGS"—your imprint is everywhere on this book. I am especially indebted to the group of students who worked diligently on this book, particularly Decker Dunlop, Jakob Salazar, Claire Halling, Atlas Pillar, Ayanna Shambe, Michaela Collins, John Payton, Carolyn Anh Thu Dang, Laisa Schweigert, and Mam Marie Sanyang. Thank you to Marie for indexing the book so thoughtfully. Thanks also to the rest of our motley crew: Madison Carlyle, Emma DiFrancesco, Crystal Zaragoza,

Laura Martinez, Natali Blazevic, Michael Karger, Kimberly Koerth, Adrielle Munger, Jax Gonzalez, Stephanie Robinson (Voelker), Rose Coursey, Chelsea Pixler Charbonneau, Corie Cisco, Elizabeth Wallace, Marisa Loiacono, Eva Sisko, Carissa Cunningham, Jennifer Bertagni, Alexis Starks, and Tatiana Crespo.

I thank my colleagues—both at Arizona State University and beyond—who have backed me up on this and many other projects. Thanks to Louis Mendoza, Todd Sandrin, Sharon Kirsch, Michael Stancliff, Gloria Cuadraz, Eduardo Pagan, Alejandra Elenes, Majia Nadesan, Julie Erfani, and Miriam Mara. Thanks also to the gang at Routledge—particularly Eleanor Reedy, Alex Howard, Jane Ussher, and Martin Pettitt—for seeing this book through to the finish line!

Thank you to my friends, whose energy, generosity, and enthusiasm reminds me that I am profoundly lucky to live and work with, around, and among them: Lori Errico-Seaman, Sean Seaman, Chris Bobel, Sara McClelland, Elizabeth Brake, Mary Dudy, Jennifer Tamir, Annika Mann, Denise Delgado, Garyn Tsuru, Jan Habarth, Marcy Winokur, Steve DuBois, Connie Hardesty, Katie Goldey, Pat Hart, Karen Swank-Fitch, Diana Álvarez, and Sadie Mohler. Thanks to my mother, who never tells me if my work scandalizes her, and who always showers me with abundant love—I am so grateful for you. To Kristen, Simon, Ryan, and Fiona, you are a part of all that I do. Finally, I dedicate this book to Eric Swank, for his careful (and game-changing) readings of my work, his boundless generosity of time and spirit, and for renewing in me again and again a belief in love as a source of creative and transformative power.

Note that an earlier version of Chapter 2 appeared in *Feminist Formations* 28.3 (2016), 46–69 (with Eric Swank) and is reprinted with permission by Johns Hopkins University Press. An earlier version of Chapter 3 appeared in *Feminism & Psychology* 27.3 (2017), 280–297 and is reprinted with permission by Sage. An earlier version of Chapter 5 appeared in *The Feminist Wire* in 2014. Chapter 6 is reprinted with permission from Waveland Press from *Lectures on the Psychology of Women, 5th Edition* (2018), 213–236, edited by Joan Chrisler and Carla Golden. Finally, an earlier version of Chapter 11 appeared in *Sexualities* 17.3 (2014), 267–290 and is reprinted with permission by Sage.

INDEX

Made in the USA
Middletown, DE
19 January 2022

59149665R00130